MW01608172

KEEP SMILING-
KEEP THINKING.
GOOD LUCK!

Jesus

A Man For All Time

A Provocative Look at the Meaning of Jesus

By
Samuel H. Fountain

Eloquent Books
New York, New York

Copyright 2008
All rights reserved – Samuel H. Fountain

No part of this book may be reproduced or transmitted in any form or by any means, graphic, electronic, or mechanical, including photocopying, recording, taping, or by any information storage retrieval system, without the permission, in writing, from the publisher.

Eloquent Books
An imprint of AEG Publishing Group
845 Third Avenue, 6th Floor - 6016
New York, NY 10022
www.eloquentbooks.com

ISBN 978-1-60693-091-5   1-60693-091-5

Printed in the United States of America

Book Design: Linda W. Rigsbee

TABLE OF CONTENTS

INTRODUCTION

Each year Christianity celebrates the high points of faith. These celebrations are scattered throughout the year and placed as close as possible to the date reflected in the Bible. For example, Easter, celebrated on the first Sunday of the full moon after the month of March, celebrates the resurrection. Lent counts backwards forty days from this date. It honors the passion of Christ, a forty-day period leading up to and including Good Friday, the crucifixion. Other holidays are based on calendar dates; Christmas always falls on December 25 or, for orthodox Christians, January 6 (twelve days after December 25). The Christian seasons provide an understanding of our faith reflected in the liturgical celebrations, but bear no relationship to the climatic seasons, that is, spring, summer, fall, and winter.

The church year celebrates different aspects of the faith such as the significant events in the life of Jesus of Nazareth and later events of the church after the life of Jesus. Together these determine what we celebrate and when.

This book looks at the life of Jesus and his impact on faith. The New Testament as a book of faith recounts the life and thought of Jesus, not as historical events, but how his life made a difference in the lives of his followers. Their memories as well as their spiritual experiences and interpretations were the source of the books of the New Testament. Jesus was not a great prophet to respectfully remember, but someone much greater who brought faith, hope, and love to generations of followers from that day to this. Jesus introduced us to the Kingdom of God (Heaven) during his lifetime.

The Kingdom, as Jesus explained it, is a state of being that Christians experience and encounter during their lifetimes. There are other sayings in the New Testament that point to the Kingdom as something that happens in the future, in life beyond death, but this has been so abused by Christians over the centuries that it raises serious questions about its true relevance. For example, American whites justified slavery and its human suffering, poverty, and indignity because in the future Heaven blacks would be saved and then in the afterlife live a glorious and happy life. Hence, a better tomorrow justifies today's pain. It may be a separate, segregated Heaven, but will still be Heaven, an eternal bliss.

The Kingdom of God is for the present age, for today, for now. Making it primarily a future event reduces the value of this life and renders it relatively meaningless. Culturally, we tend to do the same with our children. Frequently they are seen as tomorrow's hope and are given special regard so they can preserve the future. This tends to make our children our hope for tomorrow (hence the sign "Children Aboard" displayed in many automobiles), but places little value on them today. Remember the demeaning comment by adults that "children should be seen, but not heard," that is, their place in the world is in the background and not very important. Their importance can only become real and genuine when they become adults when they can speak and be heard. In the present, they are becoming humans — adults in training.

Children are more than who they will become. They are people who experience life today as much as adults do. Children have fears, dream about a better tomorrow, face conflict, and feel pain and ecstasy. They are significant and important as human beings while they are still children, today. So is the Kingdom of God a meaningful relationship today.

Or, consider the more contemporary experience of super-conservatives such as American militias masquerading as Christians. They threaten, maim, and kill minorities or anyone else they believe will menace their beliefs or their understanding of purity. The militias do violence because they believe that they have been saved for a future Kingdom. Or, worse, they do it as so-called pious acts that will ensure their place in the future Kingdom. What happens today is not important. Heaven is their future abode, which justifies today's actions. Tomorrow's Heaven is what is important.

These illustrations do little to disclaim the concept of a future heaven, but Jesus would not promise the Kingdom of God as his people endured suffering in their lives unless it promised something for their immediate living. Rather, Jesus offered something for them during their powerless and impoverished human lives, as they lived. He offered them the Kingdom of God to empower and enable while they lived. Hope was born and lived as those ancient Jews met and followed the rabbi, Jesus. To get a broader understanding of our faith, we will look at the Kingdom of God as a present experience to empower believers today, in this lifetime.

Worship has been central to Christianity since its inception. Jesus made worship an important part of his life from visiting the Jewish temples to isolating himself in the wilderness. How we bow before the greatness and wonder of God defines our worship. Do we worship to seek forgiveness or to give thanks? There is a significant difference between these. Seeking forgiveness is to gain something for ourselves. Giving thanks is recognizing what we have and that we are grateful.

A central symbol of worship is the cross. In Roman Catholicism the cross bears the body of Jesus crucified. The significance is rather straightforward the suffering of Jesus atones for our human sins and elevating Jesus to the cross raises him to Christ and to become part of the Trinitarian Godhead. This is necessary since all humans "fall short of the glory of God" (Romans 4:20). This can never be ignored, but I will stress, instead, worship as glorifying God, celebrating Christ, expressing joy because through Christ we receive and experience the Kingdom of God. Worship celebrates our salvation, given as a gift, not earned by exemplary behavior, but as a free gift to all. It is not restricted to a few who have "been saved," an elite few. We live better and freer lives when we are aware that God loves and saves us. We celebrate this by doing good for others and by taking risks for our faith rather than doing nothing because a failed risk threatens losing our spirits to sin. Salvation empowers us to live freely and fully with love in our hearts and joy in our spirits. We celebrate the Christian year in worship, formally in churches and informally in the solitude of our spirits.

———•◆•———

Christianity, a worldwide phenomenon, includes millions, who are racially and culturally diverse. Denominations separate us, Roman Catholics, Protestants, and Orthodox believers. Liberals and conservatives debate and argue heatedly. Christians are severely split concerning the meaning of our faith. Some denominations believe that their church or theology is the *only* way to salvation. Conservative Christians frequently suggest that more liberal Christians are not saved and face damnation.

Considering that Christians do not share a uniform belief, it is strange that we deny the validity of other beliefs that many non-Christians hold sacred. God is far too great to be contained in a single revelation to humanity. He is greater than the totality of human knowledge, and greater than all of the various beliefs that we know of in our rather secular world.

The issue of Christianity's relationship with world religions can only be dealt with honestly when Christians recognize there is one God but many ways to express or experience Her. This recognition of the oneness of God experienced in many ways helps to keep our faith valid and alive. Historically the Judeo-Christian communities admitted this when the Israelites claimed to be the chosen of God and, at the same time, said that there was only one God. This implies that all non-Jews had the same God but were not special. Strangely, early in the Old Testament, there were many gods, including Yahweh the God of the Jews, and Baal the god of the pagans.

These concepts will be central to helping us rethink our Christian faith stressing the positive, exploring worship to grasp a deeper understanding of our faith, and to discover a genuine ecumenical spirit, so we can share and respect all humans.

------·◈·◈·------

The structure of this book follows the seasons of the Christian year as developed by the Church over the centuries. The meaning of the Christian faith can be discovered through these seasons and offers a way to cover key aspects of faith.

The seasons cover all aspects of Christianity, because they systematically move through the important events both before and after the Resurrection. Interpreting the seasons provides a new and refreshing way to view Christian thinking or theology. This approach is not systematic theology, that is, visiting each dogma and exploring it thoroughly, but, rather, approaches our faith as Christians experience it in public and private worship.

The Christian year is a starting point to better understand our faith and sharpen our celebratory experiences. Rather than escaping problems by giving up personal responsibility and having God take care of us, we freely celebrate our faith, our Christ, and ourselves more thoroughly. We establish new highlights around the joys of faith and we strengthen our fellowship in faith rather than worrying excessively about sin and death or slipping into self-glorification by stressing personal salvation. The Cross, for example, elevates Jesus to being far more than his pain and suffering, to a living and joyful Christ. The promise is that we, too, will be lifted up and discover new, better, and more meaningful lives, and will relate to others with less selfishness and greater fellowship, *koinonia.*

The final chapters fall under "Kingdomtide," a less specific season that I use to add relevant topics not adequately covered in the other seasons. This also offers an opportunity to further explore what we can learn from the historical Jesus.

Chapter One
ADVENT, THE BEGINNING

Music surrounds us as Christmas carols announce the coming of Santa Claus and gifts for all. Ringing cash registers receiving money frequently jar the beauty of the season. Gay wrappings surround strange objects like light poles, automobiles, sides of buildings, pictures on walls, and even a few people. In some stores, sales personnel wear red, pointed, and tasseled hats trimmed with white fur. The mood is festive, at least on the surface, for amidst the joy a few show sad eyes and bowed heads, for the festive season stirs memories of not so festive events in their lives.

Thanksgiving family celebrations have just passed and colorful leaves on the trees fall swiftly to the ground to be blown into piles and burned, or placed in black plastic bags and toted away. Colorful scarves surround necks to keep warmth in while bared heads invite the cold in. It is a season of great contradictions. Chilly days split by warm Indian summer days. Excited expectations contrast with tragic memories of earlier years. Some retail businesses rely on the sales of this season to make the entire year profitable and successful.

It is Christmas for most, and Jews elevate Hanukkah so they can share the holiday mood and gifts, too. This is tragic, because a relatively unimportant Jewish holiday is elevated to compete with Christmas, which perverts a very rich Jewish tradition. Christian churches are decorated with crèches and evergreens costumed in ornaments, tinsel, and colored lights. On Sundays, the usual day to gather for worship, extra flower arrangements brighten up stern and dignified sanctuaries and special holiday offering envelopes are strategically placed in pews or chairs.

Slogans abound. "Christmas is for children." "Remember those you love." "Keep Christ in Christmas." The latter suggests that the commercialism of a religious holiday should yield to faithful worship and retooling our spiritual values.

However, the Christian Church calendar belies all this. It is not Christmas, but Advent, a season of anticipation and preparation, personal reassessment and looking ahead to a new birth. If we ponder the difference between the commercial Christmas and the traditional Advent, there is far less difference than we might think.

Commercialized Christmas celebrates giving and receiving gifts; traditional Advent celebrates the gift of new life given by birth and rebirth. Both focus on human life and bettering it. One focuses by giving and receiving gifts and the other by having faith and receiving new life.

A difficulty of Advent is that it is a mishmash of sentimentalism and powerful mythic stories. Lest this latter remark be seriously misunderstood, let us look at what myth can and should be, so that we can better understand it as a powerful concept that stretches human hearts and minds. Myth is the way that humans over many, many centuries have dealt and presently deal with Truth. Let us look at these terms.

———————

Truth is not fact. Fact is data, something that is verifiable in reality. It can be tested against what we see and by experiment and does not depend on the human mind, except as a receptor and interpreter, but exists in the world. Fact is, in a sense, scientific reality.

Truth, on the other hand, relates to human experience, to what it means to be human with thoughts, ideas, beliefs, values, fears, friends, loves, prejudices, memories, anticipations, dreams, and a myriad of other emotions and intellectual musings. Truth is, in a sense, spiritual and philosophic reality. Humans are fact only in that they exist. Beyond that we filter everything through preconditioned brains. For example, seeing children playing on a school playground, may elicit a variety of emotions from the same person or countless emotions from several people. An individual may see himself, filtered through memories, as a happy tot frolicking with friends one moment or see a frightened lad being pushed and shoved by a school bully the next. Another person may see her daughter as she was as a toddler, while still another sees a crowd of noisy, pesky brats.

The children are in the playground; this is fact. What a person sees and reacts to is quite another matter; this is truth, rather than fact, because our feelings are part of what we see and experience. This is simple truth, not verifiable, but part of who we are as thinking and feeling humans. Truth is not scientific, but tinged by emotion and memories, prejudices and fears. It is how we view and interpret life. Standing on the beach we may look out and see a stunning watery vista or we may see the reflected heat of a hot and uncomfortable day. Truth is an individual experience.

Put a capital letter in front, Truth, and we add another dimension by adding values and ideals. This elevates truth to a more universal, idealistic, and spiritual level, to Truth. Truth can be approached philosophically or religiously and, somehow, these are often parallel. For major religions and most philosophies, murder and stealing are forbidden. Other moral/ethical issues are divisive. Religions generally, but not universally, frown on homosexually, but, more and more, theologians and philosophers either ignore it or find it an acceptable and natural alternative.

Truth, as a universal, is elusive. It is different between diverse social realities, religious institutions, political philosophies, the scientific community, and sports enthusiasts. Nevertheless, Truth is a key part of our society. In modern America, politicians, especially as they campaign, carefully explain the Truth on the various issues, sometimes *ad nauseum*, as they try to convince voters that they are the best ones to ensure that their concept of Truth is enforced. However, history shows us that the most significant way to communicate Truth is through story and symbol, not lecturing or sermonizing. A simple story can evoke vivid and meaning-ful responses. Delight can be mixed with horror while compassionate tears are dried with squeals of laughter.

When we hear that someone received a raise, we share their joy. But hear the story of how that raise came to happen and we enter into the experience. With the first we may sympathize, but with the second, we may empathize, entering into the event, sharing feelings and under-standings, and uniting with the story's protagonist.

One type of story is myth. Myth is Truth shared in story and symbol. The gods and stories of Greek mythology demonstrate how effective this can be. Who knows how it began? People wondered about how the world began and why people are the way they are. They saw lightening strike and destroy a tree, and this frightened and confused them. What kind of power lay behind the lightening bolt? They did not know, but one day a story was told and circulated about a god who capriciously hurls thunder bolts. These stories evolved and covered a variety of concerns. This birthed mythology.

The mythological Greek gods are interesting because they are quite hu-manlike. These gods had husbands and wives, sexual affairs, terrible tem-pers, and did stupid things, but still had enormous power. People relate better to stories that display human characteristics. Christianity fol-lows this same pattern when its central revelation is the very human Jesus.

Myths were not frivolous stories, but critical for interpreting living. They explained the unexplainable and curried worship and awe. Many honored and worshipped mythical religions hoping that this would influence the activities of the gods for more favorable results. Myths are not exclusive to the Greeks. Modern Hinduism focuses on myth to express and interpret its faith. Today's American culture supports many myths, some imploded by recent historical research. George Washington and his cherry tree and his huge throwing arm demonstrate American myths that imploded.

Mohandas Gandhi is now truly a myth for he transcended mere earthly accomplishments to ascend to near superhuman stature. Albert Einstein, the super mind who developed marvelous theories about the universe while sitting in an office without scientific equipment, is a modern myth. Some may call these men legendary, but we raise their names as synonyms for peace and brilliance. Gandhi and Einstein have become more mythical than real. What has its seed in fact can evolve in myth. Both Gandhi and Einstein were genuine people but, by their accomplishments became far more and took on mythical characteristics by becoming bigger than life (Gandhi became almost god-like and Einstein was perceived as a mental superman as we reflect upon them.)

Christianity has created a wealth of mythical tales and people. Genesis relates two competitive stories of creation, the seven-day sequence and Adam and Eve. Both explain, in their own distinct way, the mysteries of the world and creation. One stresses the elevation of humanity over other living creatures; the other exposes the weaknesses of the human spirit. To interpret them literally destroys their power. To see them as myths is to find their power, the power to open insight and understanding, and instill faith.

The New Testament is not devoid of mythical stories. One of the most powerful is Jesus' prayer in the Garden of Gethsemane. On the evening of his trial before the Sanhedrin, Jesus goes to the Garden of Gethsemane with Peter, James, and John, three of his closest disciples and prays about his impending ordeal of being tried, convicted by the religious leaders, and crucified the next afternoon. He leaves the three disciples behind and prays alone, and his disciples fall asleep. Taken literally, the scene could have happened, but not been recorded, since the story explicitly says that Jesus was alone and those closest to him asleep. There was no one to hear and record the prayer. Also, the prayer anticipates the coming ordeal before his arrest, so-called trial, conviction, and execution. This requires knowing exactly what will happen before it happens, which makes him more than a human and, therefore, not a full partner in the total human experience. Looked at mythically, we can relate to the story as one of human agony and fear, but also triumph. Struggling to understand and accept what will happen to him, Jesus shares his agony and fear with God, then, having confessed his weaknesses, he accepts the bleak and fearful future.

———•◦•◦•———

Advent is a season for introspection, preparation, and hope. To fully understand it, let us look at Jesus' introspection, preparation, and hope as portrayed by the Gospel writers who filtered the earthly life of Jesus through the Resurrected Lord. These writers could not look at the stories of Jesus as verifiable biography or history, because their view exposed the mythical power of the stories handed down about Jesus. The writers had experienced the agony of the humiliating death of Jesus, if not personally, at least through the stories passed from generation to generation. Coupled with this sense of loss, however, they experienced a presence of their Lord of faith, the Risen Christ, the wonder of the existence in their lives of Jesus speaking to them as they lived. This meant that their immediate experience was what was most crucial to faith. They cared little about the human Jesus and more about what they were feeling. Paul substantiates this solidly with his only reference to Jesus was his explanation of the Lord's Supper, the beginning of communion. Paul makes no other reference to Jesus the man, how he lived his life or even of his transforming parables.

The result of the post resurrection experiences of the members of the early church suggests that the Gospels are a collection of powerful, faith-inducing mythical stories that reveal something about the human Jesus, but also a huge amount of the Jesus that the writers and the early church experienced through the Resurrected Lord, their faith beyond his death, and their experiences of faith years after. There may have been factual stories, but this made no difference, because they were looking to reveal the Truth. Still, these original and mythical stories of Jesus are our guides to understanding the various sides of Jesus that we now use to celebrate during the various Christian seasons.

From the evidence we have, however biographical (fact) or mythical (Truth) it may be, we do have hints of the introspective Jesus. Two stories, in particular, stand out for me as illustrative, the temptation scenes early in the Gospels and the prayer in the Garden of Gethsemane.

Although the temptations are recorded as a dialog with Satan, it appears to me to be more revealing when we see the parallels between the story and the temptations we all face, from time-to-time, in our own lives. Including the very wealthy, most of us want more money to spend and enjoy. Frequently, this means that we have to choose between what we believe is right, moral, and ethical and the temptations to cheat on our taxes, keep the extra money that a cashier gave us by mistake (as the computer age continues, this is less frequent than when cashiers had to calculate the change themselves), cheating people with false or misleading statements or advertising, or putting out shoddy workmanship to add to the profit margin. For a peasant like Jesus, food (bread) was money. Jesus had to consider the options and possibilities. He chose to refuse the temptation and go with the way of God, the right, the moral, and the ethical.

This illustrates both the introspection and preparation that highlight the meaning of Advent. There is also hope. Having made a decision, Jesus looked ahead with satisfaction and joy because he renewed his relationship to God affirmatively and confidently.

Such is the meaning of Advent. It looks ahead, but cannot do so without both introspection and preparation. To understand this better, I want to look at hope or anticipation first.

Advent points to several things at the same time, the birth of Jesus, the coming of Christ (the Second Coming), and human rebirth. These are inextricably linked and distinctly different. Only Luke and Matthew tell the fascinating story of the birth of Jesus; nowhere else in the New Testament is this story told. The account in Luke recalls the dramatic birth of Jesus that caused great rejoicing. The child born was unique and filled with promise. His uniqueness is buttressed by the account of Jesus at age twelve showing hints of his wisdom at the temple, a wisdom that promises to increase with age.

Matthew in contrast portrays the birth as tragic, causing the family of Jesus to flee to save the newborn's life threatened by the evil intrigue of Herod.

Jesus lived in an oppressive culture, born into an oppressive society ruled by absentee landlord, Caesar from distant Rome. In the first century, the lower classes, peasants, artisans, and merchants, were relatively powerless. It was a culture dominated by wealth and royalty, a dominance characterized by great injustice and economic inequality.

Enough is known about the culture and economy of Jesus' time in Israel and the general Mediterranean region from several historical sources that we can make some inferences. The most significant ones are the oppression of peasants like Jesus, the politics of survival, the Jewish resistance to religious absorption by Rome or the regional religions that competed with Judaism, and the economics of social stratification and domination. We know that the peasant son of an artisan and his youthful wife were born among them, but little about his childhood or youth or the actual conditions of his home, education, and preparation for adulthood.

I am convinced that the primary mission of the human Jesus, the magnetic and rebellious roving teacher, was to offer the Kingdom of God to all people, but primarily to his social and economic peers who were oppressed, hungry, fearful, and frequently hopeless. When the contemporaries of Jesus recalled stories about him, they heard stories of hope and fulfillment in a hostile world. Their dreams were far more modest than ours today. They wanted enough food and the opportunity to own land that could not be stolen by greedy nobles. There they could grow their own food and, perhaps, have a little left over to sell. Contrary to the way many portray him today, Jesus was not militaristic or violent; therefore he could not offer his contemporaries a physically won freedom by warfare or even armed skirmishes from the occupying Roman legions or the traitorous Jewish leaders who worked with the Romans (the Herods, for example). Another approach was needed that embraced the people without violating God's principles.

Jesus offered them, instead, the Kingdom of God. He offered friendship to the friendless, straightened backs bent by oppression, replaced frowns with smiles, inspired a zest for life in hopeless ones, and brought salvation to the forgotten. This was not some pie-in-the-sky dream for something in the far future such as after death, but the Kingdom of God in their lives as they lived.

———•◦•———

The Kingdom of God (Heaven) is a central theme of Jesus of Nazareth. He begins most of his parables with "The Kingdom of God is like…." In my opinion, the Kingdom of God defies simple interpretations. For centuries, religious thinkers have tried to define it precisely, but Jesus did not want the Kingdom of God to be easily or dogmatically interpreted. He uses story to define it, and all of his stories are different, allowing the Kingdom to be interpreted by each individual listener by inviting a story, teaching, or saying to reach into her mind and heart. Hearing a story evokes conscious thoughts, memories, experiences, fantasies, dreams, fears, hopes, doubts, ideas, and even thoughts that are buried deep in our unconscious. Hence, a story can be understood or interpreted differently by each listener.

The Kingdom of God is not a place, but a condition of the human spirit. When his audiences heard a parable of Jesus, they could of course ignore it, or they could let it enter their psyches to shatter preconceptions and prejudices, and to wrestle with their conscious thoughts, memories, experiences, fantasies, dreams, fears, hopes, doubts, ideas, and even thoughts buried deep in their unconscious. This had the power to change who they were, however dramatic or subtle the change may have been.

Today, we tend to seek the Kingdom of God to relieve our fear of spending eternity in Hell. We focus on what we may become after death, wanting to safely pass through the gates of Heaven. Although we are trapped in the present, we hope for a future with God in bliss and contentment and where oppressive domination no longer exists. Jesus understood the ongoing pain of his neighbors and friends, the impoverished and wealthy, and the powerless and the powerful. They did not seek some future relief after death; instead they desired to find and tap into something right then, in the midst of their lives that freed them to reach for God and human dignity, to transform hopelessness into hope, lift up broken spirits and heal them, show the lost the way, and transform hope into a reality for their day. They had problems that assailed them daily, and for them, sin was less of a problem than being sinned against by the "powers and principalities," by a political and religious system that dominated their world and removed justice and equity, principles in which Jesus deeply believed.

Modern people are plagued with a psychological state of mind called guilt, as opposed to sin, that may or may not relate to an ill deed or ill will. Guilt may be better identified by today's science, but it has existed throughout human history, even though we have only identified the feeling scientifically in the modern age. Today we confess to God in order to find absolution or freedom from feeling guilty about our sinful acts so that we will be worthy to enter the Kingdom of God.

Jesus thought a bit differently. He reached into people's hearts and minds to show their worthiness in their immediate lives, not in some far distant future. "The Kingdom of God is within you," he said. Jesus presented them Heaven on earth as he showed them the resources within themselves to raise their self-esteem, lift bowed heads, and transform hesitant and fearful attitudes into self-confidence. The peasants may not have been wealthy but, perhaps for the first time, they knew that the value of their lives was as great as any king, wealthy landowner, arrogant religious leader, or even Caesar. Before, they had walked with crushed spirits; Jesus taught them to walk side-by-side with him and, therefore, with God.

———————

This interpretation changes Advent. Jesus offers us salvation, the Kingdom of God, as today's reality. We no longer have to look to the future for salvation; we have it. Now we look ahead to how we can respond to the gift that Jesus and God have given us. We anticipate a new thrill to live and to live in such a way that we bring honor to God and to ourselves. Good deeds are no longer selfishly designed to win us Heaven, but as thanksgiving for the Kingdom of God that is ours now.

We still look forward to celebrating the birth of Jesus, the Second Coming, and rebirth, not because they will come, but because they have already come. Before Jesus helped us to discover the Kingdom within ourselves, we lived today as a preparation for tomorrow. Now we live today so that we can make tomorrow better, take risks for justice, embrace the ugly, heal the sick, lift up the beaten and forgotten, promote peace for our world, pacify violence, share with the poor, and befriend the friendless.

Advent reminds us of the life of Jesus and the power of the Resurrected Lord as our own faithful potential fully realized. We anticipate tomorrow because today is so marvelous for those who have met Jesus and experienced the Christ.

When I was a child, my parents made Christmas so full that each year my anticipation was uncontainable. Each Christmas Eve, I walked up the stairs to my bedroom with eyes glued to the living room rearranged for Santa Claus, who would come, tinsel the tree with decorations and lights, create a snowbound village, and place gifts so happily wrapped that I knew I would never sleep. I was always anxious. What if Santa Claus never came? Or, what if Santa left everyone gifts but me, naughty me?

My anxiety was wasted, for upon arising in the morning a fantasy world occupied our living room. The tree was gaudy and beautiful, the village only needing people walking around to make it real, and far too many gifts. I can never remember being disappointed. Never!

Christmas Eve was my childish Advent, my anticipation of finding a new world the next day. A world that only truly lasted a few brief days until life became normal and routine again. The Christian Advent is more like Christmas morning when the child delights in the beauty and wonder of the day. Except, and this is critical, Advent is not external with fanciful trees and villages, and scads of gifts. Christian Advent is internal, a magical revision of who we are, not perfection, but imperfect people of faith who wear the robes of the Master.

———•◆•———

Wearing the robes of the Master is a pretentious remark that requires explaining. Most of what we know about him is from the New Testament, primarily the four Gospels. However, the Gospels were written several generations after his crucifixion, not by his original followers but by those removed by a generation or more. Memories of Jesus came to them by way of those elders who knew Jesus and their spiritual descendents. There was another critically important factor: these anecdotal memories and stories about Jesus were buttressed by the writers who had themselves experienced the Resurrected Lord.

After Jesus died, those of the earliest church encountered him in a uniquely different way. Reflections of this are recorded in the Gospels, most sharply in Luke's Gospel in the road to Emmaus meeting. Luke tells the story of two of the disciples/apostles walking on the road on the way to Emmaus talking about the death of Jesus when they were joined by Jesus, whom they did not recognize. They told him about the events of his death. Jesus explained to them the reason behind the events, and they still did not know who he was. The disciples arrived at the village where they were to stay and invited him to stay with them, since it was late in the day. While dining with them, he reenacted the last supper causing them to recognize him and he disappeared.

If we look at this literally, word-for-word, we find a magical and miraculous encounter. If we see this as a parable told by the church to express what is truly inexpressible by normal human speech, then we find ourselves meeting a new kind of miracle. To grasp this latter reality, we must use our imaginations and recreate, to some extent, what it must have been like to have met Jesus and what that encounter meant.

Jesus, a very special person, had an extraordinary relationship with God. Jesus' relationship with his contemporaries, from what we can determine from the Gospels, was also extraordinary. Jesus befriended the powerless and impoverished, those who in return had no power to help and protect him from arrest and execution. He frequently healed without asking for faith. Some healings appeared to be generated by the individual's faith, and without reference to faith in Jesus. When Jesus was absent, as when he sent his disciples on a mission, his disciples could do much that Jesus did. What was the basis and source of their strength, healing, and wisdom? It does not appear that He gave it to them, but, rather, that he taught them to use the inner resources already available within them. He demonstrated this by using the power within him as an example. Jesus empowered those around him, neither by touch nor word, neither by ordaining nor by anointing them, but by example.

Jesus understood the power within him, though not perfectly, because he was a human, not God dressed in human skin and clothing. He understood this power better than others because of his special relationship with God. Jesus accepted that he was the son of man, a human, a gift of God. As a genuine human he related to other human beings, those he had contact with, the Twelve, the followers who walked with him, and the larger audiences who went to him when he visited their villages. He was one of them, not separate or above them. God had not sent Jesus to be an elitist, to dominate others, or to have greater powers, but to be one of them.

As such, the edge he had was that he knew the image of God was in him, that he could tap resources within himself of which most of the faithful were completely unaware. Jesus embraced those who knew and accepted him by giving them a glimpse of who they truly were and how they could realize and use the powers that God had already given to them, what Genesis called the image of God. This new awareness transformed those who surrounded Jesus. Not only did Jesus give them dignity in a world that viewed them as low-lifes, but he also gave them hope that awoke their insights, vision, and power to deepen the quality of their lives.

Walking in the robes of the Master was accepting and using the power of the image of God in them that Jesus had exposed. Without Jesus, they were ignorant and blind to this image, but Jesus enabled them to be aware of their Godly image. After Jesus brought out the image of God within them, they donned the robes of the Master. They no longer awaited something marvelous to happen in the future, but already had found it in their present lives.

This power is also our power. We, too, can know Jesus, experience the image of God that he experienced, and be transformed to know, feel, and use the power that Jesus has shown us.

This is like children waking up on Christmas Eve and finding that Santa Claus had already been there, and they no longer anticipate the excitement of the next day. They live the excitement of the day the gifts become theirs. The genuine Christmas gift is the teachings, stories, and memories of Jesus. As adult Christians we understand that Santa Claus is a childish hope, but we wear the robes of the Master, experience what Jesus set free in us, and realize the image of God within. Tomorrow becomes today, and our potential is immediately realized. Faith frees us to be.

To celebrate the Christian season of Advent is to live today what we thought was reserved for the future.

Chapter Two
CHRISTMAS, THE BIRTH

Roman Catholics celebrate Christmas Eve Midnight Mass, freeing families to be together on Christmas morning. Protestants tend not to have Christmas day worship unless it falls on a Sunday. This suggests what Christmas means to most American Christians: that the family, gift giving and receiving, and Santa Claus are central to celebrating Christmas.

Some suggest that the origin of giving gifts at Christmas is Matthew's account of the birth and the Magi showering gifts on the infant child. This is probably true, especially if we look at gift giving to children, though this does not account for the huge popularity of Santa Claus (the Coca-Cola® version of a jolly white-bearded man in a red suit). Clements's poem, "T'was the Night before Christmas," reinforces this focus on children at Christmas. Taken together these have birthed a Christmas myth. The myth, as Truth, expresses the joy of Christmas as found in children. After all, "Christmas is for children."

The early church created a Christmas myth when it recorded the two stories of the birth of Jesus that headed in different directions. Together they give Jesus god-like qualities. His birth brought foreign sages offering gifts for the child, frightening a king, and causing angels to sing sweetly to shepherds in the fields. Jesus' birth was portrayed as extremely low and humble in a Bethlehem manger, and at the same time as very high and regal, receiving kingly gifts and causing King Herod to intrigue against the child. Tradition merged these images together in crèches with kings taking gifts to the grungy animal shelter and laboring sheep herders kneeling in worship. Logically, these stories are contradictory, but when viewed together Jesus becomes a mythical figure of holiness more closely related to the post-resurrection Christ, the Risen Lord than to Jesus, the fragile human infant warmed by the body heat of barn animals or royally born as

Matthew suggests. This gap between the human Jesus and the risen Lord is critical in understanding our faith. The human Jesus gave us some specific teachings and guidance and stories. The Risen Lord gives Christians individual and collective experiences with the Lord beyond the grave. Christmas offers insights into the meaning of both, but, most clearly, a human Jesus.

At Christmas, Christians reflect on what their faith means. The possibilities are, of course, far more than we can effectively deal with here. Still, there are some that jump out because they are so common. These can be seen in the contrasts: foreigners bearing gifts for the child, a frightened king plotting evil, angels singing, a lowly manger, and kings in an unkempt stable.

———•◦•———

Transforming Christmas into a commercial affair that neglects or forgets its spiritual values outrages many Christians. Nevertheless, this transformation reveals our non-religious expectations for Christmas. We want to see people, especially children, happy. Christmas gifts make people happy. As we carefully or carelessly rip gift wrappings from packages holding secret prizes, we anticipate what surprises the wrappings hide, and this excites us. Small children sometimes belie this because colored paper, carefully tied ribbons, and tinseled decorations dazzle their eyes. Not too many years later they realize that the disguised surprises are more important than the festooned packages.

Gift givers watch excitedly to see whether their gifts are appreciated; so their hearts warm as nerves twitch. They want their hours of shopping, accepting and rejecting ideas, spending, and daydreaming about how wonderful the gift is, to be appreciated. This excitement and anticipation are powerful emotions; after all giving a gift may change a person's mood, fulfill their expectations, and create laughter and tears.

The ancient people, as they composed the New Testament, understood the birth of Jesus as a gift given them. If they had personally encountered the man Jesus, they looked back from this encounter to see Jesus' birth as the sign of what kind of a man he would become. If modern Christians could only emulate the ancient ones, we, too, could see Jesus as a man. Ah, to see Jesus with children on his knee rather than a heavenly and angelic chorus, Jesus embracing a body made ugly with open sores rather than a haloed saintly head, Jesus complimenting a wizened old woman rather than a sacred glimmering vision ascending, or Jesus walking on dusty roads accompanied by friends rather than a white robed apparition floating serenely in heavenly clouds.

The infant Jesus should remind Christians of our own humanity and the wonder that we can see God in a human and a human in God. The incarnation is not some empty thought that pictures God in the skin and clothing of a human, but that we see the image of God in all humans. Jesus becomes the window for us to see God within us. The infant Jesus does not reveal an ethereal, mysterious God but the genuine presence of the holy in all of us. Looking at the infant Jesus tells us that we have a relationship that is more than prayer or adoration, but union, becoming one, both frail human and divine, realizing the holiness within each of us.

As we celebrate Christmas, we need to see the humanity behind it, not just the divinity. When we look at the divinity, we tend to look for divine intervention, for God to take over, to remove personal responsibility, and to do for us what we feel powerless to do for ourselves. My e-mail is constantly deluged with prayers asking for God to do something for us. Worse, the e-mails are frequently converted from prayer to pure and obnoxious superstition by promising that if we forward this particular e-mail to a certain number of people, we will be blessed, guaranteed.

This is pathetic for it transforms the God of Jesus of Nazareth into a modern Merlin whom we control. When something is guaranteed certain and when we follow the correct formula, in this case forwarding the e-mail, and God must respond and obey us; we humans are completely in control. Some Christians believe that salvation is identical; that is, if we follow the correct way or path, we will be saved. This path is based on faith and obedience. The reward for faithfulness and obedience is salvation. In other words, okay God, I did my part, now you do yours. This is a struggle for power between the praying person and God.

The face of the infant Jesus, through Christmas, takes another path. Instead of humans forcing God to act, God, in Jesus and in each of us, empowers us to act. Jesus spoke, and the lame man walked; Jesus did not walk for him. Jesus beckoned, and Peter walked on water, at least until he saw himself as weak and phony, then Peter forgot or ignored the God within and began to sink. Christmas celebrates our becoming who we can be when we let the divine image within us come to the fore and empower us. Jesus showed us this when he walked among us; he healed, taught religious truths, told parables to disturb us, and showed us who we can be when we let ourselves free the God within.

An infant is powerless. This may appear strange when discussing Jesus of Nazareth. Look at an infant, especially a new-born. There is nearly total powerlessness. The infant relies on parents to meet every need. Adults feed, clothe, clean, comfort, and love. About all an infant can do is complain and gurgle — that is, cry when hungry, fuss when dirty, and coo when comforted.

This is a great way to view God, as a powerless infant, unable to condemn or punish, strike out in anger or revile. An infant will neither sentence us to hell nor welcome us to heaven. The fantastic influence of an infant is to pull from us the best within. Infants evoke our love and caring, our vulnerabilities and strengths, and our dreams and fears.

An infant is potential. Looking at a tiny infant, we see what will be. Her blank mind will fill with knowledge, good and evil; empty eyes will see beauty and ugliness; unused ears will hear the cooing of a loving mother and the ubiquitous cautions, "No! No!" As important to many parents are the visions and dreams to be fulfilled, bodies garbed with graduation gowns and caps, gratifying careers, and laughing and adoring grandchildren.

It is, also, our potential. All of us have potential not yet realized. Too often we limit ourselves to past experience and do not broaden our appreciation of what can be. An accountant may not see the potential of becoming a scientist; a scientist may believe that accounting is boring and so cut off any potential for it; a man may see himself as ugly and not see any personal potential for attractiveness; a woman may see herself as a homemaker and not envision any potential for clothing design. Lost potential limits life. Realized potential enhances life.

The infant Jesus shows us potential realized. Born a peasant impoverished in a world dominated by Rome and local Jewish leaders who grabbed their leadership by bowing before Caesar, the infant Jesus was powerless. His parents, Mary and Joseph, saw something completely different. They saw what was to be: chubby arms would become muscled and strong; the cooing sound from between his lips would speak clearly; pudgy fingers would touch and embrace with love; kicking legs would grow long to carry him swiftly in his passage through life; and innocent eyes would see the love and concern given him as they would show love and concern for others.

Upon reflection, his followers would see a once helpless infant as a man who dared to disagree with religious, political, and economic authorities; a man with a gentle voice who told delightful and difficult stories as well as speaking wisdom boldly; a man who would die rather than compromise the holy principles on which he based his life; a man who embraced the ugly and diseased fearlessly; and a man who loved the unlovable like the despicable tax-gathers.

There's another side to the perspective of the infant Jesus that is too often neglected. As much as he gave as an adult, he received as a child. He was not a child-god walking on earth performing miracles and healings.

Unlike modern comic strip heroes, he could neither fly nor destroy his enemies. Rather, according to Matthew, the holy family fled to Egypt because they could not face or survive the injustice of Herod. Also, Jesus was fed by his mother, taught a trade by his father, learned wisdom from his parents and the local religious leaders, and was befriended by neighborhood children. What happened to the years when he "became an adult" at thirteen and when he began his ministry at around thirty? Thirty was relatively old in those days, and well beyond the age when a person chose a career. There is no evidence anywhere about these missing years, but I like to believe that he was preparing for what was to come. He may not have been conscious of his preparation as he gathered more knowledge and experience. His awakening appears to come late in his growth and development.

There is some evidence that he followed John the Baptist as a disciple. This opens more questions than we have answers. Was the gap between sitting at the feet of John and initiating his ministry long enough for him to absorb John's teachings and grow beyond them? Others argue that Jesus accepted and used some of the teachings of the Buddha. For some this is repugnant, but for Jesus to accept, adapt, and integrate effective and wise teachings from the philosophies of those before him makes sense.

Regardless, Jesus was a helpless infant and experienced the teenage traumas of maturing as did his friends and neighbors. For me, at least, this is one of his characteristics most endearing and important. The idea that my Lord was a super child chills my thoughts and faith. Basing my faith on the supernatural well beyond human experience belies the values and revelation of Jesus of Nazareth. Christmas is a reminder that the divine is not some abstract and out-there concept, but that God in Christ entered into our world to share our experiences and become real like us. Jesus did not come to be remote from us, but to join with us.

Christmas is a reminder that God reaches out to us, not with a booming and forbidding voice of chastisement, but as a reality that merges with our living and being. The infant Jesus was as fragile as we; the child, as impish as any child in our generation. He grew into an adult who shifted from the thought and faith of John the Baptist to develop new thoughts and a new faith that went beyond his Jewish roots and his lessons from the Baptizer.

Christmas destroys the old debate that raged centuries and lingers today that Jesus was totally God in human form. Nonsense, Jesus was totally human who was given godliness to reveal the spark of the divine to us all. A helpless and dependent infant does not contain the wholeness of God. Rather, he gained the wisdom of God in his work with fellow human beings.

Luke tells a tender birth story filled with exaltation tempered with humble surroundings. Matthew paints of picture of adoration and evil royal intrigue. Both are fascinating narratives that share a reality of the human encounter with the divine. A cursory look at religions worldwide reveals the tendency to view the gods as royalty. Christianity is chief among them with liturgical pageantry of elaborate and rich garments for the clergy, throne-like chairs (cathedrals) in the altar or communion table area, and Pope-mobiles to display the royally robed Pope while protecting him. One of the titles of Christ Jesus is King of Kings.

The adoration of the Magi that Matthew narrates elevates the infant Jesus above earthly royalty as the three kings (magi/wise men) bowed before him and offered gifts to the new king. Matthew looked backwards (he actually penned his Gospel several years after the fall of Jerusalem in 70 CE)[1] to see the glory of the adult Jesus reflected in the face of a baby.

Luke's visit of the shepherds at the animal stable portrays the scene as one of poverty and humility, of ordinary men visiting a baby born beneath their own social station because Jesus was born among domesticated animals that were tamed and cowed. Even in those ancient days of

[1] To respect people of all religions scholars now use CE (Common Era) rather than AD, a Christian reference

primitive living, birthing a child in a stable with its smells of animal droppings and unclean environment was the antithesis of Matthew.

As history, these contradictory accounts are seriously flawed. However, as theology they are magnificent for the universality of Jesus is clearly sketched. Jesus was not and is not the exclusive property of a particular part of culture, but belongs to all. Modern religious thinkers would explain this *ad nauseum*, but the Gospels tend to imitate the parables of Jesus by sharing Truth through story and narrative.

How marvelous it is for Christmas to offer so much insight into the nature of Jesus and his ministry. The crèche, although beautified with color and reverence, points to the humanity of Jesus, his vulnerability, his poverty and wealth. He was an infant who was totally dependent upon others, no magical cape to wear as he shot through the sky, no super powers that easily vanquished his enemies, and no bigger than life brain that permitted him to read minds and anticipate events.

The child in the manger with straw as a mattress is venerated today by Christians and many others because he entered our world as frail as we, needing love and care in order to grow and mature. Later, he would leave an indelible mark upon his and future generations, which distorts our perspective of the tiny and vulnerable baby.

It is this vulnerability that freed him to become totally part of the human experience, to know pain and failure as well as love and support, to experience despair and elation, to participate in the ups and downs that comprise our human journey through life. This sharing of our humanity at every level freed Jesus to become the compassionate and virile man who lived to save and free us.

This is the meaning of Christmas, not the commercial success to help our economy, not the jolly fat man giving gifts, and not the sweet Christmas carols that fill the air, but the descent into the world of God in Jesus, the Savior who can lift us from our worst in this world to offer fulfillment and hope. The fragile baby in a manger is God's Christmas gift to us.

Chapter Three
EPIPHANY, THE SHOWING

Epiphany (appearance or manifestation) follows Christmas and celebrates the arrival of the Magi in Bethlehem. Some Christians such as most Orthodox churches celebrate Christmas on Epiphany. Still, for most of us, we celebrate Epiphany with little concern for its meaning. After all, we have been celebrating Christmas during Advent and removing our Christmas decorations, including the crèche, the day after.

Traditionally, Epiphany ends the twelve days of Christmas to mark the length of time it took the Magi to reach Bethlehem. To come from the eastern areas was a grueling and punishing journey; it certainly took far longer than twelve days. So, how did the twelve days become the tradition? There were the twelve tribes of Israel and the twelve disciples of Jesus. Of course the number of days that the Magi traveled is nowhere to be found in the New Testament. So, the faithful, who gradually developed the traditions and tenets of our faith and those who followed and helped mold the growing church, probably selected twelve days to honor the biblical significance of the number.

This directs us to a reality of our faith. The church over the centuries developed traditions that remain with us today, although not all are universally shared. Celibacy grew out of the monastic movement, but has been rejected by most, but not all, Protestant churches. Prohibition changed wine into grape juice for communion, but only for the more "pious" American denominations. Academic gowns worn by clergy to lead worship symbolize an educated clergy and became the norm for pulpit-oriented denominations. The painting, Salmon's Head of Christ, reinforced an image of a serene and well-groomed Western man rather than an Eastern Jew. American Christians relate more closely when Jesus looks like us.

Developing new traditions began with the Bible. A careful reading of the New Testament Gospels reveals some interesting passages added by the church to confirm the traditions developed early in the life of the church. Matthew 18, for example, concerns many issues that confronted the church; some are rather institutional and helped establish church order and authority such as excommunicating rowdy, crass, or doctrinally wrong followers. However, all we read in the New Testament about Jesus, his teachings and stories, suggest that excommunication would not have been an issue for him. He invited the dregs of society to follow him. He rejected no one, although some left him on their own initiative. Jesus simply would not have formalized a method to "excommunicate" anyone. He welcomed everyone, especially those whom society found lacking for whatever reason. The culture of Jesus' day would have cast from their villages those with ugly festering sores (lepers), but Jesus embraced them.

The sequence of the events in Jesus' life is not consistent between the Gospels. The best example of this is the episode in the Temple where Jesus upsets the money-changers table. In John this occurs early in the ministry of Jesus, in Chapter two. Mark puts it happening just before the passion, late in the Gospel. One Gospel explains that speaking in parables is the best way to communicate with people. Another Gospel writes that the parables confuse and hide the truth from the disciples. Mark appears to dislike the Apostles by repeatedly showing that they did not understand the teachings or words of Jesus. Matthew and Luke soften this until the Apostles become very solid in their understanding of what Jesus said to them. The Lord's Prayer in Matthew and Luke are not identical; the genealogies record different families. Matthew stresses the lineage of Mary and Luke, Joseph.

The so-called little Apocalypse (Mark 13) and the major Apocalypse (Revelation) appear to be quite different from the teachings of Jesus, the gentle persuasive man who preached, healed, told stories, and welcomed harlots and a hated tax-gatherer. Apocalypses talk of violence and death, of agonizing punishments, and good triumphing only with the power of war. This confirms the gap between the life of Jesus and the church that created the Gospels. Jesus died somewhere around 30 CE (AD). Paul wrote 1 Thessalonians about 50 CE, and the Evangelists wrote the Gospels after the fall of Israel in 70 AD. The Christian church was founded after Jesus' crucifixion.

Contrary to those who claim that these discrepancies between historical events and developed traditions cannot exist because the Bible is holy and, therefore, completely true, the discrepancies are a reality of our faith. These inconsistencies add to the holiness of the Bible. It is not the Book of Mormon, dictated by God or an angel to a robotic transcriber; it is a book of faith. If this human aspect were missing, then there would be no genuine relationship between the holy and the human. Those many people of faith, most of whom remain anonymous, wrote from their faith and religious experiences. They did not write to compose a holy book of faith. This distinction was bestowed by the Church three centuries later.

After the crucifixion, the church developed and grew among people who believed that Jesus, the man, had been resurrected into a Being they could feel inside themselves and experience together among gathered believers. Faithfulness meant that the God within them and the God within Jesus came to life in a transforming way. The awakened God within them was not a creature possessing them, but a presence inspiring them; not an alien taking over their minds, but a spirit encouraging individual thinking; not a puppeteer directing every movement, but a motivating guide.

Faithful humans were not prey to a "voice of God" speaking to them, but a presence of God enabling them to be more human, as Jesus was human. This presence creates thoughtful people who make choices, though not necessarily perfect choices. Skeptics often challenge religious experiences as if they are delusional or insane. This presupposes that the posture and understanding of the skeptic are correct and that of a religious person wrong. This is a huge intellectual leap with a touch of arrogance added. Certainly, some people have delusions based on neurosis or psychosis, but others, quite sane, have mystical experiences that cannot be tested by empirical methods. We must be cautious that because we do not share another's personal experience that they are wrong. They may be wrong for us, not for them. So it was and is with Christians and other people of faith, our experiences within our faith are genuine and real. Just because something appears not to make sense does not render it senseless.

Jesus understood this in his own life and ministry. His parables seemed to contradict cultural standards, apparently not making logical sense: some were enigmatic; some were confusing; some were challenging; all were thought provoking. Jesus did not point to one path as Paul later did, but to multiple paths that stirred and disturbed complacency and thinking and, therefore, stimulated the spirits of Jesus' listeners and challenged their ethical and moral values. He recognized difference of mind and perceptions and gave his audiences an opportunity to be different, they heard different clues in his stories and reacted quite differently and still were faithful to his message. We need to relearn that message of individual freedom of mind and interpretation.

The writers of the New Testament were faithful people who made free choices and dealt with aggravating problems. They felt and experienced God in Jesus, not as a psychological neurosis or a delusional voice, but a presence that guided and directed sane and faithful minds. The Gospels beautifully illustrate the faithfulness of their writers, each of whom responded to his own faith, the contemporary historical conditions, the general situations of their readers, and the information available to them.

For too many years Christians have dealt with the Gospel, the entire New Testament and the Old Testament, as if they were magical books dictated word-for-word to saintly but robotic scribes. This approach seriously denigrates our faith for it makes the ancient disciples and modern Christians into mindless, weak people who rely completely on the actions of God; God takes over and relieves them of responsibility rather than offering the opportunity to be responsible.

This is the opposite of the perspective of Jesus, who encouraged thought and respected people for whom and what they were. He did not want or expect obeisance, never asked anyone to bow before him, and never required anyone to suspend his or her judgment, although their values were frequently questioned and subsequently changed. Jesus never acted like an imperious god. Quite the opposite, he spoke to them to share ideas, perspectives, and faith.

The Gospel writers understood this freedom and created tiny books specifically designed to help people cope with day-to-day problems, to reduce hyperbole to more realistic perspectives, and to use familiar stories and folk tales to lead them to follow Jesus. The writers did not write biographies or history, but stories to inspire and express faith to people where and when they lived. Hence, Matthew, Mark, Luke, and John wrote for the people they encountered, broke bread with, and shared common milieus. Each stressed different things so that the four Gospels were different, not because they were intended to be different, but because the writers and each group of initial readers were different, lived in different locations, lived with different people, friends and relatives, lived in different political situations, and faced different threats. The model that Jesus established with his parables freed the Gospel writers to respond using their own minds and their own situations as they wrote.

This is why the church grew under the most horrifying conditions. Christianity was spawned in Israel, but its most rapid growth was in the Gentile's territories. There, Rome became a formidable enemy and created havoc among the Christians. The earliest Christian communities (churches) were scattered around the Mediterranean, each facing far different forms of opposition in quite different environments. The Christian movement worked its way through this, in part, because of the diversity of the Gospels, each addressing a unique situation; each recognizing the unique needs of its community; each bringing a slightly different aspect of Jesus of Nazareth; each revealing a very human Jesus; and each bringing the spirit of Jesus the Christ to their people in a way that they would know and experience him.

So, the epiphany of Jesus was not universally uniform. Rather, it met people where they were in their lives, considered where they lived, the forces that influenced them, the loves that molded them, and the politics that impacted them. This is how it should be. Any manifestation of Jesus and God in Jesus must be able to speak to a person in nearly any circumstance, and with a genuine humanness that we can effectively and faithfully relate to personally.

How marvelous it is that the New Testament is imperfect as humans are imperfect and yet it reveals perfection, an ideal to which we can strive. After all, perfection is not genuine; it is a construct of the human mind that converts what is into what should be. A look at the diverse theologies that presently coexist within Christianity illustrates this. What does perfection mean to a Roman Catholic? A Lutheran (Martin Luther)? A Presbyterian (John Calvin)? A Methodist (John Wesley)? A Mormon (Joseph Smith)? A Christian Scientist (Mary Eddy Baker)? A Jehovah's Witness? A Southern Baptist? A Primitive Baptist? A Pentecostal? To carry this even further, look at members of the same denomination in a variety of settings. A Roman Catholic in the United States does not think the same as a Roman Catholic serf in South America. A Methodist in Kansas does not have the same religious tenets as one in Sussex, England.

Jesus told his stories and shared his wisdom in the local streets, byways, and gathering places to people in specific and imperfect contexts. Perfection was not part of his formula, for he welcomed the most imperfect and related to them far better than to those who were near perfect (or thought they were). Remember that perfection is better defined by cultural rather than religious standards. Hence a "perfect" meal is quite different in Mexico compared to Libya. Similarly, a perfect woman in

Sweden will not look like her counterpart in Liberia. A perfectly well-dressed person in India will not wear the same clothing as one in Argentina. The same is true for moral and ethical standards. A moral person is not the same in fundamental Islam than in the rest of Islam, or in fundamental Christianity than in mainline churches. The difference can be quite startling.

Since only God is perfect, let's take another approach. Who are the elite? For most Americans the elite are those with wealth and power, the movers and shakers, those who have access to the highest in the land such as access to the President. Other elites are celebrities, sport stars, singers, actors, and other well-known people. No one expects them to be perfect, but they have, rather, a more perfect life. At least, this is the popular perspective. Popular though it may be, the Betty Ford Clinic is populated with the rich and famous and the powerful. This trend is bothersome for it highlights the wrong values. Justice is strongly slanted towards the haves. Economics are kept imbalanced. Equality does not exist.

In complete contrast, Jesus focused on those he would call the elite, the poor, the abused, the sick, the powerless, and the outcasts. These were the center of his relationships and the heart of his values. He told them stories and trusted them to understand and find meaning in them, shared his wisdom to broaden their enlightenment, and they broke bread together for them to draw closer to each other. Jesus believed in the quality of the human heart as the measure of the cream of society, not wealth and power.

To ensure we are talking the same language, let me define what I mean by "heart." This word is so badly abused and romanticized that its meaning is sometimes vague. It has multiple meanings from a physical muscle pumping blood to dreamy, emotional love. It also means inner strength, courage, and wisdom. This use of love is a relatively modern innovation. The Bible used a much less glamorous word, "bowels," to describe the same thing.

Let me go one step further and suggest that heart is more than inner strength, courage, and wisdom. Heart is who we are inside, our hopes and fears, our experiences and beliefs, our courage and our timidity, our values or lack of them, tolerances and prejudices, loves and hates. Our heart is often hidden behind a façade of conformity. Most of us tend to conform to the culture in which we live. If we do not, society calls us deviants. As a male, for example, if I began wearing mini skirts, most would laugh and think me crazy, and some would try to institutionalize me — to protect society from me, of course.

Maybe Jesus could or could not read into the depth of the human heart, the Gospels suggest he occasionally did, but he still he reaches into our innermost being most of the time. A dirty face never bothered him, but a dirty mind did. Poverty in the pockets never bothered Jesus, poverty in the heart did. He told parables to challenge the very being of his listeners, to reach into their hearts and their heads, and to embrace the inner and outer person.

This is the Epiphany, the sudden awareness in our hearts, the center of our humanness and the deepest part of our being, where the values of Jesus displace the values of the marketplace. The tradition of the Epiphany is the Magi arriving and "beholding" the Christ child. For us, it is similar; we behold Jesus, not visually, but in our hearts, in the very core of our being; he touches us where the feelings and ideas cut through the superficial cultural values and thoughts and reach inside to grab the heart of our being.

———————•◦•———————

More and more how we look physically is one of the most important values today. Cosmetic surgery is an extreme example of this, but so are diets. Walking through the checkout line at a supermarket, one may notice that nearly every month the *Reader's Digest* offers another diet used by a well-known celebrity. Youth change their styles to maintain status with peers and to look like everyone else in their age group. There appears to be endless advertisements on commercial television touting hair restoration from painting scalps to using drugs and scalp surgery.

Religion is no different. Churches reflect the values of their interpretation of faith, written or unwritten. High gothic ceilings suggest the vastness of God and point towards heaven, somber furnishings suggest God's solemnity, crosses and crucifixes symbolize God's great sacrifice, and kneeling benches reflect our human piety. The list is far longer, of course, and includes Sunday dress-up and carrying Bibles.

How does the modern church in America want to be seen? There are no obvious answers, but a plethora of many reflecting religious, cultural, and even political values. Compare an Episcopal cathedral with the simple architecture of a Jehovah's Witness kingdom hall, a Roman Catholic processional with a Pentecostal rolling in the aisles, a peace vigil with armed people pursuing heretics.

Churches are institutions located in certain spots and frequently have national headquarter buildings. Jesus, in contrast, had no home, no building. He went to people rather than asking them to come to him in a specific place. He never dressed to worship, but when he took his few prayer breaks from his followers, he just walked away. This is a critical difference in attitude. Nearly all religions have central places to meet and worship whether a church, synagogue, mosque, temple, or whatever. People are expected to attend these central sites. Indeed, many people experience God more in a house of worship than at home or riding in a car. Are not worship centers considered holy? When vandals vandalize a place of worship we call it desecration, a word with religious overtones. Enter a house of worship and one may either remove a head covering or put one on, a sign of respect for a holy place.

It is virtually impossible to identify how Christian churches want to appear, how they want their faith to be expressed. There are simply too many varieties to pick enough similar traits that are meaningful. Architecture can be a key to how worship houses should look, if the attitude of Jesus is to be seriously considered.

Worship houses can begin to recognize the orientation of Jesus toward people, especially those on the lower rungs of the cultural hierarchy. Jesus celebrated people. He praised a poor widow, dined with a hated tax-gatherer, put dirty and dusty children on his knees, befriended a prostitute, touched a leper, and healed a madman. To emulate this attitude is difficult, because we isolate the poor and powerless no less than did the ancient people of Jesus' day. We no longer have poor houses, but we have those who live in cardboard boxes, we allow them to hold all their possessions in stolen supermarket carts, and when we offer them shelter, we try to keep these shelters far away from our neighborhoods.

To develop worship houses that echo the standards and ethics of Jesus, we have to find a way to find love for everyone. Perhaps we should draw our inspiration from the inner city missions where the poor and homeless are offered enriching food and humble shelter. We don't have to follow the theology of most missions that serve the poor to convert them. We can just serve them. It is time to worship the God within us, who nurtures us and who welcomes us no matter who or what we are. This is the way of Jesus. Our places of worship need to be humble and inviting so we can share with others by offering them respect as well as love. Rather than vaulted ceilings that point to God, let's find symbols that point to us, the children of God having the image of God deep within. Let our worship centers represent the earth that Jesus inhabited rather than an idealized heaven that we know so little about, at best. For example, let us get rid of altars, pulpits, and clerical garb that tend to make it look so heavenly.

Jesus was startlingly different. He had no building or headquarters, no holy place. He treated Jewish temples with great respect and gathered with his disciples in them. He met his people on the streets of their villages, in private homes, in private places (the Upper Room), anywhere he could and often in hostile environments where his enemies or those who felt threatened by him challenged him.

We may believe that this is the inevitable result of his death and resurrection. Without his human physical presence, his followers could not perform in the same way as Jesus did. There were "twelve Apostles" and they needed to constantly communicate with each other. It is reasonable to think that they needed a central place to work from and where they could be contacted by each other and receive believers. Also, as time passed the Christian movement adopted some of the cultural customs it encountered, and structures inevitably followed. Matthew's Gospel, the Acts of the Apostles, and the letters of Paul strongly suggest that, as the number of Christians grew the need for order and discipline grew. Leaders were chosen in the different communities where a church existed or was expanded. These new leaders needed a base to work from.

If the rapid development of an institution with a specific location is a logical progression, comparing the ministry of Jesus with the modern movement is forbidding. Yet, there are some characteristics of Jesus' style that are useful to pursue and recapture. The intimacy of walking and talking with people one-to-one is enviable. Jesus did this regularly and the religious leaders today like to do the same with personal (pastoral) visits and small groups. It is at the next level where the difference is notable. He almost always met with small groups where he could engage them and respond to their questions. Now, congregations gather for worship. Some are quite small and intimate while others are large and forbidding.

— • • • —

We need to reestablish intimacy as the central way believers encounter each other and their leaders, pastors, rabbis, imams, priests, gurus, or elders. Notice the word leader. Jesus became a leader in a unique and

significant way. He earned the respect of people by respecting them. In the
Sermon on the Mount (Matthew) and the Sermon on the Plain (Luke)
Jesus offered guidelines to his audiences on how to act and gave them
specific rules to follow. This appears to conflict with my thesis that the
parables demonstrate the primary way that Jesus communicated by
showing his listeners respect. He trusted their potential to listen and chose
a way that suited their own lifestyles and experiences. This does not mean
that he communicated only in parables, that he was never specific, or that
he did not respond to questions. He did.

Of course, these sermons, closely related, were probably not presented
the way that Matthew and Luke presented them. For example, look more
closely at the Sermon on the Mount. The quantity of topics and ideas
expressed is huge. There is no way that listeners could have grasped them
all. The Beatitudes offer succinct statements that appear quite difficult to
comprehend such as "The meek shall inherit the earth." Throughout the
centuries of Christianity, scholars and believers have debated the meaning
of the Beatitudes and still have never come to a consensus.

It is far more likely that Matthew gathered many sayings of Jesus from
Jesus' entire ministry in many different settings. To put all that he said in
their proper contexts, even if the extended memory of the Christians
decades after Jesus' death was accurate, the length of the Gospel would
be as large as the entire New Testament, or greater.

The most significant examples of the words of Jesus are the parables.
They are unique. Although Jesus did not invent the parable form, he
mastered it. Storytelling is a rather intimate exercise. When telling stories,
unlike sermons and discourse, stories intimately draw in an audience.
Children demonstrate this best. They listen with rapt attention, clinging
to every word and feeling every emotion. Stories almost never pontificate,
except for Aesop and his fables. Rather, stories engage the listeners, their
minds and their emotions. A listener relates personally.

Most important, stories free listeners to interpret the story from their own individual experiences, values, and environments. In an audience of 100, it is possible there will 100 different interpretations, however subtle some of the interpretations may be. Sermons do not allow this freedom. Also, television is our primary source of stories today. However, they do not, cannot, have the same impact as stories that are told in person. Television and motion pictures rob the audience of much of their imaginations. No longer can an audience visualize an image. Instead, the actors become their characters, whom we now visualize as the characters portrayed. Somehow, Moses looks like Charlton Heston.

Similarly, set designers and directors firmly establish the setting of a story, which denies us viewing the scene from our own imaginations. Jesus let his listeners use their own imaginations to create the characters and settings of his parables. His stories are nearly skeletons compared to modern literature that frequently describes a scene in great detail, sometimes pages and pages of it. Jesus totally freed his listeners to use their imaginations, to add details from their own experiences, picture someone from their own memories, or distort characters and scenes as their fanciful or pained minds led them.

Put a bit differently, Jesus trusted his listeners with his stories. A listener could fit a story into her own experiences or visualize them with rich imagination. Jesus encouraged his listeners to hear his stories from their own biases, their victories and defeats, their joys and hurts, their confidences and fears, positive and negative attitudes. He did not demand that his parables be understood literally, metaphorically, or symbolically. They could be all or each. He respected his audiences.

Generally, Jesus' audiences were not very well educated, had little leisure time, probably ate poorly, owned very little, if anything at all, held no high positions religiously, politically, or financially. Throughout history these kinds of people are not respected or their advice sought. Mostly, they were ignored, scoffed at, or ridiculed. In a way, Jesus respected and trusted the unrespectable and untrustworthy.

This raises some interesting questions such as why did Jesus trust those who could not be trusted to interpret, evaluate, and understand his parables? We certainly cannot read the mind of Jesus, but we can interpret his behavior and words. There is a reason that Jesus associated with the "have-nots" of his time. He was one of them. He was not born to wealth, even if the Gospels called him a king; he was not a part of the power structure; he was not a leader of his faith, Judaism; and he was not highly educated. At that time, he, too, may have been illiterate.

His ideas about faith were radical and mostly revolutionary. He was not part of the establishment and offered strong suggestions that the establishment was moving in the wrong direction, suppressing the poor, insensitive to the sick, contemptuous of lawbreakers, and making religion empty.

His friends and followers were oppressed and had little hope of shedding poverty and ascending the cultural ladder. Many had been landowners, although poor, and able to feed their families. As the entrenched power took over farm after farm for indebtedness, farm owners became tenant farmers and many fell into severe poverty and moved to villages hoping to find other work.

Jesus brought hope to those on the edges of society. He preached the Kingdom of God (Heaven) to them as a present reality — something that changed them immediately, not as a future hope in another world. The New Testament talks mightily of the Kingdom of God in the next world (Heaven), but Jesus seldom did. Indeed, he said that the Kingdom of God is among us, within us, and lives for us in our present reality.

What the Kingdom of God means is hard to pin down. Jesus intended it to be this way. He opens his parables with "The Kingdom of God is like…." Since the parables are extremely diverse, the meaning of the Kingdom of God is elusive. If people of faith want to have everything wrapped in neat and clear definitions, they need to look elsewhere than Jesus. He provided a diverse definition, if he offered one at all.

Still, the Kingdom was a present reality. His friends and followers were not looking for salvation in a far away place and time. They needed food to feed their souls while they lived. The alternative would be despair, a complete loss of hope. So, we cannot define the Kingdom precisely, but we can speculate on its impact on Jesus' people. The poor had little dignity and less self-esteem. Jesus offered them both with his gentle way, touching the untouchables, embracing the dirty and smelly people he met, championing the widows and prisoners, loving without conditions, and opposing the established religious and political powers.

Jesus gave them back their humanity. He appeared to them, not as a mystical vision, but as the love of God incarnate. In Jesus, they saw God, the God in Jesus and the God within themselves. This is the ultimate Kingdom of God, God in Jesus and God in humans. Jesus redefined humanity by restoring the ancient biblical portrayal of the image of God living in humans.

Jesus offered the Kingdom of God to the people he lived and walked with in the struggle for life in a harsh and brutal age. He returned their human dignity to them. Remember that he also lived in an age of religious pluralism. The Hebrew God Jesus worshipped was the God of Israel. Beyond the immediate borders of Israel, Caesar elevated himself to be a god of Rome. There were many mythical gods inherited from Greece as well as Baal, a god of life and fertility who reigned nearby competed with the God of Israel, Yahweh, as did Zoroastrianism in Persia, and to the east Buddhism and Hinduism provided religious nurturing and faith to millions.

He did not interact with these other religious communities, remaining throughout his life in Israel. Did he encounter other religions? Surely. The

Roman military occupation forces were not Jewish and, probably worshiped Caesar as a sign of patriotism. Israel was located in the "fertile crescent" and on the trade routes between eastern countries, Rome and Egypt. In addition, the area was thoroughly Hellenized by the pervasiveness of Greek influences. Although he seldom visited cities, except for Jerusalem and then only once, maybe twice if you count the experience at age twelve, Jesus must have felt the influence of these competing religions. None of the sources about Jesus hint of any comments or confrontations about other religions. He was only interested in the people around him. It is not only possible but probable that he was not particularly interested in all of the other religions represented. His concern was with people, especially the disenfranchised. He did not challenge Judaism, only its abuses during a period when the purity of the faith was low and corruption relatively widespread, when injustice dominated and inequity ruled.

Everything indicates that if Jesus had been transplanted to India, his concerns for ordinary people would have remained consistent. The Kingdom he offered would not have changed, for it restored dignity to those without any. It is doubtful that he would have challenged the teachings of Buddha unless his followers corrupted those teachings in ways that impoverished people physically, economically, and spiritually. Jesus cared for people not religious doctrines; he loved human beings not rigid rules; and embraced God as a relationship who personally touched without specific images and not as a super person claiming to be god.

It is a puzzle that rigid beliefs have gotten between people today. Ethnic groups frequently hate other groups who disagree or have other beliefs. Religious intolerance rages as bigotry and hatred. Jesus could not have acted this way. He loved people, not their beliefs. Much has been written here about the respect Jesus had for people, allowing them to interpret his parables freely. He never demanded conformity to religious tenets, but to faith and humane conduct.

Those who hate others because of their beliefs have never encountered Jesus. From what we can put together in the New Testament, Jesus not only loved but sought out those whom most of society shunned. We tend to love, admire, and emulate popular icons like athletes and entertainers. Jesus taught us differently.

Chapter Four
LENT, THE PASSION

She had a black cross crudely drawn on her forehead to celebrate Ash Wednesday, the beginning of Lent, and a season of sacrifice, spiritual reflection, piety, repentance, and renewal. Ash Wednesday initiates the Lenten season as worshippers, in some denominations, have the ashes of burnt palm fronds applied as a cross to signify piety and repentance.

Lent celebrates the passion of Christ. For forty days, the pious faithful deny themselves something from their lives, usually a food, but not always. There is no direct biblical reference to this pious Christian tradition. The forty days may trace themselves back to the forty days that Jesus spent in the wilderness fasting and that ended with the satanic temptations. This is conjecture, since there is no biblical justification for the forty days of Lent. There is no direct link between Lent and the life of Jesus. This is not unusual, since many Christian traditions developed during the history of the church long after the scribing of the New Testament.

If, indeed, Lent, as fasting and contemplation in preparation for the victory of Easter, is to be understood as an imitation of an episode within the life of Jesus, we understand it as a symbolic or metaphorical relationship. The forty days in the wilderness is not a literal event, but a story that illustrates a quality of Jesus as understood by the church that followed him. The forty days echo the forty years the children of Israel spent in the wilderness before establishing their own homeland. This is as it should be. The early Christians contemplated the life of Jesus, not as biography or human history, but to understand and validate their encounters with the resurrected Lord, the Lord of their faith. It is what we all do; we look back upon what we have done and experienced to better understand the events and experiences of our lives today. This means, however, that memories are, more often than not, seriously flawed. Details are filtered through subjective memory that skews things to reflect today's values, fears, dreams, loves, hates, opinions, religious beliefs, and forces that mold us. Yesterday becomes tainted by today.

It was the same for those Christians who composed and collected the books of the New Testament. They looked upon the Gospels as stories that supported their day-to-day living. As long as we are human and not automatons or robots, this is how it is and must be. To look at the events in Jesus' life and reconstruct them as accurately as possible, we must look at sources as close to the time of Jesus as possible and that reflect his life. We must also realize that we will never find an absolute reconstruction. It will always be filtered through who Jesus was, who his earliest followers were, who the Christians over the centuries were, and who we are.

To search and find the human Jesus is always a difficult and inaccurate process, for it implies that the scenes in the life of Jesus as presented by the Gospels may not be precisely exact. A comparison of the Gospels using a Gospel parallel, a book that puts the text of Matthew, Mark, and Luke side-by-side, reveals that the events as written are not exactly the same. Sometimes the context has changed slightly and other times, the events are enhanced, slightly changed or added to in order to suit the writers' situations. Mark is short and terse, while Matthew and Luke add greater detail to the same material, frequently softening it to conform to the faith and sensitivities of the authors' readers. An excellent example of this is when the brothers, James and John, vie to be closer to Jesus than the other twelve disciples. In the shorter story the brothers ask directly whom Jesus favors. The longer story softens their efforts to be more favorable; the mother of the brothers asks rather than the brothers themselves. It is almost as if Matthew and Luke want to save the later reputation of the brothers. After all, any mother would do the same. Asking for Jesus' favor for themselves would certainly not show them as humble followers of Jesus, but as seekers of special favor, but when their mother asks, the situation changes considerably.

These inconsistencies suggest that another perspective, the perspective of Jesus, would be more accurate and reliable than that of the Gospel storytellers. This depends on learning, as best we can, not the precise events in the life of Jesus, but what Jesus said and taught as well as what he did. Since the Gospel narratives differ on the details of Jesus' life, it seems far better to look at what he said. Discovering words and deeds that are less tainted by the Gospel writers is no easy task and will have some of the same pitfalls as interpreting the events as presented by the different writers. Still it is a worthy and faithful venture. Some sayings of Jesus are more universal and found in the teachings of other religions and philosophies. While he certainly could have uttered these universal sayings, they are not distinctive enough to reveal the uniqueness of Jesus. The "Golden Rule" is found in many religions, sometimes worded a bit differently, but the intent is clearly the same. Jesus certainly may have taught the Golden Rule, but since so many others also did, it reveals nothing distinctive and unique about him.

The parables are the best evidence of what Jesus actually said, although his sayings are not exclusively contained in the parables. Still the parables are distinctive and unique. Some are so unique that Christians, over the centuries, have not been able to agree on their meaning. The parable of a landowner who hired casual labor throughout the day, from early morning until twilight illustrates this uniqueness. Those hired early who had worked a full day and those who had worked only an hour or so were each paid a full day's pay. This violates convention, and Christians struggle with this discordant idea. For Jews, even today, consider the parable of the Good Samaritan as anti-Semitic since it portrays Jewish religious leaders in an extremely poor light and a much-despised Samaritan portrayed as the good guy. These parables, among others, shocked their listeners. None had an expected or even an acceptable ending. They were certainly distinctive, unique, and thought-provoking.

I am not going to interpret any parables. This is for another day. The parables strongly point to the relationship that Jesus had with the people around him. The general attitude of the Gospels points to a gentle, concerned, trusting, and warm human being which supports the theme of the parables. Note, however, that neither the parables nor the Gospels suggest that Jesus was weak. Gentle and weak are not synonyms.

With this said, our knowledge of Jesus tells us nearly nothing about Lent. Lent is built upon the idea that people are degenerate sinners who need to realize how imperfect we are. The blood sacrifice tradition in ancient Judaism illustrates this; we are so evil that only a blood sacrifice can save us, so, rather than offering animals for slaughter or killing some of us from time-to-time, Jesus was offered as the final and most perfect blood sacrifice. So, the horrible ugly crucifixion, a relatively bloodless execution except that the soldiers stabbed him and blood did flow, becomes a living sacrifice. Paul supports this thinking.

This is a terrible, terrible theology; a terrible, terrible portrait of God. As human parents, few if any of us would kill one of our children or even a pet dog or cat as a blood sacrifice for the imperfections of our other children. More closely to the point, no leader of a large clan would sacrifice their favorite cousin as a human blood sacrifice for the sins of the other clan members and future members. The clan would be considered barbaric and murderous.

We cannot portray our God as so vengeful he would give up his favorite son to die for the rest of humanity. If we want to find the true God, look at Jesus of Nazareth, the son of God who best reflects the characteristics of his Father, not physically, of course, but in attitude, compassion, love, and forgiveness. God did not send Jesus to his death. The Romans killed him and left him to become animal carrion, a proper end for an enemy of the people, a renegade, and not a very important one at that. Crucifixion was limited to the peasant class or below. Those higher on the social, religious, and political ladder were given far more dignified executions and were buried, not left in the open to painfully die alone and to be carrion for animals. Jesus, as the Gospels tell us, was buried by friends, not by the authorities of Rome.

This execution will be considered in greater detail in the Good Friday discussion.

Jesus offers an alternative to this rather gory portrayal of the human condition. Jesus did not view his people as degenerate sinners, but people he respected and loved. He was certainly willing to die for his people, but not as a living, human, blood sacrifice, but as a champion for his people. He would have died in their stead, if this had been possible. Jesus loved his people and his love was based not on human sinfulness but human dignity, not on imperfection but human fragility, not on pity but respect, and not on weakness but strength. He saw his people as those with huge potential. It is interesting to note that Jesus did not see his followers as so frail that only divine intervention would make a difference, but as strong people needing a gentle push and loving support to realize their potential. The divine intervention was the life and ministry of Jesus.

The road to the cross for Jesus was not filled with grief and sadness but with a confident celebration of life. He went to Jerusalem knowing that Rome feared those who worked with and helped the have-nots and who could possibly mobilize them into a resistance movement. The Roman authorities thought that Jesus posed a threat to Rome, perhaps similar to the Maccabees who resisted and defeated the Syrian occupiers nearly two centuries earlier and reclaimed their country, restored the temple, and reestablished their Jewish heritage. They were successful, if only for a short time.

To Rome, Israel was a particularly contentious country that maintained its Jewish identity far better than most of the countries Rome had conquered. Jesus did not attempt to start an insurrection to overthrow the religious establishment, but as a leader of peasants could have been perceived as a threat. There was an implied threat that Jesus would recruit for subversive reasons, to raise an army to revolt. Peasants were poor and frequently willing to rebel against those who dominated them with cruelty and poverty. Rome considered Jesus an enemy of the state, but not a significant one.

What Rome thought of Jesus is far less important than what Jesus thought of people. There is no question that Jesus viewed people as filled with huge potential, the potential to become the best kind of human beings, but also with the potential to fail and fall into sinfulness.

The tension between these is critical. Traditional Christianity stresses the powerlessness of people to conquer their sinful natures. Jesus, to the contrary, had enough faith in the people he encountered to believe that they could make good choices, could think clearly even when overcome by negative circumstances, and could conquer their own base tendencies. When Jesus proclaimed the Kingdom of God, he did not proclaim a future made possible only by his shameful death, but that by allowing the provocative ideas of Jesus to embrace people, letting his stimulating stories challenge their thoughts, prejudices, and beliefs, and permitting his style of life to influence them, those surrounding him could and would experience the Kingdom of God as a reality in their lives. Any of them could have chosen to ignore the provocative ideas by calling them strange and out-of-tune with the commonly held ideas, chosen to hear the stimulating stories as perverse, or viewed the lifestyle of Jesus as idealistic and unrealistic. And some did.

This was part of the trust that Jesus had in the people. People did not have to robotically react the way Jesus wanted, but could react as they chose from their own faith, experiences, knowledge, and hopes. This is a huge amount of freedom for people who were usually told directly what and how to think by workplace supervisors as well as religious and secular leaders. Jesus had a huge amount of faith in people. From the perspective of his teachings, Jesus trusted his audiences to hear what he had to say even when it conflicted with the popular religious, philosophical, and political ideas of his day. From the perspective of his stories, Jesus trusted his audiences to listen and to let their own experiences influence how they interpreted his stories, so the stories would reach far more deeply into their hearts and minds.

As humans we struggle with demons within and without. Jesus understood this clearly. Much of the myth that developed surrounding his life, death, and resurrection focused on these demons. The Gospels relate stories of faith healing and cleansing believers. Jesus put spittle on a man's eyes to heal his blindness. The demoniacs were driven out and fell to their deaths. Conquering the internal demons is best illustrated by Jesus' faith healing and driving evil out; they could use the God within when Jesus opened their inner eyes. The Gospels show Jesus responding with, "Your faith has set you free."

Because Lent is the period in the Christian year that centers most clearly on these demons, this is an excellent time to deal with human sin. The Old Testament suggests that sin became a part of human nature during the "fall" of Adam and Eve, the second creation story in Genesis and a story of yielding to temptation. There are two stories of creation in Genesis, the seven-day sequence of creation and the more dramatic story of Adam and Eve. There are several contradictions between these accounts, but for our purposes, the contradiction with the perspective of humans is quite informative. The younger story is told first in Genesis 1:1 forward. This story describes humans, male and female, as made in the image of God and given responsibility (dominion) for all the earth. This portrayal is significant because it portrays human beings as fundamentally good and worthy of responsibility for the animals and plants in the world. Humans were created as capable and responsible. Sin and evil are not dealt with at all. Indeed, after this sequence of creation is concluded, God pronounced it good.

Then the older story begins with male dominance (Eve was made from the "rib" of Adam), a lustful seeking to be like God (eating from the fruit of the tree of knowledge), seduction by a snake, awareness of nudity, and the rapid decline of humans after their ejection from Eden, the death of Abel and denial of Cain. This is truly an ugly portrayal of the origin of humans. They are portrayed as deceitful, conniving, egotistical, and murderous. This account is powerful and set the mood for the Old Testament and the later New Testament. The Old Testament wrote of covenants made and broken, of cruel punishments and vengeful acts, of wars won and lost, of the LORD abandoning his people, of seduction and murder (David and Bathsheba), of good kings and bad kings, of captivity in a foreign land, and of famines. The original covenant was established with the Mosaic Law and broken by unfaithfulness resulting in the flood described in the story of Noah. Later, the people were taken to Babylonia and held captive there. The list is long and exposes human evil as pervasive and on-going.

The New Testament continued this demonizing of humanity. John the Baptist harangues his listeners with the contemptibility of their sinfulness (Christians call him the last of the Old Testament), and John of Patmos, author of the Book of Revelation, the Apocalypse, and a Christian imprisoned by Rome on the island of Patmos, speaks of hell fire and brimstone, of monsters, and the final conflict that destroys more people than it saves.

These dramatic revelations of the despicableness of humanity are not without corroboration by the history of humanity beyond the Bible. Christians initiated the Spanish Inquisition, conducted the Crusades against eastern heathens, and wiped out tribes of American Indians by converting their ways to more "Christian" (Western) ones. These examples are within the Christian movement. Beyond it there have been monsters like Adolf Hitler, Idi Amin, and Saddam Hussein. All of these are extreme examples of sin, of evil, and of the demonic. More common are the simple daily sins we commit as well as the aberrant behavior seen commonly in such diseases as alcoholism and drug addiction that cause other related problems.

These realities explain, in part, why Jesus, in total contrast, chose to trust his people rather than condemn them. Traditional Christianity condemns humans as sinners with no ability to save themselves. This is the definition of grace or, in Paul's ideology we are saved only by grace. Good deeds are useless. Faith accepts our helplessness and puts our trust in Christ (faith) as our only hope. Works are of little value. Of course, Protestant and Roman Catholic Christianity do not agree on this either. Generally, Protestant Christians rely totally on grace and call for confession to show our reliance on this grace. Roman Catholic Christians put more value in good works, i.e., what we say and what we do truly make a difference, venal and mortal sins. Confession is mandatory for both Protestants and Roman Catholics to rid us of the burden of our sin and free us to respond with lives lived better.

In spite of this difference, Protestant and Roman Catholics remain essentially the same. Protestants rely on grace, the influence of a forgiving God outside of themselves. Roman Catholics rely on the forgiveness or absolution of the church as given by a priest. In both cases, the individual is fundamentally powerless without serious help. As Christians meditate on their own sinfulness during Lent, living lives of repentance, and seeking forgiveness, they seek purification by God, either directly or as mediated by a priest, because our flaws are the primary characteristics of being human.

Jesus understood humans as flawed, but not fatally so. The Christian tradition sees humans as fatally flawed and only the Holiest of Holies can redeem them. Jesus trusted humans to be capable of responding to his words, ideas, and stories and to use the divine inside them without additional outside divine intervention. This trust is huge for it shifts the focus of the entire history of the Christian movement from its inception following the death of Jesus to the modern age. We shift from condemnation to acceptance. Responding to Jesus' words and stories demanded allowing mindsets to become unsettled, beliefs to become tentative, and values rethought. Jesus opted for the seven-day creation sequence in Genesis that proclaimed humans as made in the image of God who gave them dominion over all the earth. Jesus found the spark of God in each of us rather finding a treacherous snake.

The significance is critical, for when Jesus offered the Kingdom of God, he did not offer something earned by God in a final conflict with evil, but an immediate human relationship with God for all who accepted the life and words of Jesus, his ways and teachings, as serious possibilities. Evil was not done away with, but put into perspective. Believers, those who accepted the Kingdom of God that Jesus offered, knew how to choose right from wrong and how to win the inner battle that so many others lose. Believers made difficult life choices in response to the Kingdom of God rather than as an attempt to win it. Christians live good lives, not perfect, because they embrace the Kingdom of God as they live, not as a reward to enter the Kingdom later. Salvation is an immediate graduation rather than an entrance examination. We have it now instead of looking for it at some future time.

Salvation is immediate empowerment, not a later escape from eternal damnation, from Hell, or from exclusion from God. Focusing on the death of Jesus and the spilling of his blood as necessary for forgiveness and salvation turns the life of Jesus upside down. This makes little sense when viewed from the perspective of what we know and understand about the life and words of Jesus. Rather, death and blood reflect the despair and helplessness of people who do not believe in themselves and do not believe that the image of God lives within them. This powerless leads to despair. Extreme poverty, for example, renders one powerless, without resources to effectively struggle for justice; enemies become powerful and have the ability to help or harm the powerless.

When feeling powerless, the only recourse is to find a champion with power to overcome and destroy the powerful enemies. John of Patmos experienced this kind of despair against Rome and against the powers that allowed the evil Roman Empire to act with such malevolence. John needed to transform despair into hope and did it by writing the Book of Revelation. Revelation, symbolically, talks of the powers of evil and their potential and offsets this with the confrontation between good and evil, the battle of Armageddon. God, good, destroys the evil powers and casts them into eternal punishment.

In this way, God does for John and other Christians beleaguered by Rome and the earthly forces of evil what they cannot do for themselves. God destroys the evil power. John was desperate and powerless, so he relied on God, the Almighty, to vanquish the evil and malicious enemy. The cross became the sign of the powerful doing for the powerless; the spilled blood compensated for the anemic ones with no ability and without power and washed away sin. It is ironic that the cross, more accurately a sign of powerless before the awesome power of Rome, became a sign of power.

Powerlessness, hopelessness, and despair transformed the message of Jesus into something completely different; people were viewed as pathetically inept and in need of complete assistance. In contrast, Jesus respected people as having potential with minds that think and hearts that embrace. The Kingdom of God was not a future haven for frightened and despairing people, but a reality that lifted them from the agony of their impoverished human lives into new beings in their day, immediately, not only potentially. They could live successful lives today in spite of the problems engulfing them, powerful enemies or poverty. Salvation gave them the personal power within to live successful lives respecting themselves and others, not letting the world overpower them. They had within them the Kingdom of God.

People's own inner resources opened their minds to the words of Jesus and opened their hearts to the human Jesus and how he lived his life. The life and words of Jesus impacted them and their lives. Ironically, they gained dignity from their own indignity, felt empowered rather than powerless, found confidence to overcome fear, and walked boldly instead of timidly.

Jesus led the way. His life, lived in poverty and without a permanent home to shelter him, was successful. It was not a failure that demanded a crucifixion and resurrection to justify it. Jesus helped the people he met to change their lives and to empower them to carry the onerous burdens life had thrust upon them. Jesus died as a criminal, but the life he led leading up to the cross was as successful as any life can possibly be.

The world had not dramatically changed. There was still injustice and poverty, and the politically powerful and powerless, but perceptions of the world had changed. Impoverished followers of Jesus had more spring to their steps, a lively twinkle in their eyes, broken bodies healed, crazy minds became sane, and the impossible barriers before them seemed less ominous and prohibitive. Rome considered these people considerably more dangerous than before they met and knew Jesus. They had cringed before authority, trembled when threatened, cowered in front of the powerful. Despair yielded to self-confidence and the timid became assertive. Jesus had transformed a handful of those who opened their minds and hearts into a radically different kind of people.

Good Friday celebrates the execution of Jesus, merely a political gadfly to the Romans. It should have been expected. For years scholars have offered reasons why Jesus, who appeared timid and kindly, as opposed to aggressive and harsh, threatened Rome. Perhaps, it was not as much what Jesus did politically but how he transformed those who followed him. Passive peasants became energetically reinvigorated, and this hinted at danger for both Rome and the Jewish leaders who cooperated with the occupying forces.

Consider who is more threatening, someone with head bowed, back bent, eyes cast downward, shuffling tired feet, and cringing to avoid any physical contact or someone standing erect, eyes meeting yours without flinching or wavering, strides when walking without flinching or wavering. To use a hated war analogy, a retreating battalion is nowhere near as dangerous as an attacking platoon.

So it was during the times of Jesus. Those with power and who demanded obeisance from subordinates walking the roads of the ancient world expected the "ordinary" citizen to move out of their way. Those challenging power often were met with immediate reprisals such as vigorously whipped by a rope or clubbed by a walking staff. These weapons became far less intimidating to those who did not fear the powerful who carried the ropes and staffs, the economic and political elite.

Everything suggests that Jesus, by offering the Kingdom of God to his followers, transformed them, not into an army, but into more confident and self-assured people who posed an implied threat to the politically and economically powerful. Ironically, the Gospels constantly portray the enemies of Jesus as those who were insecure in their power. Self-assured authorities seldom worry too much about covert threats, but worried about overt threats. But for those less secure such as Matthew's Herod, the birth of Jesus, a covert threat at best, threatened him. No armies had been committed to the infant and not a single dignitary looked to the infant for leadership. Still Herod reacted violently. He feared, at best, a covert threat, and at worst a non-existing threat.

The political threat of Jesus was covert. No armies gathered behind him, and no warrior bands followed him. The threat was covert, found only in the changed attitudes of his followers and in his words and stories that challenged the status quo. There was one possible exception, the "cleansing of the temple." This episode recounted by the Gospels is similar to the parables in that it violated ordinary thinking and traditional values held by pious Jews. The merchants were supposed to be in the temple.

Nowhere else could the faithful access and buy the animals required for their blood sacrifices to be made in the Temple. Nowhere else could the faithful bring their lowly wares to trade and barter for the sacrificial animals. Sacrifice was how they atoned for their sins of the past year. It was how they annually resparked their spiritual lives.

Attacking the temple merchants attacked one of the foundations of Judaism at that particular time in history. It was not disruptive as much as it violated accepted religious behavior. The attack in the temple by Jesus as recorded in the Gospels violated the portrait of Jesus as a mild and gentle man. Violence is not a trait of a peaceful person. The words were biting and stinging, far from the kind words usually uttered.

Attacking the merchants intending to physically hurt them does not appear to fit Jesus, but attacking a repugnant idea does. The parables and other thoughts of Jesus opposed the common ideas and thoughts of the day. Opposing animal sacrifice to appease God clearly fits within the character of Jesus. Indeed, it goes another huge step. Opposing animal sacrifice also opposes human sacrifice, that is, the self-sacrifice of Jesus to appease God. The ideas of Jesus did not include thoughts about God offering his son as a living sacrifice.

This challenges the heart of much Christian thought, that Jesus was the ultimate and final sacrifice. This is the heart of Lent and Good Friday, the meaning of the cross. Indeed, any who challenge the traditional thinking are in danger of being dubbed heretics. Heretic is not necessarily a completely negative title. Heretic means that many Christian thinkers came together in huge meetings, councils, and declared what was, is, and shall be called proper Christian thought. Anything in opposition to this was heretical. The most critical of these is the Trinity, God as three persons. This is reviewed in the chapter on the Trinity. So, it appears, Jesus was a heretic, he argued against what was considered proper religious thought.

This prompts a different discussion. As we think through our faith, in particular, the Christian faith, where do we put authority and its significance? From my perspective, there are four primary authorities that Christians have relied on throughout the centuries: the Holy Scriptures, tradition, revelation, and the words and life of Jesus of Nazareth.

For our purposes here, Scriptures and the words and life of Jesus of Nazareth are our major concerns. The words and life of Jesus of Nazareth are the subject of this book, although Scriptures will be briefly discussed.

For most Protestants Holy Scripture is the key authority and base this authority on the Bible's holiness. Some extend this to mean that the Bible is absolute and totally without error. This absoluteness follows the wrong path for it elevates the many writers of the Bible to a state of holiness rivaling that of Christ, the one experienced as the Resurrected Lord. The Bible is not a substitute for God. Making it inerrant, that is, without error, and absolute equates it with the most Holy. This inerrancy can have the opposite effect for it becomes permanent and unchanging. This makes the Bible rigid and unyielding. Anything that is completely rigid and unyielding is usually dead. I assure you that God is not dead.

The Bible is more than this. It is a bridge between God and humans. The human writers wrote of their experiences of God and the holy. They took the mundane, in many cases, and elevated it to become part of their spiritual lives. One of the most infamous Old Testament stories, David and Bathsheba, illustrates this well. David is motivated by lust to kill Bathsheba's husband and marry her, and is reprimanded for it by his counselor. This rather ugly little story points to a transformation of the worst in human action to become part of the religious and spiritual history of ancient Judaism and, by extension, Christianity. This extraordinary example of unethical and immoral behavior confuses many. The question raised is how can such obvious depraved behavior be supported and sustained by the holiest of books. I do not believe it can be.

This question becomes urgent to any who believe that the Bible is the inerrant Word of God. Anything that contradicts error-free Scripture also contradicts faith. The answer is clearer when we view the Bible as a book of faith rather than the absolutely true and inerrant Word. We call it the Holy Bible, but we dare not measure its holiness against the holiness of God. When the Bible becomes as holy as God, then God and the Bible are frozen in time by their words, visions, images, stories, events, and pronouncements. This means that God cannot grow or that our human perceptions of God cannot grow and change as time passes and the world changes.

The Bible of Jesus, the Hebrew Bible or the Old Testament, and the Bible of the Christians, the New and Old Testaments together, arose in an ancient world devoid of computers, weapons of mass destruction, instant communication throughout the entire planet, aircraft that make travel swift and comfortable, entertainment boxed in living rooms, widespread literacy, a world where a substantial middle-income class influence political events, and broad religious tolerance (ecumenism) lives side-by-side with intense religious intolerance. Yesterday cannot share these modern experiences, but yesterday and today do share good and evil, class distinctions that degrade the poor, ethnic distinctions that spawn and encourage bigotry, political aristocracy led by a powerful few, and oppression of the poor.

Ancient Scriptures cannot account for these cultural differences and their impact on human life. Today a debate rages over same-sex marriage yet pre-New Testament times accepted homosexuality as a natural part of living in the golden age of Greece. Some argue that the Bible forbids any behavior that is not heterosexual, but this may not be completely accurate because it offers many stories of aberrant sexual behavior. It tells the story of incest and the seduction of a father by his daughters in Genesis as well as the later story of David and Bathsheba. Sexual relationships are somewhat vague. The New Testament does a bit better, although Paul would like to see the whole subject go away. The Bible is not consistent and to make a few passages that appear to refer to aberrant behavior key to its interpretation misconstrues the biblical message.

The Bible is not inerrant. It does have values and practices that are not acceptable to religious sensitivities, then and now. War and pestilence predominate in sections of both the Old and New Testaments, injustice in other sections (see Job), and elitism in still others (Jews are favored by Yahweh over other human beings). The Bible does not always easily adapt to the changing years and the shifting of environments and values. Slavery is an acceptable social value in the Bible, yet is nearly universally rejected in the modern world. The Bible does not change to reflect this. In many ways, Scripture is static. There are, beneath its vagaries, wisdom and spirituality that transcend all ages, but this is not always apparent and takes some digging and interpretation to find.

God, however, has adapted to changes. God is with us yesterday, today, and tomorrow and is not dependent on "forever" values. God knows us in a space capsule circling the earth or bound for the moon as well as he knew our ancestors as they walked dusty pathways. God knows us as we gather as families around television as well as around a fire telling stories.

A cliché from years ago suggests that God is the same at any time in history, yesterday, today, and forever. This truth is based on the premise that God is perfect and cannot be made better and is, therefore, always the same. This is not a Truth as much as it is the human failure or inability to conceive of perfection. To use a logical approach, if humans are imperfect and still constantly change, God cannot be less than mere humans; therefore, God should constantly change. In opposition to this, of course, is that God is already perfect, therefore, God has no need to change. Never to change is to remain static, always the same and without growth. There is a hairline between never changing and death. All of life is change, God does change which is necessary to his own creative judgment. How God changes is beyond human imagination, but this does not mean it does not happen.

God is not a static being, unchanging and immutable, but something far greater. The Bible, as wonderful as it truly is, is not God but it is static. Because it is static, it cannot be forever absolute and true. This contradicts God's wisdom and how the world truly is, forever changing. Indeed, because it shares the humanness of its writers, it is prone to the same weaknesses as humans.

Maundy Thursday is an important celebration that, in its own way, reveals the nature of Jesus. It is the meal that opens an absolutely marvelous insight into Jesus. In the Gospel narratives there is the "Last Supper" that we celebrate on Maundy Thursday. As we celebrate the Last Supper, communion, the Eucharist, we must always remember the banquet parables. These make little sense until we understand the social, economic, and religious implications of sharing a meal at the time of the historical Jesus. Eating was and is a necessary factor for human survival. Without food, we die. For most societies, however, eating has other values, especially social relationships.

It begins with what we eat, moves to how we eat, and then to with whom we eat. The dietary laws of Judaism are well known. Probably these laws were initially established to keep the Jews from eating food that would cause illness and death. Pork, for example, was prone to spread parasitic diseases and was extremely dangerous. Pork was forbidden food, not to be eaten by pious Jews. Dietary laws were born. Eventually, simple safety precautions evolved into more complex rules that became distinctive of religious piety and spiritual purity.

Food was more than nourishment; it was also a sign of religious identity. Jews ate food that complied with religious law. This piety also became a sign of belonging. As the Jews ate together and observed the ritual laws, they bonded. Just participating in these meals demonstrated that they shared more than food but also faith and fraternity. Sharing a meal was like being in a family. Those who were not members of the family could not share the family meal. Eating together showed their unity and ethnic identity. Jews shared meals with Jews and not with non-Jews, those unfamiliar with and not observers of the dietary laws and other signs of Judaism.

Eating together extended this sense of belonging and ethnic identity. Who performed what ritualistic acts within the meal, who sat in the most honored position, who served, how things were shared and what role accompanied sharing, what was permitted, and what was banned, defined the meal and those who shared it. All of these factors combined to elevate the meal to a central part of the Jewish life at that time. The Gospels illustrated this with the brothers, while dining with Jesus and the others of the Twelve, vying to sit at the right and left of Jesus, i.e., in positions of honor expressing a special relationship with Jesus. This could most adequately be shown by where each sat while eating.

Paul elevated the Lord's Supper of the Gospels into a love feast (*agapé*) and communion, a holy sacrament (the biblical difference between these is obscure). Jesus added another dimension or twist with a parable, the banquet, a simple story of a man holding a feast and inviting specific guests to share it with him. Unfortunately, excuse upon excuse decimated the ranks of the invited guests until none were left.

At the Jewish meals of the time, Jews only ate with those who were ritualistically clean and who ate the proper food. So, those who were invited to the banquet were other Jews, friends, and relatives. Individually, the excuses not to attend appear legitimate. Cumulatively, they become rejections of the man who invited them. Some interpreters of this parable argue that this was a metaphor for the Jews who rejected Christ. This is an interesting interpretation except for the reality that it is a parable of Jesus, not one told later after his death and resurrection. The Christian church did not exist, *per se*, during the life of Jesus.

The parable points in a slightly different direction than the Gospel account of the Lord's Supper or Paul's interpretation. The parable opened the banquet to the uninvited, similar to what Jesus did in his ministry. He walked among the poor and downtrodden, the diseased and disfigured, the unloved and the hated, and the powerless and the defeated. This sharply contrasted with most aspiring leaders who associated with their peers, other economic, religious, and political leaders and identified more closely with power brokers, those who could make things happen. Jesus repudiated this by identifying with their opposites, the have-nots.

As pointed out above, the parables of Jesus did not follow expected directions; the parables took unexpected turns, departed from conventions, surprised listeners, stimulated thought and imagination, and generally teased minds to open up new possibilities.

Opening the banquet to riff-raff was a dramatic new possibility. It was not, however, something that Jews welcomed. It was repulsive, ugly, and impious. By indiscriminately rounding up people off the streets he invited the unclean, physically, emotionally, and spiritually, threatened to welcome foreigners and non-Jews who were forbidden to eat with Jews, threatened to mix wealthy and poor, educated and uneducated, sophisticated and unsophisticated, and threatened to degrade those who had first been invited. After all, their seats at the table were taken by the unworthy.

There is another strong positive implication that has meaning for how we interpret the Lord's Supper. Sharing the banquet meal, as hinted at in the parable, were those who may have been starving, those who would eat anything regardless of religious cleanliness or dietary laws, those who slobbered food on their clothing and sifted drink through unkempt beards, those whose body sores kept them isolated from others, and those who were hated such as the Jews who gathered taxes for Rome.

Jesus transformed eating from an exclusive club of the initiated to an open meal for anyone to share. Breaking bread broke stereotypes and traditions. The modern tradition of barring from communion those who do not belong among those religiously initiated violates the teaching of Jesus to admit anyone and everyone. We should do more than admitting everyone: we should invite them. By this standard, modern communion should mean extending fellowship to those beyond membership, rubbing elbows with the ugly and others we normally do not associate with, breaking down class, race, and economic barriers. In a sense, it is opening faith and the Kingdom of God to the world, especially those in our own small and limited world where we can actually invite them in the name of Jesus.

Sharing communion in the modern world is sharing and uniting with those we do not normally associate with, even in church. It is easy for a wealthy person to act nobly and generously with the poor and to give alms and support charities, but to recognize and acknowledge them as equals in every way, socially, politically, economically, and physically is extremely difficult. Yet, this is what Jesus suggested in his parables and lifestyle.

The Lord's Supper reflects the meal shared by Jesus with those closest to him in an upper room in Jerusalem, and it reflects Paul's elevating it to a love feast and a sacred event. This cannot and should not be discarded in our search for spiritual meaning. Yet, it still must be rethought in light of the teachings of Jesus in his stories and preaching, although this can be difficult sometimes. Rather than concentrating on this sacrament as eating his body and blood in a literal or spiritual sense, it should be viewed in a more symbolic way. Of course, there are many who argue that this waters down the meaning of the Lord's Supper, rendering it a mere shadow of its meaning. This is simply not true.

To better understand this, look more closely at the meal as explained in the Gospel accounts. Jesus dines with the Twelve, takes bread, says it is his body, and passes it to them to eat. He then follows up by passing the cup of wine as his blood for them to drink. Jesus uses his hands, his flesh, to pass the bread and wine. Obviously, he neither suggested that the Twelve gnaw at his flesh nor that they cut his flesh to spill enough blood for each to have a sip. This is a caricature of the scene that focuses on betrayal.

Note a couple of important points. Although Jesus talks about the betrayal, in John's Gospel Jesus passed the bread and wine before sending Judas on his way of betrayal. Judas was not excluded from the meal of friendship. Friend and foe, the faithful and the betrayer shared the fellowship meal. The meal was not exclusive for the eleven faithful disciples but included the betrayer.

The bread and wine jogged memories. Every time the Twelve ate bread or sipped wine as part of their meals, especially shared meals, they were reminded of Jesus and the upper room meal they shared. It had not yet become a sacred sharing. We can debate long over how Jesus knew he was soon to die. It follows that this would have been on his mind. His enemies had long tried to trap him into something that would cause his arrest and conviction. Now he brazenly entered the city where the nation's religious leaders resided; he walked into the midst of his enemies. Then, even more brazenly, he challenged the legitimacy of the merchants in the temple area. This act alone was enough to be named an enemy of the faith and, by implication, a political troublemaker. His arrest was a natural consequence of his acts strengthened by the poor history between him and many of the authorities.

Paul added a sacramental dimension years after the crucifixion and resurrection of Christ that is not historical but spiritual and has little to do with the scene in the upper room or with Jesus' parables. This dimension will be discussed in the chapter on Easter. Here, we are interested primarily in the approach to faith used by Jesus as he walked side-by-side with the Twelve and the hundreds of disciples who heard and followed him.

At his point, however, we will stress the gift of memory and the wonder of loving everyone. Jesus gave his most intimate friends something ordinary and routine to stir their memories of him and all that his life meant to them, the personal relationships, the quiet teachings, the stories and healings, befriending the ugly and beautiful, the old and young, rich and poor, the powerful and powerless, the sick and well, the popular and unpopular, the faithful and unfaithful. Bolster these rich and vivid memories with intimate private meals, evening campfires, personal conversations, and loving embraces. The memories ran deep and extended far beyond the walls of the upper room in Jerusalem. These memories inspired spirits and embraced hearts. To remember Jesus was to remember the Kingdom of God.

Meals were also, according to Jesus, times of incredible acceptance and love. The New Testament word for Christian love is *agapé*. Although in non-theological Greek, the three words for love, *eros*, *philos*, and *agapé*, can be easily interchanged. To better understand the New Testament, *agapé* expresses the uniqueness of Christian love. *Agapé* means selfless love. This love does not depend on receiving love in return, not upon our feeling good about giving love, not upon reward, not upon success, and not upon gaining salvation. It is love that is given anonymously, without personal gain, and because it is the right thing to do. It can be given to a poster child or a war victim, a lonely widow or a bride, a humane cause or a worthy reason, when it makes a difference to the giver or benefits the receiver. One does not have to like someone to *agapé* them. We can love those we do not know.

Such is the love of the Lord's Supper. It is filled with love, a love that surpasses human reward or reason, extends beyond gratification, and always leaves a winner, the recipient. As we touch elbows at the communion meal, we give and receive love. Mix this love with memories of Jesus, and our world will be richer, more beautiful, spirit filled, ennobling, and filled with the Kingdom of God.

Good Friday ends the season of Lent. Good Friday, a dark and ugly day, ended the life of Jesus, snatched hope from the fleeing Twelve, and suggested the end of the Kingdom of God. Taken by itself, it is one of the most agonizing scenes in history, especially as vividly portrayed in the motion picture, *The Passion of Christ*. The scene, as pictured in the Gospels, has creative and mind-blowing symbolism that reflects much I have discussed.

Jesus was hung between two thieves, the scum of society, and he uttered both defiant and submissive words, mocked with a crown of thorns, humiliated as they cast dice for his clothing, intensified his pain as a spear penetrated his side, belittled when they eased his thirst with vinegar, and dishonored as they derided him with words. Scholars have written volumes discussing the nature of Roman crucifixion and the biology of his death.

Reduce this to its simplest exposes a grotesque scene. The death of Jesus is described as an act of a benevolent God sacrificing his son for the sins of the world. The ugly scene becomes beautiful when forgiveness showers our sinful souls. History tries to deny this by alternately blaming the Jews and the Romans for the death of Jesus. Christianity has long argued that this was the final act to free humans from the captivity of our own sinful inclinations.

If this is true, then neither Jew nor Roman can be blamed for the crucifixion of Jesus. It was the inevitable act of God demonstrating his love for us. God killed to save.

Jesus disputes this with his words and deeds. He showed a huge respect for sinful people. He trusted their ability to think and believe knowing that some would fail and all would struggle with temptation and making choices. The cross is the great symbol of forgiveness, but it does not eliminate temptation. The cross promises salvation as a gracious act of God without cost and unmerited. Jesus already offered the Kingdom of God to tormented people because he loved unconditionally.

The cross purifies sinners in preparation for salvation; Jesus offered the Kingdom of God without purification, an interesting contrast. The contrast is significant, for Jesus offers the Kingdom of God to all who are open and receptive without purification and with genuine love – *agapé*. The teachings and stories of Jesus leave little room for a parent who sends a child to his own painful and degrading execution so that vast hordes of sinners can win heaven. Rather it is more closely akin to the story about Jesus and the little children. The Twelve chastise Jesus for allowing the pesky children to sit at his feet, or as frequently portrayed, sit on his knee. Jesus rebutted the Twelve suggesting that being childlike is the better way to be. Those children were not tiny angels dancing around with perfection. To the contrary, children can be quite evil. They pull the wings from insects, call other children by dirty, ugly, and hurtful names, yank on the ears of family pets, and so forth. Today's newspaper comic strips re-enforce the images of children doing their not-so-innocent deeds, strips like "Dennis the Menace" and "Peanuts" (Peanuts does an excellent job of showing this because the strip has a religious basis).

The God of Jesus would not actively send his son to suffer and die, nor would he allow it to happen. Yet, this is the way the New Testament appears to stage the scene. Is it possible that the early Christians were dealing with some very difficult issues that motivated the writers of the New Testament to respond in this manner to these issues? This is a logical assumption, but not provable. Still, there has to be a reason that the early church moved so quickly away from the teachings and stories of Jesus.

Somehow the gift of the Kingdom of God is lost and never again mentioned in the New Testament, not even in the Acts of the Apostles, an extension of Luke's Gospel. Of course the writers of Matthew and Luke take much of their material from Mark, and the Kingdom of God was used in

Mark and Luke. Matthew used the Kingdom of Heaven. These are the same, no difference between them. Using this term is important because the term is pregnant with meaning. It is the gift that Jesus gave directly to those who accepted it from him. As he strode the roads and footpaths of the ancient world, he told stories, taught lessons, hugged the untouchables, liked the unlikables, strengthened the weak, empowered the powerless, and gave them the Kingdom of God that transformed them into new beings who found their own inner divinity, perhaps, for the first time.

We do not hear of the Kingdom of God after the three Gospels Matthew, Mark, and Luke. No one has traced why this happened, at least as far as I know. My guess is that the world changed for the Christians. While Jesus lived, he walked among them, respected them, and gave them the Kingdom of God. After his death, the Christians relied on a different Jesus, the Resurrected Christ. This was different because the memories of the human Jesus faded to be replaced by a spiritual presence filtered through their life experiences. Paul, for example, never met the human Jesus, but on the road to Damascus he experienced the Resurrected Christ who took the Jewish radical conservative and transformed this energy into apostleship. Paul had hunted down Christians as criminals, then he became one of their strongest leaders.

Filtering the message through life experiences provides the foundation and a continuing inspiration for the Christian movement throughout the centuries. It explains some of the differences in the New Testament, i.e., Paul rejects salvation by doing good deeds and James encourages it. Most frequently, Christians attempt to harmonize the discrepancies, but this threatens the integrity of the New Testament, of the entire Bible. Perfection is not the core of biblical Truth. The core Truth is faithful people expressing their understanding of God from their own experiences. This will be discussed more thoroughly in the chapter on Easter. For now it is enough to say that the genuine experiences of faith that Christians encounter and, for that matter, people of all religions, are not the same.

However, in the words, the stories and teachings, and life of Jesus of Nazareth there is a Truth that transcends all others. Later Christian interpretations of faith tend to come from the experiences of faithful individuals. All are important, but what can be traced back to Jesus is more fundamental and transcends disparaging experiences and interpretations that might otherwise disrupt faith.

Today, the huge differences between denominations and their teachings, the internal differences within denominations, and the individuals offering diverse interpretations of what the meaning of Christianity illustrates the lack of cohesion when the human factor overcomes the core Truth found in Jesus himself.

Jesus, as he has revealed himself, never suggested that a parent sacrifice a child for the good and welfare of humanity. Countries do this all the time when issuing a call to arms against an enemy, genuine or imagined, but not Jesus. In an age of terrible injustice aggravated by the Roman occupation, Jesus did not develop a military presence however small. He did not call on his followers to slay the enemy, but to live with dignity and courage in spite of enemies. Jesus led a movement of passive resistance where armaments were not lifted, but the people found meaning in their lives in spite of the dominance of Rome and those religious leaders who bowed before Caesar.

To return to Jesus and look at the cross from what we can discern from him is not an easy task, but there are some clues. Jesus respected humans, but did not expect perfection. Rather, he offered them the Kingdom of God, God's reign. This is not an empty gift and offered an interesting alternative to a huge sacrifice for our sinfulness.

Living in God's reign means living imperfectly while embraced by the perfect. As long as we live within this scope, within the reign of God, we can err as humans while constantly striving to conduct our lives as if we live in the reign or grace of God. We are not perfect, but we constantly struggle to live better with more purity. Just as Jesus trusted his people to respond in spite of the overwhelming odds against them, we move beyond our sin because we have the same gifts that his original followers did; we have the Kingdom of God. This is the cross that Jesus gave us, not as a grave burden, but as an exhilarating opportunity.

The cross of Calvary was an historical event brought about by authorities who feared Jesus because he was different, because he loved those whom the authorities held in contempt, and because he found nobility in the poor while the authorities degraded them. Hanging Jesus on the cross was despicable, wrong, and political. It was not a divine act, but a human act. People killed Jesus, not God.

We do not need to find a supernatural way to rid ourselves of sin because we are loved and have already received the Kingdom of God. The Reign of God transforms us. We do not need to have Jesus suffer greatly for he, as he lived, gave us the ultimate gift, the **Kingdom of God**, a gift for all time.

Chapter Five
EASTER RESURRECTION

Slowly crimson breaks the darkness, promising the dawn. A small group of eighteen or nineteen stand bundled in winter boots and overcoats in near freezing temperature at a Vermont lakeside to celebrate the rising of the sun (Son). Easter sunrise service in Vermont, at least, mixes the joy of resurrection with the pain of rising too early with weather that is not yet spring-like. The Christian season is much the same. The joy of resurrection is tempered by the centuries where the excitement of meeting the Christ meets the human desire to extend our lives into eternity.

Easter is the opposite or antithesis of death. Jesus died ignobly on a cross to claim victory over death and rise in new life, resurrection. This resurrection is the heart of the Christian faith. There is nothing else that quite compares to it. We modern American Christians celebrate more vigorously at Christmas, but Christmas pales compared to the importance of Easter on the Christian calendar. Because Easter celebrates victory over death, it also celebrates victory over sin. This ties the season into the basic quest of humankind to live forever. Humans simply do not like to die.

Death is not merely the cessation of life; it is the denial of life and its meaning. For some death renders our human existence as a worthless waste of time. A common illustration of this is the cliché, "You can't take it with you." Most frequently, this refers to money and wealth, but it can have other meanings as well. A great writer, Shakespeare, left a legacy of extraordinarily fine poetic plays, but the acclaim over the centuries is not for him to enjoy. Death separated him from the fame for his genius. But, he lives on in his writing.

In contrast, others write in order to leave part of themselves to posterity and beyond the length of their lives. The same can also be said for breeding and bearing children. Our genes live beyond us. Or, our children will remember and pass memories of us to the following generations. Regardless of whom we are, a Shakespeare leaving a strong written heritage behind or someone who leaves a son or daughter as her heritage, death separates them. This raises some unacceptable questions that we want to deny by, somehow, extending life beyond death.

This human aspect vigorously denies death. Death denies the denial. To our knowledge, all living things die. Most religions, in some way, participate in the denial of death by offering life after death. This may be the greatest conceit. To believe we must live forever and to have meaningful lives now suggests that we truly believe ourselves incredibly important — important enough to defy the laws of nature and the normal course of biological life. To better understand this and find greater meaning in resurrection, we can look at what we know of Jesus of Nazareth, the man.

Jesus resisted death, as do we. As he spoke from the cross, as the Gospels report it, he shouted angrily at God, "Father, why have you forsaken me?" A human question from an agonized human, but he backed away from it with the additional words, "Not my will, but yours." These words of resignation offer some insights into Jesus. True, these words were probably constructed by the Church many years later, but they were not created without a context. Somehow, these words written after the resurrection reflect a characteristic of Jesus living in the collective memory of the Church. Stories passed from those who knew Jesus personally to the next generation who only had these stories to recreate a picture of the human Jesus. Through generations of believers, stories were reconstructed to meet their needs and conform to the doctrines as they had developed.

From these memories the Gospels were born and nurtured. Some memories were distorted by time, circumstance, and beliefs. Matthew 18 is an excellent example of this because it deals with church order, that is, how to keep the people of faith acting properly and believing correctly, and the consequences of failing in one or both of these. Matthew explains how to cast from their numbers those who did not meet the right standards. This section of Matthew, although Jesus is a key participant, could not have reflected an actual event in the life of Jesus. Church order was a function of the Church after his death and resurrection.

Still, the Church attempted to recreate, if not actual events, events that accurately reflected the life of Jesus. How well the Church accomplished this depends on many factors, mostly the Church based its interpretations on the structure and doctrines of its beliefs. For us in this volume, we return to earlier times before the New Testament and the stories and words of Jesus for our guidance.

As discussed earlier, the ministry of Jesus focused on the lives of his followers. He gave them the Kingdom of God to use in their earthly lives, not as a gift to be realized in some future life. Indeed, we Americans historically used the promise of Heaven as a way to control slaves. It was okay to suffer during their lives because in their lives to come, in the afterlife, they will be marvelously glorious; pain and servitude will be behind them. Jesus never did this.

This was not the approach of Jesus. He offered the Kingdom in this life to radically change lives immediately. This change was not to don some ultra-white garments and grow a pair of fluffy wings. No. No. The change was to change the inner spirit of a person so that living and coping today, in the immediate present, can be acts of courageous faith instilling dignity where there was none. More important, it was not important to Jesus for this change to be visible to all, although more erect postures and confident gazes may have been characteristics of the presence of the Kingdom within a person. It was more than enough for the person to feel better about herself and to live with greater strength and self-assurance. The gift of the Kingdom was not a prize to display for all to see; it was not a trophy. It was a human conversion that transformed individuals in their hearts and minds. It made life possible in ugly conditions so that when change was possible, they were ready to accept responsibility. They lived under the reign of God (the Kingdom of God) rather than the reign of Herod or Caesar.

Jesus was a healer. The large quantity of healing stories in the Gospels strongly suggests that this perception is accurate. Healing is not an event for the future, for life after death in Heaven, but an immediate event for continuing and preserving life. The Gospels have Jesus restoring life, such as raising Lazarus from death. This becomes a logical problem as well as one of the spirit. Healing and restoring life places the greatest value on life. If life after death or Heaven is the ultimate gift of God, then Jesus denies this by emphasizing life during our human existence. Jesus gave sanity to the demoniac, sight to the blind, sound to the deaf, and health to the sick. This is not a future reward, but an instant reward; promise becomes fulfillment.

The parables also suggest the immediacy of the Kingdom of God. A son is restored to his father, a laborer is paid for his daily work, people share a meal, the shepherd leaves his herd to find the one lost sheep, the mustard seed becomes a large bush, and flowers display all their beauty. Resurrection is not for tomorrow but for today.

———————•◆•———————

Jesus transforms Easter into tomorrow's promise kept today. There is another perspective to be considered: the impact of the resurrection on the later Church and on today's Christians. It is critical to recognize that Jesus offered the Kingdom to his friends and followers and to strangers and wanderers, not as reward in some far off future life in a blissful Heaven, but as something realized in their present existence. It is another thing to consider how Jesus became real in the lives of people who lived after his crucifixion and death.

Resurrection is Jesus being present and offering the Kingdom of God to us, now, today, in this lifetime. Easter celebrates Jesus reaching over time to embrace and offer us the Kingdom of God. Jesus reaches us now much the same as he did his original friends and followers, by giving us his stories, words, and life. Traditionally, Christians constructed a different way to express this, the Trinity, i.e., the Holy Spirit, the presence of God as we experience our faith. We tried to make sense of the apparent contradiction between God as a human in Jesus and the presence of God today after the death of Jesus.

Ever notice that our experience of faith spikes when something stimulates our consciousness. A revival preacher elicits a response when he or she exposes and exacerbates our guilt feelings and, then, offers an escape. Someone else sits quietly reading and meditating on a passage of Scripture; an idea or thought intrudes and spikes his experience of faith. A grief strickened family watches helplessly as a young child lies in a coma. Their helplessness stirs them to reach for the divine, a power beyond their own powerlessness. Those involved in "Twelve-step" programs, alcoholics and drug addicts, seek a power stronger than themselves to help them conquer what they cannot conquer by themselves.

In all of these illustrations when something or someone who touches our hearts, the emotional depths of our being, our experience of faith spikes. These touches empower something within that is mysterious and fragile. The stories, words, and life of Jesus touch the deepest part of us because they embrace the God within us, the image of God that Genesis wrote about and a link that others might call a genetic link that leaps the years in strange ways. Modern science has a parallel concept in quantum physics where time and distance are not barriers to simultaneously influencing the smallest of particles that are nearby or separated by vast distances. The spiritual and scientific are certainly not the same; however, it is interesting that a parallel concept does exist between them, even if their interpretations are vastly different.

Most of us want scientific or empirical verification, but by reaching beyond death through time resurrection offers a mystery that we can only speculate about and never know. Resurrection embraces the God within and invites Jesus of Nazareth to become part of us, to share the special space of the divine, so that we can be sensitive to and respond to his stories, words, and life. In a marvelous and wonderful way, the past reaches into the present to offer us the Kingdom of God. The Jesus who walked with friends and followers once again walks with friends and followers; we modern Christians open the divine within ourselves to the spirit of yesterday's Jesus for us.

———•·•·•———

We must be cautious, for our ache for the divine can also expose us to the demonic. As our emotional and spiritual hearts reach for fulfillment, false christs can entice us. Groups of people can become lynch mobs as shouts for "justice" corrupt minds and hearts. Motivational speakers can sell us overpriced, undervalued, and substandard merchandise. They simply expose our inner yearnings using exciting but misused words to arouse our emotions.

This is the value of Scripture, the Bible. It can become the baseline to keep our inner yearnings uncorrupted. For example, Jesus trusted his friends and followers to think and make good decisions when given good information and stimulation. Those who attempt to make emotional robots of us, that is, follow ideas and teachings without the freedom to think clearly and rationally, are far, far away from the teachings of Jesus. Blind obedience is not truly part of the stories, words, and life of Jesus. The Kingdom of God that Jesus gives us is not a prison for our minds and hearts, but a liberating reality. A Christian church or denomination that demands unquestioned obedience to an idea or tenet does not follow Jesus and, therefore, does not offer the Kingdom of God. Unquestioned obedience is not a resurrection experience, but the opposite, an experience of death. This is like nailing one to the cross, not freeing one from it.

We dare not trust just anything that *feels* good. It may not be the voice of Jesus reaching over the years, but evil violating our inner spirit. To discern the difference between the voice of Jesus and any other voice turn to the anchor of faith, the Bible. In this particular case to validate the voice of Jesus, compare the voice to what we know of Jesus, his stories, words, and life. We have all read headlines that tell of someone obeying the "Holy Spirit" and killing a family to protect them from a coming disaster. This is so obviously against all that we know of Jesus that it can be rejected quickly, however, not necessarily easily.

This is where the trust that Jesus gives us is critical. Jesus trusts our minds and our hearts even though some abuse or ignore this trust. We have the freedom to choose unwisely, to choose evil rather than the Kingdom of God. We may hear conflicting voices and must choose between them. We have the image of God within us; God is a part of each of us, even the most corrupt. This does not mean we are God or even a god. We are fully and truly human. We are Jesus walking with his friends and followers and we are Adam and Eve nibbling from the forbidden fruit of the tree of knowledge; we are Sister Theresa tending the destitute and we are the sniper indiscriminately killing innocents; we are a child gently caressing a crying infant and the little boy yanking a dog's ear. Humans are the world's most conflicted beings, seeking good and yielding to evil.

Why Jesus trusted us, and still does, defies human logic. Perhaps, it is because he was a human and conflicted as we are. He healed the sick and was frustrated and short tempered with Peter; he loved the despised Zacheaus and fussed with James and John, his disciples who asked for special favor. The temptation scene in Matthew, Mark, and Luke depicts Jesus dealing with demonic temptation and maintaining his primary allegiance to God, the Father. The later Church vigorously debated the humanity of Jesus and finally resolved it in a major church council by declaring that Jesus was fully human and fully divine, one hundred percent human and one hundred percent part of the Godhead. This was so complicated that the debate finally resulted in the development of the Trinity, that is, three in one, one God with three persons, a logical brain-buster.

Mark wrote well before the Church created these mysterious dogmas, but the issue was still there. So, Mark, as he collected, edited, and wrote the stories about the life of Jesus for his readers, found an existing oral tradition that showed how Jesus dealt with the weak side of his humanity. The temptations scene beautifully shows this. It becomes the initiation of his human ministry. Mark symbolized the inner conflicts of Jesus by removing the conflict from within and putting it outside of Jesus. The inner conflicts became Satan challenging the perfect person, the divine one.

In any event, Jesus personally dealt with his own inner conflicts. Mark transformed the conflicts of Jesus into a terse and powerful mythical event, but Jesus had to deal with inner conflict day-to-day much like the rest of us. He knew that when his friends and followers accepted the contradictions in his parables, the ideals in his teachings, and the model of his living they recognized themselves as well. For Jesus to trust them was not as difficult as it may seem at first thought, for he experienced the same conflicts. His trust for them freed them to choose both yes and no to the Kingdom he offered. Jesus trusted Judas who betrayed him.

Resurrection is not some spirit floating around in the world ready to gently pounce on anyone and speak to their inner being, but a concrete reality of Jesus communicating over the years as he touches the God within us to create a holy experience. Anchoring these experiences in the stories, words, and life of Jesus is a modern experience of faith. Bringing faith into our lives today is resurrection.

Religious thinkers often refer to the Holy Spirit as if it were a separate entity rather than an integrated part of the human experience of faith. Resurrection puts this into a completely different perspective. The linkage between the past and present, between Jesus and us today, is not an ineffable spirit, but the creative reality of the God in us. This linkage spans generations and defies accepted time barriers. The Holy Spirit links to the image of God within each human being.

------•◦•------

In the Gospels, Jesus is called Jesus. The Apostle Paul refers to him as Christ Jesus. The title Christ most frequently refers to the Resurrected Lord, the Jesus we experience after his death and who is not limited to time and space. As used here, Jesus refers to the human and Christ refers to our experience of faith and our experience of Jesus beyond his death. Christ is, then, Jesus resurrected; Jesus raised; Jesus experienced in the contemporary and modern age. Christ is the name of Jesus leaping across the barrier of death into life with his friends and followers of all ages. Christ speaks to us today and offers the Kingdom of God today.

To illustrate this, let us look at a single parable, the parable of the prodigal son. As recorded in Luke, this parable begins with the phrase, "The Kingdom of God is like...." The gift of the Kingdom of God is offered to those who listen carefully to the parable and are open to letting the parable speak to them. We know not the specific setting when the parable was first told to a live audience, but the parable was retold, in the name of Jesus, to audiences long before Luke wrote it in his Gospel. Indeed, it is from these retellings that Luke was able to capture it in written form as he struggled to share it with Christians some 50 or 60 years after the crucifixion. The Kingdom of God is offered to all of generations of believers.

The story is simple and well known. A greedy and impatient second son of a wealthy landowner and farmer wants to receive his inheritance ahead of time. He did not want to wait for his father's death to receive his fortune. His promised inheritance was half the size of his older brother's, but that was of no importance. What was important was to get his inheritance immediately.

Like many who suddenly become wealthy, he knew not how to manage it. Instead, he squandered it on all the wrong things. Soon, without money, he had to scrounge for a living. He was without funds when a famine struck. Now he was without food, too. He got a job slopping pigs. This is about as ugly as life can get. Jews consider pigs unclean and not edible; they were filthy and caused illness. Along with the ugly and religiously unclean job, the young son had so little food; he was willing to eat pig food. As he starves, memories of excellent meals and comfortable living crowd his mind. As he reflects on his life, he realizes that even the unclean and contemptuous swine eat better than he did.

Memories of home crowd other thoughts. He slopped pigs for a living and had little to eat. At home, things were so much better. His father's servants ate grandly compared to him. His gastric juices flooded his stomach as he recalled sumptuous meals shared with companionable diners. Now he dined inadequately with pigs for tablemates. How much worse can it get? His greed and ambition led him to his present plight, now it was time for him to plan his escape and restoration. As one who slops pigs, becoming one of his father's servants was a huge social and economic leap. Surely, his father would hire him. Surely!

This could be an opportunity to improve his status, to become adequately paid and well fed. He carefully implemented his plan by rehearsing his speech to persuade his father to hire him. The younger son plans carefully beginning with a line about how wrong he was to show that he would never revert to his former greed and bad habits. After all, his father would not give him a break if his attitude had not changed.

As he nears home, his father sees his youngest son and rushes to greet the lad who quickly began his well-rehearsed speech. His father cut off the speech, welcomed his son, and ordered the fatted calf for the welcome back celebration.

Ah! The older brother was angered by the celebration and jealously chastised his father for never rewarding him, the older and faithful brother, for not taking his inheritance and fleeing the father and the farm. He remained at home working with his father to improve and make things better. The older brother was the reliable son. The father responded that they always had each other. This had not changed.

This is an interesting parable that breaks several rules of that day. To give the younger son his inheritance, the farm would have had to be split up and part of it sold to make the assets liquid. It is questionable whether there would be enough cash available to give the younger son his share. Sales like this would not be easy to make. In any case, giving an ungrateful son his assets so early was not customary. This was especially true when the son left his native Jewish lands for alien and religiously unclean lands.

A Jewish lad moving to non-Jewish lands by himself was rare, for it required moving to and associating with unclean people. This seriously worsened his situation when he was forced to slop hogs, forbidden animals for Jews. An audience hearing this story would not have accepted for themselves the religious, moral, and emotional price the younger son paid. For later generations, this price becomes lower and lower until today few pay attention to the disaster of leaving the Jewish religious and ethnic environment. Still, the price of leaving adds a touch of unreality to the story making it a bit incredulous to a Jewish audience. The Jewish listeners would not have been forgiving for such flagrant violation of the faith.

For many years, Christian thinkers have suggested that the main theme of this parable was the repentance of the younger son. This does not work. As the parable unfolds he is not repentant but continues to plan for his own well-being. His repentance speech was planned and rehearsed too carefully.

Big brother acted the way most expected. The younger, unrepentant, and conniving brother had earned nothing, while he, the older brother, had been faithful, honest, and hard working, yet unrewarded. This follows conventional thinking. It would be truer today, perhaps, than in Jesus' time because we live in a world dominated by competitiveness; it is the capitalistic way.

The point of this over-simplified look at the parable of the Prodigal Son is that the energy of Jesus telling this story remains when we listen carefully and without too many traditional interpretations prejudicing our perspectives. When we remove the clutter in our own minds, we are free to let these inconsistencies tantalize our minds and hearts so that the possibility of transformation becomes genuine. This parable violates "conventional wisdom" enough to force an open and receptive mind to discover something new and different and, possibly, the Kingdom of God.

This is the Easter experience, opening ourselves to the voice of Jesus as it reaches across the centuries and gives us the Kingdom of God.

———◆•◆•◆———

Easter is also our personal resurrection. Many live today to enjoy tomorrow. Retirees. Students. Parents. This list goes on and on. Easter is often seen as the doorway to Heaven, the rite of passage into a perfect and satisfactory life to escape the torments of today. The question Jesus posed with his stories, words, and life questions this. Certainly, we can only live for the future, because this present instant is immediately gone. We have nothing but the future. Still, Jesus improved the lives of his friends and followers as they lived out their lives without promising Heaven tomorrow as a reward for today's suffering. Jesus offered an immediate life changing Kingdom of God rather than a promise for the distant future beyond death.

Easter is living our faith, not waiting for it. When Jesus offered the Kingdom of God, there were immediate changes in his friends and followers who accepted it. Fears fled, hope sparked, spirits rose, illnesses healed, and empowerment happened. Put a bit differently, life was lived with vigor and courage, faith and fulfillment. Living an Easter/resurrection life is living free and unencumbered. An elderly woman lived in quiet seclusion. When invited to participate in a religious festival, she said no, "I don't want to do anything that will jeopardize my future in Heaven with my Christ. I don't want to accidentally commit a sin." This is life denied. This is passivity, doing nothing; living as if dead.

Jesus, on the other hand, offered strength for the day to live, not die. Having the Kingdom of God frees a person to risk, to dare to live, and to boldly approach choices and make them. Christians live for others; they risk death, when appropriate, for others. The woman in the last paragraph did not live for others, but for herself. Her personal salvation was the only thing that truly mattered to her. She found little joy in living. But salvation, interpreted here as possessing the Kingdom of God, frees us to lose that selfish preoccupation with self and risk for others as we find joy and fulfillment in living.

The crucifixion was an ugly event choreographed by Rome to rid itself of minor political threats and lowlife criminals. Although God the Father did not sacrifice his son, the cross did happen, and Jesus did not run away to escape and did not argue strongly against it, but accepted it. We could ask why, but it seems obvious. His lifestyle promoted the Kingdom of God for others. To retreat from this would have denied the stories, words, and life he lived for his friends and followers. He could not deny them, no matter the cost. Many of those he gave the Kingdom of God lived harsh lives and were threatened by death every day. By giving them the Kingdom of God, he gave them the strength to live as they faced the severe hardships life offered them.

Easter does not promise life, it gives it. Those who experience the Easter Christ live in the present. Living with courage is the reward of Easter and the Kingdom of God. Christian courage is willing to risk infection by serving HIV patients, speaking out for justice for an enemy when most others want revenge, offering a newly freed prisoner an opportunity against popular trends never to hire a "con," befriending a psychotic when others think he is "crazy," seeking peaceful solutions rather than war, making friends with gays and lesbians rather than disdaining them, defending our environment rather than exploiting it, using money as a resource for good rather than an object of greed, embracing the homeless rather than avoiding them, defending those we strongly disagree with rather than silencing their voices, etc. These acts celebrate and honor Jesus' Kingdom of God.

Christian courage, a gift of Easter, permits making the human mistakes that demonstrates our weaknesses and fallibilities; it is living and doing. This may be the most significant characteristic, as many consider good behavior as passivity, the absence of doing evil. The cliché, "Children should be seen, not heard," illustrates this childishly. Do nothing to be good. Jesus never did "nothing." He challenged those in authority, debated their spokespersons, and questioned generally accepted principles. Jesus championed the have-nots of his day, argued with lawyers, and protested injustice.

The Kingdom of God challenges us to be aggressive for the ideals taught by Jesus. Strangely, Christians possessing the Kingdom of God never concern themselves with personal salvation. It is not important because they own the gift of Easter, therefore they are saved. Hell is not a concern; living today is what matters. God transcends the years through the wonder of Jesus of Nazareth, his stories, words, and life. God embraces us through the marvel of Easter. The Kingdom of God empowers us to live strong meaningful lives that willingly take risks.

When embraced by Easter and the Kingdom of God, we can stumble and know that we will not fall; we can err in the cause of good and know that we are safe, we can live for others as Jesus did, and we can be the daughters and sons of God because love holds us close.

Easter gives us the victory over death, not because we are promised eternal life, but because we are not afraid of death; we are too filled with life. Death holds no sting because we are made complete by the love of God. The victory of Easter becomes our victory when we experience Jesus in our lives now.

Do not fear death, for there is nothing to fear. Death is a mystery that engulfs us because we do not know or understand it. The promise of eternal life confronts death by denying it. Jesus faced death by accepting it. The idea of Heaven promises that death is better than life. To the contrary, Jesus lived his life as if it were better than death. He did not fear the unknown, but paid little attention to it and did not heed it as he gave his full attention to living and offered his friends and followers the Kingdom of God as a genuine reality of their lives.

———— • ✦ • ————

For centuries, religious thinkers have debated the "problem of evil." This problem attempts to answer the questions raised by evil in the world, especially natural evil such as deadly tornados, disease that adds pain to life, mental disease that reduces life, evil people who have little respect for life (except their own), floods that drown life, and fires that horribly burn life. These are fundamentally the evils we cannot explain or that appear to deny that God loves or even cares for us. The question is: can a loving God permit these disasters to strike humans?

This raises many issues far beyond the scope of this volume. Here are a couple of extremely brief questions. God is a loving God, but does she love humans more than other living creatures? Similarly, does God love living creatures more than inanimate objects? For example, does God give the earth as a planet less, the same as, or more than the beings that inhabit it? Indeed, some have persuasively argued that the earth, *Gaia*, is a living being. Human ego suggests that we are above all else because we are sensate, thinking, and feeling beings.

If God loves all beings, alive or not, evenly, then the natural disasters tend to maintain all things in more perfect balance and health. Forests cannot thrive without fire. Disease permits life forms that are the enemies of humans to live and thrive. Humans want to believe that we are very special. Science fiction novels tend to make the protagonists human-like. Alternate life-forms more often than not display distinctly humanlike shapes.

Part of this debate then is more accurately a discussion of human psychology or gross species egotism, that is, we love ourselves too much. Still, humans are more aware of themselves than any other living form that we know. At the same time, we are the thinkers, we are the species of which Jesus belonged and so we must deal with our own realities, not the reality of others. We cannot relate to or think like *Gaia* the living earth. We can only deal with ourselves and our human condition. Easter expresses this.

Easter becomes the human victory over adversity and the uncontrollable evil in the world. Jesus worked and lived in a harsh world, perhaps far harsher than ours. The difference is not of degrees, but of kind. They are just different. As Jesus related more closely to those with the least and suffering the most, the perspective focused on what could be controlled, not on what could not be controlled. Jesus led his people to survive in these harsh conditions. The conditions included abuse by humans, unfair social standards, elitist religious values, and political suppression as well as plagues and famines, disease and severe hot and cold.

The Kingdom of God does not empower people to overcome evil but live victoriously in spite of evil. Easter does not control the weather, but gives life meaning and purpose regardless of the weather. The resurrection does not conquer death, but gives us the strength to live great lives anyway.

Ours is the victory over the mental, emotional, and spiritual enemies that haunt us.

Ours is the victory.

Chapter Six
PENTECOST, A FIERY BEGINNING

Luke tells the story of Pentecost in the Acts of the Apostles. It is the first major story following the crucifixion and resurrection and the first account where the human Jesus of Nazareth does not participate. Pentecost announces the birth of the church, the union of believers blessed by the Holy Spirit.

The Acts of the Apostles is an extension of Luke's Gospel. Together they form a two-volume narrative, a story of Jesus and a story of the Christian movement after the execution of Jesus. The Pentecostal event received the power of the Holy Spirit, bonded together the first Christians, and immediately preceded the formation of the institutional church. Pentecost authenticates the beginning of the church as a spiritual union of believers.

To take the story of the church's birth literally destroys its Truth. It becomes mere history and interpreted history at that. Instead, the power of this mythic story demonstrates the Truth of the Church as a universal reality and as a collection of people who want to preserve the Truth of the faith. It is not merely the birth of the Church, however crucial this is, but it is also where the followers of Jesus take personal responsibility for the Truth of the message and mission of Jesus. To better understand the wonder of Christian responsibility and the marvel of empowerment, we need to look at the story with faithful imagination. Retelling Pentecost and the ensuing events in an imaginative way opens genuine insight into how the church formed. Merging this with the authenticating account in Acts offers a refreshing and different perspective. Retelling the story demands faith; it also demands reconstructing what the culture was like during that ancient age. We can never know for certain, but only make intelligent reconstructions based on available evidence and applying faith.

Jesus was dead. He died in a grossly humiliating and physically painful way; killed according to the law of the Roman occupying forces. The Gospels suggest that his closest followers hid in fear, a likely possibility. No one wanted to suffer an ugly, degrading, and painful death by crucifixion. Remaining at his side would not have helped Jesus. The Roman army would have still crucified him along with those other minor threats to the Roman Empire and low level criminals and may have added the faithful followers of Jesus to crosses of their own. To honor Jesus, his followers had to live and keep his memory alive, to communicate his stories, words, and life so others would be touched by them. The Twelve (a name for those closest to Jesus during his life ministry) and the other followers gathered in secret at Pentecost so that Rome could not easily find them.

Retelling stories about and by Jesus comforted and inspired them. Together they found strength and solace in Jesus and in each other as they bonded in faith. This togetherness is the key to the birth of the Church, for it led to both a common experience of Jesus and of the Holy Spirit.

Sharing Jesus and their own personal stories confirmed faith and strengthened them all. The same is true for us centuries later. When we live in isolation, we tend to wither. For example, isolating a prisoner in "solitary confinement" punishes them severely. An infant who is denied touching is emotionally stunted, perhaps for the rest of her life. Few, if any, can manage intense loneliness. Loneliness intensifies even more when, for whatever reason, society deems someone a deviant. Minorities tend to be called deviants, that is, they diverge from what is generally considered normal. Our culture considers criminals, the insane, drug addicts, religious fanatics, the homeless, political radicals, and those with different sexual orientations deviants. To protect itself and its ideas, society isolates deviants. They are ostracized from the mainline culture. Deviants who unite with other deviants are frequently considered dangerous. We fear gangs of criminals; institutionalize the insane; jail drug addicts; shun religious fanatics; frown on the homeless; challenge political radicals; and publicly list convicted sexual offenders on the Internet. However dangerous deviants may be when they unite and organize, it eases their loneliness and thereby strengthens them. Not all deviants are evil or dangerous, but society tends to treat them poorly regardless.

So it was for the followers of Jesus. Jesus had been executed as a criminal, so society would have considered his followers criminals at worst and deviants at best. Alone, each individual had limited and unsupported resources. Together, their individual resources were dramatically increased, and they supported and drew strength from each other. In addition to strengthened resources, they supported each other emotionally, spiritually, and intellectually. Collectively, it was a synergistic relationship where the whole was greater than its parts. Simplistically, it is like one plus one equals more than two. Together they were stronger than each of them individually. Among themselves, they gained additional strength to deal with public derision, being ostracized, and persecution.

There is also an aspect of "revival psychology." It is easier to feel and react to a "hell's fire and brimstone" sermon while a part of a congregation. Each participant supports the feelings and reactions of the others. Normally timid people boldly walk to the front of the congregation where everyone can see them as they respond to the emotion of the moment. "Revival psychology" may pervert the synergy of people bonded together in a mutual belief or cause, because it can manipulate people. It is a close relative to mob psychology which can produce very poor results. The wisdom of Christianity moved well beyond the negatives of revival psychology and found strength in their shared faith, purpose, and mutual cause. They spread the wonder of Jesus among those who neither understood about Jesus nor experienced his wonder.

Regardless, coming together synergistically is one of the marvelous experiences of participating in a church or religious movement. Those who share similar beliefs and values talk more openly and freely, and, thereby, grow and mature spiritually and emotionally. Intimacy thrives, and lives benefit.

This is the environment that the followers of Jesus shared immediately following his ignoble death. They huddled together from fear but gained spoken and unspoken support from each other. They became a group that would later be called a church. The spiritual foundation for the group was the common belief that Jesus of Nazareth gave them the Kingdom of God. Salvation became an event for the moment. This gave them the strength, courage, and wisdom to persevere despite genuine barriers and dangers from Rome.

Together their fears dissipated, replaced by self-assurance mutually sustained; doubts disappeared, replaced by confidence; fearful people felt their spirits lift and their hope restored. It was like being engulfed by a gentle warming flame. Holding hands secured each to the others. Individuals molded into a cohesive group sharing, reinforcing, and encouraging each other so they could speak freely amongst themselves on mutual concerns and faith. This initial "church" had no organization or structure. These developed very quickly as those who knew Jesus well lifted voices to remember Jesus and inspire each other.

Joy reached out and hugged each individual and quickly spread to reinforce the group. This unbounded joy pushed them to share this joy with others and birthed church growth. Peter and Paul and James, the brother of Jesus, became the early leaders who struggled with what Jesus truly meant to them and to the world. In a world growing more and more hostile, the bond of faith tied them together and strong leadership became critically important. From this grew an institution with structure and a developing dogma. The New Testament books are the initial writings that resulted in the early doctrine as well as sharing memories and stories. Paul strongly averred a theology that was uniquely his own, although informed by his experience of the Risen Lord. Paul stressed "salvation by faith." A few years later the writer of James (certainly not the James who was a member of the Twelve as reported in the Gospels) preached "salvation by works," an opposing view from Paul.

The four Gospels were directed to four different readerships. Each stressed faith a bit differently from the others because each separate community had different issues and leaders. The dogma derived from them varied and contributed to the whole Christian community. The dogma, as it developed, was not uniform. Relative uniformity would come late, at least two hundred years later when the books of the New Testament were canonized, that is, set as the final books of the Bible. Even then, uniformity was dramatically short-lived as denominations and different movements grew; each had a slightly different understanding of the Bible. Diversity ruled. The message of Jesus as handed down was not simplistically uniform, but nearly as diverse as the believers inspired by it.

There was also an unifying glue that held everything together, that transcended the diversity, and that enabled a church to develop and grow in a milieu made hostile by Roman antagonism, Greek pluralism, and Jewish protectionism. Rome wanted the Caesars lionized; the Greeks wanted their mystery religions to thrive; and the Jews wanted to keep their Hebrew roots pure and uncorrupted by this new Jewish-Christian movement. This hostility helped glue the earliest Christians together, for only in unity and mutual support could they exist and prosper.

I believe that the strongest glue bonding them together was the Kingdom of God. Although not mentioned outside the Gospels and using two names, the Kingdom of God and the Kingdom of Heaven (John's Gospel uses the term Eternal Life for essentially the same thing, but John is so different that the implications are not the same. Little material is shared with Matthew, Mark, and Luke while John is more mystical). The Kingdom of God was the gift that Jesus gave his followers. It was immediate, life-empowering, life-saving and, more than a promise for the future. In the Kingdom the present became more meaningful, powerful, and fulfilling.

Most often, Jesus gave this gift of the Kingdom by telling his marvelous and enigmatic stories. His followers retold the stories and sometimes expanded them. As they huddled in fear, they retold his stories and added stories about Jesus himself and stories about how their lives were changed as they encountered these stories. It was like passing the Holy Spirit to the next generations by stories and fellowship.

In the Acts of the Apostles, Luke graphically shows how the church began among a group of fearful followers of Jesus. This tiny group of faithful followers were empowered by a sound like the rushing wind, each touched by a tongue of flame and embraced by the Holy Spirit. Then, they spoke in foreign languages that were understood by the alien onlookers. This is interesting and startling imagery that, if taken literally, is an intrusion by natural forces in an unnatural way. The rush of a mighty wind can be deafening, shutting out everything else or, better, blowing other sounds away.

Taken more figuratively, the voice of Jesus overwhelms everything else. His human voice was stilled by the cross, but his continuing voice was not stilled by death but strengthened. The human accomplishments by Jesus during his lifetime were relatively modest. His influence was local and limited. But his continuing influence after death is anything but modest. Jesus conquered a world as his voice was echoed and strengthened by his followers for many centuries and into the modern age.

Noise or interference distorted his voice when human egos encroached. Human sin became louder and louder, muffling and distorting the voice of Jesus, sometimes nearly drowning it out. As humans became more and more preoccupied with their own human frailty, apparent powerlessness, and propensity to sin, the need for forgiveness became more and more important. The Kingdom of God that Jesus gave seemed unattainable. As the voice of Jesus became fainter and fainter and the din of the noise of human frailty grew louder and louder, the message of Jesus of the immediate empowerment in the face of gigantic adversity became distorted.

Rather than accepting the Kingdom of God and its parallel gift of responsibility, Christians began to rely more and more on the future Kingdom of God and dodged personal responsibility by returning it to God. Today's failures would be redeemed by tomorrow's victory led by the armies of God.

This is certainly the trend today. Today's message is clear: rely on God. Indeed, in some areas this has been reduced to mere superstition. E-mail on the Internet suggests that special blessings and improved luck happen when an e-mail is forwarded to others. Often, this is enhanced by even better luck and greater blessings when one sends out more than the specified minimum number of e-mails. This denigrates God and turns God into a humanly controlled superstition. To respond to this mentality denies genuine faith. We look for "God gimmicks" to overcome our human sense of helplessness.

Similarly, we believe ourselves to be so "wretched" that we cannot earn forgiveness; it must be given by a graceful God. Of course, ironically, we contradict our sense of wretchedness because we believe that we can earn forgiveness by giving our hearts to Christ. This requires that, when we give ourselves to Christ, God *must* respond by offering us salvation.

In contrast, rather than demanding that his followers rely totally on him, Jesus offered them the Kingdom of God and immediate empowerment to be responsible for their own lives. It is a strange quirk in the development and history of Christianity that a near complete reversal of Jesus' ministry happened. Yet, this appears to be the case. Today we prefer to rely on the Cross to forgive our wretched condition. This condition is based upon the terribleness of humans, especially when compared to the holiness and perfection of God. This denies the biblical account of creation where the theological foundation of humanity as those deemed worthy to have "dominion" (authority) over the other creatures. God trusted and gave responsibility to humans in the biblical account of creation.

The second creation story paints a far more brutal picture of humanity who, through Adam and Eve, aspired to be like God, to have all knowledge of good and evil. This is not a portrait of wretchedness. It is a portrait of humans who are not godlike and tend to yield to temptation and greed. They wanted to be godlike, but, ironically, their egotistical aspirations made them less godlike. In spite of this Old Testament portrait, Jesus offered the gift of the Kingdom of God and empowerment. This is not an easy gift for humans to accept. It is far easier to rely on the grace of God than to be responsible for ourselves.

Jesus empowered us to take responsibility for ourselves, to make difficult choices, to stand firm in the face of temptation and greed, and to push aside tendencies to cringe in fear and beg for mercy (forgiveness) rather than face the consequences of our choices. The voice of Jesus still shouts over the centuries as his stories and teachings live. To hear them is difficult. We wear faith as if to muffle and silence the competing sounds of church traditions, their theologies, fearful piety, a world captivated by war, and our human greed — the selfish factors. But we can hear his voice. This is the wonder and power of resurrection. Resurrection is divine empowerment of the human spirit. It is the continual reenactment of the relationship between Jesus and his followers many centuries ago. Jesus lives anew as we are made new. This is the ideal of the church.

We have been so preoccupied with sin and decadence that the good that Jesus saw in his followers has been lost, blurred and made indistinct. Some argue that Jesus gave up his life for the hopelessness of the human condition. However, even the Cross does not spell hopelessness, but is filled with hope. Jesus understood this long before any others. He saw hope in his followers and responded to them while he and they both lived. He "preached" the Kingdom of God and then confirmed it with his willingness to sacrifice himself for those he trusted rather than deny death.

Resurrection has come to mean that Jesus was physically raised to heaven and that he lives. The resurrection of the body has been questioned by many, but is a specific part of the dogma of many Christian denominations. I am convinced that the bodily resurrection is more of a human aspiration than a spiritual reality. Humans tend to want to live forever. This is supported by our fear of death and the attempt to extend our lives through bearing our children to continue our lives through them. The fear of death is mitigated by a belief in life after death. Life appears to have little meaning if we struggle to succeed, leave children, live active lives, and, finally, die and our accomplishments fade through death into nothingness. This has spawned cryogenics, freezing our bodies until a cure for the disease that killed us is found and, therefore, cure the disease, restore life, and overcome death. Cryogenic denies life after death in heaven in favor of extending human life on earth.

Eternal life and resurrection are human conceits that each individual should never die, but live forever. This echoes the human flaw graphically exposed in the Adam and Eve story in Genesis. The quest for the knowledge of good and evil, that is, having the knowledge of God, is what theology calls original sin (or disobeying God to gain the knowledge of good and evil), the original or innate craving of humans to be more than we are — to know all things and be like God. Mere mortals do not condemn our children for wanting to be like us; we want our children to be like us and, perhaps, improve a wee bit, too. Through our seed (children) we live again. It is difficult to believe that God would cast us off because we want to be godlike as the Adam and Eve myth suggests. Imitating a parent seldom drives a wedge between parent and child, but flatters and draws them closer together.

These are similar — wanting to live forever and wanting to be godlike. Both reflect our human ego stretching its limits. Although there are certainly notable aberrations like Adolf Hitler and Sadam Hussein, humans are not the wretches that some Christians would have us be. There appears to be in most humans a kindness, tenderness, and goodness that belies basic perversity. The image of God embraces it and Jesus enhances it with the Kingdom of God. Here is where resurrection takes on great meaning. Resurrection is when the image of God within us meets the Kingdom of God.

The image of God within us is our potential to be more than we are. Within is a divine spark — God within the human being. This spark is not something implanted as a physical part of our being as some searched for years ago, suggesting, for example, that it was located in the pituitary gland. It is the potential that we all have to reach beyond our limited physical, mental, and emotional being. It is not a rare characteristic, but far more common than we would believe. The image is stirred when new insights are born, the "aha" experience that psychologists call gestalt. It is stirred when we discover good in someone we thought evil; when we shed an unexpected tear over someone's misfortune; when we understand someone who appears unreasonable; when we defend someone we strongly disagree with; when we offer love rather than pity; when we take up a cause and sacrifice for it. The magic of the image within is its ability to smile at our personal discomfort and feel compassion over another's because we see her pain. The image of God stirs when our self-centered egos fade and nobleness rises. It is in all of us, a gift of creation.

―――――――・◆・――――――

The Kingdom of God is God's gift through Jesus. Jesus told his stories and preached his sermons; he healed the sick and befriended the unworthy. The God within him reached out to his friends and to us to stir minds and rouse feelings; to embrace the image within and transform our being. This happens today, not tomorrow, although it makes our tomorrows far better and more meaningful. Resurrection is for living, not for dying.

The Kingdom of God did not die with Jesus, but lives with Jesus and with us. We have so stressed conquering death physically that the spiritual value of reaching beyond the barrier of death and time has been neglected. When we can move beyond our human need to live forever and never die, perhaps, we can look at the resurrection of Jesus as a spiritual reality. To do this effectively, let us look at Jesus. As mentioned earlier, the most reliable information on Jesus is contained in his words, his sayings and stories. The narrative material about him probably reflects his life to some extent, but is so overlaid with reflections by and concerns of the early church that historical information is extraordinarily difficult to reconstruct, if not impossible.

Still his words, especially his parables, most accurately reflect the person behind them, his interests and concerns. His parables are particularly important because they clearly reveal his respect for people, their ability to think and react. Jesus gave them the Kingdom of God to embrace them while they lived, to strengthen their living, and to inspire their lives. Jesus was far more interested in his followers while they lived. This suggests an important value for Jesus; he was more concerned for his followers, and all people, while they lived and we live.

This was apparently true even for himself. Although never afraid of death, Jesus struggled to live and to share his life with others. He did not live to die, but to make life more meaningful and rich, to snatch victory from defeat, to confront life rather hide from it. His model for us was to live fully, richly, and victoriously. He never healed to prepare someone for death or even afterlife; he healed to restore full and rich lives. Jesus embraced children because they were at the beginning of life, not the end; he offered the Kingdom to immediately enhance life, not endure until the next world. Jesus does not elevate the next life above the present one. To the contrary, he elevated *this life* above all else.

Resurrection is not some future hope, but a present reality. It is Jesus hurdling across time and death to speak to us, to touch and enrich our living, and to embrace us as his friends and followers. The life of Jesus was not frozen to a few short years, but spans all time and any other barriers between him and us.

To experience Jesus, we do not have to die. This would be like imitating God in Jesus who truly spans eternity. Rather, we hear a word preached and feel it reaching inside and touching our hearts and minds; we sit and reflect on a passage of Scripture and feel our spirits raising; we quietly reflect on life and feel our lives being refreshed; we think about something Jesus said and feel the weight of life lifting; we close our eyes and visualize Jesus reaching for us and feel strength and power surging through our bodies and souls. There are so many ways to feel the power of resurrection grip us in love and faith that no list can contain them.

Sometimes we just relax and let our minds go blank so that God in Jesus can embrace us. Other times, we feel the full power of stress or pain attack us only to experience Jesus lending us his strength to empower our strength. Read the daily headlines shouting human weakness and foolishness and, in contrast, feel the wisdom of Jesus raise questions, suggest answers, and prod our thinking.

Resurrection is such a marvelously positive experience that to add cautions seems wrong, but, as Mark 13 suggests, there are those people and ideas that come disguised as Jesus but are false and deceptive, misleading people with easy answers and rigid thought. Jesus stirred imaginations but never raised a voice to hurt or injure another. Jesus tickled our minds, never offered absolutes to fossilize thinking. He touched to heal, never to kill. He always loved, never hated.

We must be alert to those who promote teachings that conflict with what we know about Jesus. Some lift the name of Jesus Christ to support racial superiority, ethnic purity, economic injustice, political extremism, religious elitism, and radical nationalism. These are not consistent with the Jesus of the Gospels or the original Christian faith. Christians seek truth and enlightenment, compassion and caring, peace and justice among all people. This leaves Christians with some choices to make. This is one of the delights of Christianity, we can make choices. There is no easy and clearly marked road map to faith that guides us to make better choices. Jesus told stories to urge us to freely make choices. He did not preach rigid and unyielding thoughts for us to blindly follow. Rather, he encouraged thoughtfulness and imagination. Thoughtfulness can reach inside and change us and our consciences. Imagination pushes the edges of the ordinary and common to reveal the extraordinary and unique. Christians dare not accept anything that is preached as absolutely true about our faith. There are false prophets among us — many of them.

Christian conscience is tricky. It is not something we develop as a result of our encounter with Jesus, although this seriously influences it. Rather, conscience is a subjective value unconsciously created from all of our experiences and knowledge. The uniqueness of human beings strongly suggests that the conscience of each individual differs from every other person because each of us is unique and from different environments. Conscience does not measure absolute justice or righteousness. It measures the mind-set and values of the individual as preconditioned by parents, church, teachers, friends, school, and the other influences that move us toward adulthood. Conscience is the repository of our values that influences our thoughts and actions, our beliefs and faith. It works both consciously and unconsciously. Consciously, it helps us to choose what is right. Unconsciously, it plants guilt.

As our values change with new experiences and influences, our conscience also changes. Jesus clearly approached his followers to change them internally, to stir their consciences as well as their conscious thoughts. His parables provoked, challenged, stirred, disturbed, and delighted them and us. He never demanded total conformity, but freed us to choose and change. Notice that Jesus freed us to change, did not force it or try to make us uniform and make all people the same. As each individual is unique, so each change is unique. However, the standards of Jesus are not limitless. He did not kill or maim, did not corrupt or insult, and did not demand robotic conformity. Jesus recognized the talents and abilities of his followers and encouraged free and inspired thinking. Still, there are limits to what can be called Christian.

Be cautious when considering something said to be part of Christian conscience. This can dangerously mislead. Jesus offered us choices. False christs offer limited perspectives, limited points-of-view, and a rigidity that belies the stories of Jesus.

A wise man once said that "truth is more important than sincerity." In contrast, a delightful woman commenting on a televangelist said, "He is just so sincere." Sincerity is illusory, an appearance that can deceive. Another televangelist cries on cue suggesting more sham than sincerity, but it looks sincere. For genuine faith, we must discern the difference between truth and sincerity. Believing something does not make it true. We believe in things not seen. To find faith, we must leap over the obstacles that blur our view. Indeed this is a definition of belief (faith). Sören Kiekergaard, the Danish philosopher and theologian suggested a "leap of faith." This, however, implies that we leave our minds behind and just jump.

Again, Jesus offers some models for us. They appear in parables, sayings, and deeds as recorded in the Gospels. We look for complete clarity to guide our faith, but are confused by diversity. Contrast the Sermon on the Mount with the parables. The Sermon on the Mount is mostly a collection of sayings that could be viewed as rather pedantic and rigid. This may have been Matthew's intention when he collected these sayings and put them together into a whole. Even so, the sermon strongly features a wide variety of ideas and ideals. One argument against this sermon being a single sermon is its complexity. So many ideas are discussed that no one could absorb them at one time. Tomes have been written to explore the sermon's meanings and interpretations. These voluminous works are not uniform; they do not say the same things; the interpretations are different, sometimes vastly different. It is as if simple and straightforward statements by Jesus are neither simple nor straightforward, but open to be understood differently by the individual mindsets of listeners and readers. Dogma disappears, and multiple understandings replace single-minded doctrine.

Like most of his sayings, the Sermon on the Mount frees and stimulates thoughtfulness rather than blind obedience. Christian faith is not rigid but flexible. It does not offer absolutes as much as broad guidelines. Christians find our way by thoughtfully and faithfully reacting to Jesus and, therefore, to our world, its foibles and successes. Jesus stretches our minds and imaginations so that the ordinary becomes extraordinary, the dull shines, the obtuse becomes clear, and challenges become victories. Our world can be a barrier that the illumination of our faithful minds must leap to transform cynicism into optimism. The heroes in this world are not the well-armed warriors whom we honor with statues, but caring teachers, healing physicians, concerned neighbors, compassionate friends, and helpful strangers. We seldom erect statues of them, for they do not demand it, but we honor them by recognizing the image of God in them and by emulating them.

This is not seeing the world through "rose colored glasses." Rather, it approaches the ugly knowing that beauty is there, too; it faces the demonic and overcomes it; and it confronts hopelessness and offers hope. It is the same attitude that Jesus had when considering his followers and others around him. They were not hopeless and helpless people who were destined to live in sin, but people with the potential to realize the most from the image of God within. Jesus gave them the Kingdom of God that lifted them to new and fulfilled lives. We have within us the image of God, and Jesus, reaching through time, gives us the Kingdom of God. We have new lives. We live!

Chapter Seven
TRINITY, GOD WRIT THREE

A friend takes special care and uses great skill to wrap her gifts. So special are her packages that, when seeing her gifts, the refrain is often spoken, "It's so beautiful, I hate to open it." Another friend received one of those extremely well wrapped boxes, a tiny ring sized box, and declared that she was going to keep and add it to her Christmas tree ornaments. She recognized that this would deny her the gift because she could not unwrap it without destroying it, and didn't know how to resolve her dilemma. In this instance, she chose the wrapped box. Suppose that she could find a way to have both, the gift and the wrapped gift box. This would be a far better resolution. It reminds us of the cliché, "having your cake and eating it, too."

This was the situation in the ancient world for Christians. They followed their religious roots and believed themselves to be monotheistic, believers in one God and only one God. They had a problem, however; they experienced three Gods, the Creator (Father), the Great Revealer and Savior (Messiah), and the living faith Experience (Holy Spirit). The problem of the package arose; how could Christians embrace all three understandings of God and remain monotheistic? Without going into the details of how this happened, which involved church councils, acrimonious debate, and contentious issues, especially describing the nature of Jesus, let's look at the result: the Holy Trinity.

Many argue that religion is a search for answers to the unknown. There is a seed of truth to this as demonstrated by the reality that almost all religions from Christian-Judeo traditions to primitive animism have creation stories. These answer the questions we all have when we look at the natural world in awe and at nature's power such as earthquakes, hurricanes, tornadoes, and fire. The many and greatly imaginative creation stories of indigenous peoples around the world are interesting reading, great storytelling, and mythically answer the questions about nature's power. In the same way, Christianity adopted the two Jewish creation stories preserved in Genesis about how the world came into being, its creation. These are not truly compatible and stress two distinct viewpoints. The seven-day sequence stresses the creation of the physical world which culminates in making humans superior. The Adam and Eve story stresses humans as the primary focus of God's interest but who are also tragically flawed.

As we view creation, we can be inspired by it. Something happens that is almost unexplainable. Simplistically and naively, I am still awed by a full moon hanging without visible support in the sky. Lightening strikes fear, and I run for shelter. Holding my children for the first time overwhelmed me. Creation, the making of our world and its living creatures, is a reality that is beyond my personal comprehension. I read Einstein's theories for a logical explanation of the universe and some understanding penetrates, but the vastness and diversity of the universe still stretches my imagination. Viewing the greening of the trees in spring tingles my nerves. Feeling the sudden awakening of my intellect, the "aha," is both deeply satisfying and disturbing. Where did the new insight suddenly come from?

Such is the power of creation for me. I can only speak for myself, but there appears to have been similar experiences for others throughout history; primitive religions such as animism worship creation and its mysteries. The modern debate in American education illustrates the power of creation in some Christian thinking. Evolution vs. creationism (more recently disguised as "intelligent design") still haunts many communities. Religiously, I find the debate somewhat useless.

Evolution is the best scientific explanation. Consider how much better we human beings would be if every aspect of our being was consciously the creation of God. We would have no flaws, war would not exist, human degradation would be replaced by human dignity, competition would find a way to have no losers, and death would hold no fear. Intelligent design makes no sense, for if God had consciously and carefully planned creation, then all would be in order, but it is not. Natural disasters still strike with devastating cruelty; evil does exist in the world; and a prevalent characteristic of civilization is human brutality to other humans as well as planned economic and social injustice.

The power behind creation may not be understood but as we look at the heavens and our own tiny planet and its inhabitants, it remains something truly beyond our imaginations. To blame all that is in the world and the world itself on God is misdirection. God is in and a part of the world. The concept of creation, although answering some of our more basic mysteries, puts God "out there," rather than "in here" and denies the God within and the reality of Jesus. It is not necessary to have an answer to everything. The randomness of evolution is no less inspiring in its success than finding the mind of God behind it all. Evolutionary randomness is extremely inspiring. The idea of order and intelligence emanating from randomness is totally illogical and, therefore, beyond our human ability to understand. It is a total mystery, something we humans do not like. Those who struggle with the mystery of creation forget the marvelous story of the Tree of the Knowledge of Good and Evil. Did not Adam and Eve fall from Eden precisely because they wanted to know everything, i.e., become like God. Ah, the mystery of creation is exactly that, a mystery, as God is a mystery.

The Trinitarian formula moves beyond God as creator; it is Father, Son, and Holy Spirit. Father is a synonym for Creator. God fathered the world. As a male, a father, I envied the mother of my children whose relationship with our children in birth was far, far more profound than my own. I may have provided the million or so sperms chasing a single egg, but the mother provided the egg, the nourishment, the home, and the ultimate love that brings a child into being. And after the child bursts into the world, the mother is the only one capable of continuing to nourish the infant.

112   JESUS: A MAN FOR ALL TIME

How pretentious for Christianity to create a formula that is so male dominated that it neglects its more important female characteristics. Males have larger body mass and stronger muscles suited for hunting and conflict. Females have smaller body mass and generally softer surfaces suited for caring and nourishing. Somehow bigger and stronger has erroneously been translated into better. This has been true throughout history and never more prominently than in today's world with universal steroid abuse and near hero status for sports figures. War heroes are venerated while peacemakers are perceived as intellectual fops. In Washington, DC, our nation's capital, the memorials and statuary for war far out number those for peacemakers, scientists, artists, poets, and philosophers.

This is a strange perversion. The strength of civilization lies in its female characteristics: caring for each other, nourishing the weak to make them healthier, and making peace instead of war. Stressed and injured children seek the warmth and comfort of mothers far more than fathers. Reality suggests that the male characteristics are central because we frequently hate those who are different (racism), we build weapons to destroy, and we threaten rather than negotiate. God as Father stresses the negative. A far better term would be Mother, and better still, Parent.

The Father and Mother, the Parent, is a genuine paradox. The Parent is everywhere and, at the same time, within each of us individually. Certainly, this is a logical contradiction; the third person of the trinity, the experience of the Holy Spirit validates this.

The second person is the significant one for Christians, the Son. The Romans executed Jesus somewhere around 30 CE. The Christian Church was created sometime after this, if we follow the account recorded in "The Acts of the Apostles." Jesus did not found the church named after him. His followers did. The church was founded, therefore, upon the memory of Jesus and how the first Christians experienced him. Paul, the first to write for what would later be called the New Testament, penned 1 Thessalonians about 20 years after the execution of Jesus or around 50 CE. The church was founded after the life of Jesus and before the distinctly Christian New Testament was written.

The stories about Jesus and by Jesus were told and retold until they were burned into the memories of those who followed him. Christians gathered in small groups in the homes of believers and together they created rituals around these stories and teachings and focused on the last meal Jesus shared with his followers. This meal was recreated until they internalized Jesus into their souls and spirits. Jesus lived in these faithful people and came alive in their rituals and meal sharing. Jesus not only lived within these people, he brought them a new life that sustained their faith and living.

Jesus is the genuine revelation of God, the Parent. Jesus lived among us as a complete human, but lived and spoke in such a way that revealed God. Before Jesus, God was most often characterized through his wrath rather than love. He did express love when he both renewed the covenants to bridge the alienation between humans and God and renewed the relationship established between them. At the same time, there were plagues and war, incest, political intrigue, genocide, and all manner of cruelty. The New Testament reflects some of this, especially in books like Revelation (Apocalypse) where extreme punishment (fire and brimstone) was inflicted upon the enemies of Christ and who were later vanquished in the final conflict at Armageddon.

Jesus is consistently portrayed as gentle and courageous, willing to face death rather than take a life, a healer who preserved life and never took it. This is the picture where Jesus reveals the Parent, the One who cares for people, their condition and personal value. This is how the friends and followers of Jesus met God.

The second person of the Holy Trinity was born, not in the flesh of an infant birthed by Mary, but in the lives and experiences of each generation of his followers. Jesus also brought into being the third person of the Trinity, the Holy Spirit.

The memory and spirit of Jesus animated the early Christians; Jesus' memory and spirit brought them alive. This is the same as a modern conversion experience relived again and again. Something happens to an individual that can be as unique as each person: a warm feeling, a sudden increased heart beat, an overwhelming experience of goodwill, a sense of completeness and fulfillment, a mystical consciousness of reality, or an awareness of humility mixed with fullness of heart and faith. It can be any of these, all of these, or something completely different. In any event, a person feels different and is aware that a change has taken place that is unexplainable but meaningful.

This experience is the Holy Spirit, the animating and holy reality that grabs and holds those with faith. Because it extends far beyond physical and time limitations, it is beyond our everyday knowledge, an unsolved mystery and a mystical reality.

The Holy Spirit is more than a singular event, it sustains as well as inspires. Once inspired, a person is re-inspired again and again. Also, there is no time limitation. People are embraced by the Holy Spirit today, nearly two thousand years after the events that led to and carried out the execution of Jesus of Nazareth.

The Spirit touches the holy within us to enrich and inspire. It does not act as a voice that overrides our own voice. The Holy Spirit is not a military leader issuing orders to willing troops. This violates the principles of trust that Jesus demonstrated so clearly in his storytelling and parables. Rather, the Spirit inspires but does not dictate. It inspires the discernment and wisdom that each of us has within as part of the God within us. We are embraced and, therefore, can act with ethical and moral wisdom, or not act at all.

Those who act vindictively and viciously hear a voice that is not of God and is not the Spirit within, but is from their psychological imbalances. Evil is not a genuine spiritual value or motivation, but a perverted psychological condition. Similarly, war is not a spiritual value, but a perverted psychological condition. A "holy war" contradicts any premise of God, either Christian or otherwise.

Although the purpose of this volume is to open discussion on the nature of the Son and focus on the supremacy of his humanness, there remains his divinity. An easy explanation is to parallel Jesus and the Holy Spirit, and this is a valid approach. There is more to the divinity of the Son, Jesus the Christ.

History is filled with charismatic personalities, those whose strength of personality dominates a discussion or a gathering of people. A key politician works a crowd by touching hands as she passes by; a popular singer walks on stage and a fan faints; an actor's spellbinding performance mesmerizes an audience; or a poet's rhythms enthralls listeners. Occasionally, words reach beyond the centuries to enchant moderns through the Bible or poetry. Even more rarely, a religious or moral leader attracts followers for centuries, like Buddha or Mohammed. But none but Jesus has been worshipped as God for so long. Egyptian Pharaohs and Roman Caesars were worshipped, but their divinity was forgotten shortly after their deaths.

In contrast, the divinity of Jesus was not truly recognized until after his death. His divinity grew as the years passed. The difference, to me, is that Jesus himself never claimed to be God. Even John's Gospel, the most mystical and spiritual of the four, never portrayed Jesus as God. Rather, John's Jesus always and clearly subordinated himself to the Father. John does make the relationship between Son and Father intimate and close, but never equal. The critical question is how Jesus of Nazareth, a human, became a God, the Son of the Trinity.

My argument is speculative, but follows the description of Jesus giving the Kingdom directly to his friends and followers. The people Jesus encountered throughout his walk through life were profoundly changed. Those who had been long ignored or abused found love and compassion that changed and empowered them. They became more than they were before their encounter with Jesus. They became more alive. Some experienced fear and cowered before the Romans and their religious enemies, but as they had been changed, empowered, and made more alive, they never completely returned to who they were before.

These first Christians became the seed for the larger community, the church, that soon developed. As they gathered and shared their encounters with Jesus, the importance of Jesus grew and blossomed. Themselves changed, empowered, and newly alive, Christians changed, empowered, and brought new life to others. As they told and retold stories about Jesus and the stories Jesus told, something happened, the newer Christians encountered Jesus for themselves. Changed lives became the heart of the new movement. The power that changed those lives became more and more important. For some, not all, Jesus became God. Not all Christians accepted this elevation, which prompted the debates concerning the divinity of Jesus and created the Trinity as the solution. Nevertheless, the power of the living Jesus, the Christ, to renew life, to bring inner peace, to raise personal confidence, to make whole the broken, and to sharpen spirits became a divine power worthy of worship.

The Christian Trinity is a human intellectual construct to explain the unexplainable multiple ways we experience and know God.

Chapter Eight
THE SACRAMENTS, HOLY THINGS

The Sacraments divide the Christian movement rather than unite, but they should unite. Sacraments are generally defined as those aspects of the Christian life that Jesus ordained. Roman Catholics have seven: communion, baptism, ordination, marriage, confession, last rites, and confirmation. The names of some of these have changed. Confession is now called reconciliation, for example. However, confession is more universally recognized between all denominations and some other religions, as well. So, I will use the older, more universally recognized terms. Protestants generally limit the sacraments to communion and baptism. The arguments for and against seven or two solve very little. There is much to commend all of them and good arguments for not recognizing the additional five as sacraments.

For this work, however, I will discuss primarily communion and baptism because they are universally recognized and play a major role in the life of Christians before looking briefly at the other five to seek greater understanding of their meanings and roles. We will look at baptism first.

Jesus was baptized, but never baptized others. John baptized Jesus; Jesus apparently baptized no one, although a persuasive argument can be made that he did while a disciple of John the Baptizer. However, during the ministry of Jesus as presented by the four Gospels, he did not baptize. To understand Jesus better, we need to look first at John the Baptist. He was probably a member of the Jewish sect, the Essenes, who frequently immersed themselves in large water filled baths as ritual cleansings. For them, baptism was not performed once, but often, sometimes several times a day, to keep them spiritually clean. From this background, John brought a message of sinfulness. If he followed the Essene practice of multiple baptisms to cleanse himself of sin, then his preoccupation with sin is understandable. The New Testament describes him wearing harsh and scratchy clothing, eating bugs, and screaming condemnations at people that they were sinners.

He taught that his baptism cleansed the sin from sinners and gave them new opportunities for living. His call to repentance was abusive and filled with invectives. John demanded discipline from his followers. In contrast to Jesus, John did not trust his followers, and required them to be baptized to be cleansed from sin and to carefully follow his way. All other ways were wrong. Only his way was correct. The absoluteness of John's beliefs or religious positions was set. It appears that in some instances the Christian movement carefully follows this absoluteness dogmatically.

Jesus was probably a disciple of John and learned the theology of condemnation, cleansing, disciplined obedience, and dogma. What is most startling about their relationship is that Jesus turned away from the ways of John. Jesus trusted those who followed him and offered them the Kingdom rather than condemnation and total obedience. Jesus did not demand slavish compliance with a single dogma. Rather, Jesus offered the opposite, freedom to think for themselves, liberty to choose discipleship or reject it, principles based on individual interpretations, and the burden to choose rather than have a choice thrust upon them.

Baptism in the Christian movement reflects John's thinking and Jesus' radical shift. Jesus, however, did not speak about baptism. Only his submission to John's baptism gives us any hint about what he thought about the rite preserved in all Christian movements. To understand what Jesus thought or intended we will treat the baptism of Jesus as a parable. This can be risky, since we are rethinking an event that has been for centuries treated as a literal occurrence and looking at it with new eyes that are sensitive to storytelling. The Gospel accounts are stories, loosely formed biographies that defy all modern rules for biography. The Gospels are far more interested in showing the impact of Jesus, the Christ, on the life of the Church than in the actual biographical events of the life of Jesus, the man, as demonstrated by the lack of consistency between the four Gospels and even some of the letters of Paul. However, the baptism of Jesus by John did happen.

The primary focus of the Gospels on the impact Jesus had can be quickly seen in the choice of the events that the Gospel writers chose. There is very little about his personal life except where a religious point is made. One of the better examples of this is Luke's account of the youthful encounter of Jesus, as a young lad, with the religious thinkers during a short visit to Jerusalem. In addition to revealing his great wisdom at a very young age, it portrays the youth as very callous, completely ignoring the concern of his parents for his safety. Only his immediate concerns mattered. The story also reveals a Jesus who appears more interested in the intellectual aspect of faith than in the emotional. Jesus is portrayed as superior to the adults.

Matthew, Mark, Luke, and John did not write casual biographies of a great man, but wrote documents to instill and encourage faith in Jesus by their friends and followers in the various Christian communities. They wanted to share the "good news" of their faith and the one who inspired it, Jesus of Nazareth, not so much the man who walked the earth, but the Risen Lord who directly impacted their lives decades after Jesus was executed. The Gospels were stories carefully constructed to inspire, not inform. Although the Gospels relied on other sources (Matthew and Luke relied on Mark and "Q"[2]), they were frequently read, in whole or in part, to gathered congregations. In a very genuine way, the Gospels were communicated orally, as a story read or told.

---

[2]Q refers to the material common to Matthew and Luke but not found in Mark. It is a meaningless term in itself and it is assumed that this material was found by both Gospel writers in a document that no longer exists. It was lost in antiquity.

The story is a simple one, told different ways depending on the Gospel. Jesus approaches John the Baptist at the Jordan River and submits to being baptized. Historically, because of the number of those being baptized, immersion by John usually meant the followers entered the water and immersed themselves in the river under the supervision of the Baptist. The elements of the story are unique and a bit confusing. Luke adds a unique detail when the prenatal John the Baptist leapt in the womb of his mother Elizabeth in the presence of the unborn Jesus in the womb of Mary. Later, the adult John confirms when he recognizes Jesus as greater than John, who is unworthy to baptize his younger cousin. John, the wild and ranting preacher who condemned the world, suddenly reversed himself as the one who demanded repentance from all and now accepted a subservient role. Yet, in another reversal, the Baptist never joined those who followed Jesus, but remained a competing movement.

The baptism was never portrayed as a simple event, one baptism among hundreds if not thousands, but as a spectacular event where the baptism plays an introductory role to the Holy Spirit. The Spirit descends like a dove and splits the heavens as God pronounces Jesus the "beloved son in whom I am well pleased." Wow! Jesus is truly someone who is very, very special. John the Baptist considers himself a lesser being, the Holy Spirit descends, and God, the Father, pronounces this man Jesus to be extraordinary and specially loved.

Visualize a group of people sitting at the feet of an early Christian leader and hearing this story for the first time. Storytelling is more than an auditory art. Well-told stories evince a visual response and tap our other senses as well. Listeners would see a dove descend and hear a voice from heaven. They may have visualized the Baptist in his rough hewn and forbidding clothing and Jesus focused in the light from the split heavens and dressed far more elegantly even if equally humbly.

The baptism of Jesus was not a simple sequence of brief events to those hearing it as a story, but an assault on their emotions as well as stimulating the brain. None of them would have experienced the story in exactly the same way. It was not like a small part of a biography that was interesting, but a whole scene engrossing them completely, embracing their thoughts and tantalizing their emotions. The baptism of Jesus stirred them.

We cannot know what each person felt, but they likely shared more fully in the life of this marvelous man. Some would have wanted, perhaps, to experience the baptism as Jesus did, to hear the voice of God approving them, to see the heavens split so the light of the sun dazzled them, to see the dove of the Holy Spirit touch them gently. They did not need to understand the story to participate in it. To hear the story is to participate in it and in Jesus.

The baptism was and is understood as the event that initiated the ministry of Jesus. As the church grew and time passed, baptism was part of the initiation ritual into the Christian movement. There is a close parallel — baptism initiated the ministry of Jesus, and initiated the later followers into the movement. The question this raises concerns what is the role of this sacrament. Indeed, is it a genuine sacrament?

As mentioned above, a sacrament is a rite or ritual that was blessed or endorsed by Jesus. This is a loose interpretation. For example, the wedding at Cana (John's Gospel) is the justification for wedding as a sacrament, but the Cana story stresses converting water into wine; the wedding was the context of the scene, not the focus of the scene. This is a highly suspect reason for classifying weddings as sacrament. Or, the sacrament of ordination in Roman Catholicism is not truly mentioned in the New Testament. Baptism, as demonstrated above, was never spoken about nor performed by Jesus.

The reality is that the sacraments are what the church, Roman Catholic and Protestant, deem sacred. The holy claim to biblical origins can be supported only with a large dose of imagination. On the other hand, what we believe to be sacred is a valid reason to call something a sacrament. Using this logic, we could add at least one more, meditation or the mystical experience. This is a personal experience that Jesus certainly experienced. Although forty days in the wilderness facing temptation probably refers back to the forty years the Israelites spend in the wilderness fleeing Egypt, the forty days in the wilderness still represents an extended period of time. My faith tells me that Jesus meditated while fasting and entered a mystical state. Regardless, those who have experienced mysticism have made a significant contribution to the Christian movement from Meister Eckerd and Saint Bernadette to modern Pentecostals.

We cannot leave this brief discussion without acknowledging that a mystical experience can be drug induced and is frequently used to manipulate others. LSD and marijuana induce experiences that are certainly not holy experiences. Although a southwestern tribe of Native Americans use Peyote as part of their spiritual rituals.

Baptism does not cleanse us from sin, ala the Baptist. This smacks more of magic than faith or a regeneration of our spirits. Water and soap may wash away a great deal of dirt, but does not penetrate beneath the skin into our inner being. However, those receptive to the meaning of the baptism of Jesus can be energized into a new life as Jesus entered into a new phase of his own life, his ministry.

For some, especially immersion, emulates dying to sin and rising to new life, a sin-free life. This is great as a symbol; unfortunately it does not generally work in real life. A newly baptized individual seldom has a sudden personality change. This happens only when a person is open and ready for a major change.

Baptism should be considered a sacrament because it is a major experience of holiness for adults being baptized and for the families of baptized children. Like the ancient sacrament, it is a ritual of initiation for children and adults. It marks the passage into the community of faith. This is important, for it moves beyond a personal experience and includes the community of faith. If baptism is initiation into the community, then the community must, in some way, respond by welcoming the newcomer.

There is responsibility for both, the one baptized and the community. A newly baptized child becomes part of the community and, therefore, the community takes partial responsibility of the nurturing of the child.

Baptism is also a sign of one's humble submission to faith and holiness. This is most obvious in immersion by an aware youth or adult, but is also present in infant baptism by the presentation of the child and the application of water. A humble submission also suggests a willingness to change, however subtly. This is not change, of course, but willingness and a will to change.

We dare not neglect baptism as the forgiveness of sins. The Roman Catholic tradition considers infant baptism as fundamental to the Christian life because it washes from the child the inherited sins from past generations. This is based on the Old Testament narrative that cites that the sins of the fathers will be visited upon their children for generations to come. This makes for good storytelling, but does it mean that sin is passed like a gene from parents to children, the grandchildren, and so forth? Hardly. There is certainly a propensity for humans to sin or do evil, however minor, but this cannot translate in the sins of generations ago staining our newly-born infants. We do a great job, as we raise them, of passing on bad habits and evil thoughts.

To listen to Jesus explain this is to take what little we know of him and recognize that he loved all people, children as well, and saw in humanity a huge potential for growth and possibilities.

Communion is another sacrament recognized by all facets of the Christian movement, except Friends, Quakers, who may consider meditation and mysticism as sacraments. Regardless, the evidence in the New Testament sustains the sacrament in a variety of ways, primarily the

Last Supper, a key part of the end of the life of Jesus. Paul attests to it in his letter, especially Romans, and the parables of Jesus also support it with the Parable of the Great Banquet.

The practice of communion is diverse, not only how the meal is served, but what the meal means. At one end of the spectrum are the Roman Catholic Church and some Orthodox Churches that the communion elements (bread and wine) become the literal body and blood of Jesus. The prayer of consecration by the priest transforms simple bread into divine flesh, and common wine (fruit of the grape) into holy blood. The actual substance becomes a new substance.

The opposite end of the spectrum is communion as a memorial. There is no change of substance, bread does not become flesh and wine does not become blood. The bread and wine stir memories in the faithful of the Last Supper and the great life that Jesus lived on our behalf.

In between are denominations that believe that the bread and wine are spiritually the body and blood of Jesus. No physical transformation takes place. The spirit of the Christ is present in both bread and wine.

All of these options miss a critical point. At the Last Supper, Jesus shares a final meal with his closest associates, his friends. It is an intimate meal where Jesus shares his fear that the end of his life is near, initiated a way for his friends to remember him, and exposed a betrayer. Note an interesting detail — in Luke Jesus shares his meal of remembrance with the Twelve before exposing the betrayer. In Matthew and Mark, he exposes the betrayer, but does not ask him to leave the intimate fellowship of the meal. This is a totally unexpected twist on the events. We have read this story so frequently that this detail is often neglected. It is a critical detail in understanding Jesus' approach to sharing at a dining table.

Jesus does not exclude anyone from sharing a meal even with the despicable betrayer, Judas Iscariot. Most often we would think that he should exclude Judas before sharing the meal, not after, especially an intimate meal. Jesus never dismisses Judas. Like the parables of Jesus, this event turns "normal" conventions upside down. Jesus shares an intimate experience with someone he knew was to betray him. The betrayal had already been set into motion. It needed only the final kiss to complete it.

To understand this strange event, we turn to one of the parables, the Banquet. A man wants to celebrate, so he plans a banquet and invites his friends to share it with him. One by one, they decline and offer legitimate excuses for not attending. The man is left with a banquet, lots and lots of food, but no one to share it with him. To understand this dynamic of this parable, we need to have some understanding of the traditions of sharing food for Jews of that day. Ritual cleanliness was mandatory. The dietary laws were strict, but just as important were the cleanliness of the participants. No Jew shared a meal with someone who did not meet the ritual cleanliness criteria. Jews were generous to strangers and warm to travelers, but unless the strangers and travelers were Jewish and obeyed the dietary laws, shared meals were forbidden. Like all generations of cultures, equals tended to work and socialize together.

This is the backdrop of the Parable of the Banquet. The host invited his friends and associates to share a meal with him. When none accepted the invitation, the host went to the streets and invited everyone to share his banquet. This would be the shocker, this break with convention, moving well beyond the expected. He invited the riffraff and unclean non-Jews.

It has been my contention, based on the groundwork of many religious thinkers and scholars before me, that this is the core of the meaning of the parables of Jesus, an unexpected turn in the stories that startles or shocks the hearers or readers and causes them to think and to open themselves to alternate views. In a world, as was the world of Jesus, with many confusing images, religions, and morals surrounding them from the Jewish, Greek, Roman, oriental, and other cultures that passed through Israel, the ability to think and choose was frequently muted. The parables tended to remove the mute and restore thinking and choosing. This was a wonder of Jesus and his parables.

Admittedly, Jesus trod through the rural parts of his homeland and only visited Jerusalem, a large urban area, toward the end of his life. Those followers he most frequently met and spoke to knew little of the rich cultural mix of the cities. They were steeped in more traditional beliefs and teachings. The parables pushed their thinking and believing, pushed their values and morals, and left them wondering and reevaluating it all.

The Parable of the Banquet twisted these traditional and day-to-day values and stirred them. Some rejected the stories of Jesus and, perhaps, felt indignation or even intense anger. This is the usual response to alternate values. So it was with this parable. It revealed an alternate way. Although the first hearers of this parable may have come to completely different understandings of what Jesus meant, there is implied that sharing a meal was a critical part of life as Jesus understood it. Jesus' approach to sharing meals departed from the usual tradition and opened a path to new friends and relationships based on different values. Jesus invited the unwanted to dine.

This, to me, is the heart of communion. Not the sacrifice of a human for our sins, but the invitations to the unwanted to share a meal and, therefore, to share intimacy.

The Last Supper in the upper room was a sharing between intimates, not just sharing with Jesus, but sharing with each other. The Parable of the Feast invites those well beyond the intimate inner circle to share a meal. The Christian movement over many centuries has taught that communion is eating and drinking the body and blood of Jesus, the resurrected Christ. What if, alternately, the teachings of Jesus point in a very different direction, a marvelous extension of our intimacy with others. Faith is more than a relationship between an individual and God, but an extended relationship between God and others. Faith is not selfishly gaining salvation, but offering the Kingdom of God to those around us, including our enemies and those we normally would avoid. We become, as it were, Jesus offering what only he could, the Kingdom of God right now, in present reality.

In my protestant tradition, we kneel to receive the sacrament of the Lord's Supper, heads are bowed and a spiritual presence sought. If we look at Jesus, however, it might be more important to eat the bread and drink the cup while rubbing shoulders and then embracing each other, friends, those we dislike, and those we do not know, and to share the meal equally between all. We suspend judgment on others in a sacrament of acceptance and love. It is not the bread and wine that are sacred, but human relationships shared with each other in the presence of God in Jesus. By following the lead of Jesus, he, too, becomes a part of communion, not his literal body and blood, but the presence of the mind of Jesus, of his values for spiritual living, of his gift of the Kingdom. Jesus lives in the communion, touching us all with what he believed and taught, embracing us with a spirit that spans centuries to live with us and in us.

It is not an accident that Jesus shares bread and wine; it adds to our ability to receive him. Rather than using primarily hearing and reading, he added touching, taste, and smell to seeing and hearing. All of our senses participate in this shared meal. There's more, for the bread and wine move from outside our bodies to become an inner reality, not only spiritual presence but a physical presence as well. Ah, the wonder of communion!

The sacredness of baptism is becoming a member of the family of faith. The sacredness of communion is living within the family of faith. The first consciously and reverently obligates us to the community of faith. The second consciously enacts the intimacy of the fellowship of faith with each other and Jesus of Nazareth. Jesus leaps across the centuries to become the Lord of life and the Christ of faith.

This puts sacredness in a different perspective. It no long relates to "up there" or a "divine being" such as God the Father (parent) or Jesus the

Christ. Seen in relationship to community and intimacy, sacredness becomes something new; it becomes how we respond to the God in each person, the wholly other God and the God within. Sacredness is moved from external to the internal. Sacredness transforms itself into feelings, how we experience divinity in ourselves and in others.

The sacraments need redefining. Instead of being based on something Jesus specifically recognized as revealed in the Bible (Protestant) or even adding tradition as an authority (Roman Catholic), we need to look again at the foundations of sacredness. For me it is looking more closely at what Jesus held sacred.

This becomes a bit sticky because we know so much and so little. The Gospels give us much that combine stories about Jesus and stories by Jesus with the reflections the church added including the needs of the people at that time and any immediate spiritual, institutional, or political crises as well as traditions developed as the church matured. The Gospels were not written in isolation from faith but with the moods, hopes, and fears of the writers influenced deeply by those who surrounded them in faith. The search for the Jesus of history began a century ago. Albert Schweitzer in the early twentieth century argued that the historical Jesus cannot be found in the New Testament because all of the narratives about Jesus are from the perspective of faith in the Risen Lord, the divine Christ. The divine Christ overshadows and dims the human Jesus.

The struggle to find the historical Jesus continues today, more openly than before, but it is a vigorous search nonetheless. The Gospel stories of Jesus portray a legendary character who walked on water, restored life to the dead, healed life-long cripples, converted ordinary water into fine wine, and was transformed into a holy being to meet with long deceased Moses and Elijah. To know the human Jesus who was an historical man in the midst of these great stories is difficult. These are not the deeds of a human but the actions of divinity.

The task became an effort by many religious thinkers from all denominations to find the man called Jesus. This demands a faith in a totally human person who shared life with his contemporaries as well as faith in the Resurrected Lord. The search, although far from complete, waded through all of the available material and concluded that in the midst of the legends and myths were some original words of Jesus.

The parables of Jesus yielded some of the most original materials because of the unique approach of Jesus as he told the great stories. The parable form preceded Jesus, but he added to a familiar form an astonishing difference by twisting familiar scenes into unexpected and, sometimes, strange endings. No responsible shepherd would abandon ninety-nine sheep to seek a single lost one. This risks losing many more, maybe all of them. As pure story this is shocking, but the Gospel writers often tempered the shock of a story like this by adding an ending that removed the challenge of thinking and experiencing. For example, the point is made that saving one lost soul was most important. The listener no longer had to wrestle with new and exciting ideas, but was told what the parable meant.

The search revealed a source of words more original than the Gospel texts. There are certainly other original words of Jesus but the parables illustrate part of the criteria for classifying the original words of Jesus. From these words we can begin to look at the values of Jesus. There is another source, the narratives of the Gospels. These are filled with allusions to the Risen Lord, but within this limitation, the Gospels reveal enough about the life of Jesus to give us some idea of the kind of person he was. Healing and associating with those on the fringes of society tells us much.

Jesus liked and respected people, even the least important. He healed the sick and fed five thousand; he sighted the blind and drove demons out; he tolerated the brash tongue of Peter and blessed him; Jesus told complex stories to the uneducated and sought children; he befriended the disliked and ate with the hated. Reality and legend mix in these illustrations, but cumulatively there can be no question that Jesus liked people, not for how he could benefit from them or how they could benefit from him, but simply because they were human beings.

His indiscriminate love of people is clearly different from John the Baptist who held people in contempt. All were filled with sin and evil until John baptized them. John of Patmos, writer of the Apocalypse, Revelation, throws most people, the unbelievers, into fire and brimstone. There are passages in the Gospel that quote Jesus talking about casting out some into the outer darkness, but these do not ring true as the genuine words of Jesus. These kinds of comments are vindictive and signs of weakness.

They are weak because these comments derive from the apocalyptic movement, grounded in the posture of hopelessness and powerlessness. When repressed people feel hopeless, they want a stronger power to rescue them. Huddled and fearful Christians, powerless against Rome, cried out in prayer for God to rescue them, to bring destruction to their enemies and to vindicate their faith. United States foreign policy echoes this "God complex" when we threaten nations that violate the human rights of their citizens. Ironically, poverty and homelessness apparently do not qualify as human rights violations. Many Americans are poor and homeless. A powerful nation (United States) steps in, like a god, to save the powerless. Jesus thought differently, as he lived and worked among the poor and homeless, he empowered the individuals. As a society and democratic nation, we must deal strongly with injustice, but, then, people of faith are not societies or nations. The U.S. is religiously diverse, so the moral sensibilities of faithful people must consider the rights of those who disagree.

Jesus walked among the humblest of people and empowered them. He did not empower them to become strong and warlike, but to become individuals able to face and live victoriously within the oppressiveness of their culture or society. The individuals who accepted the message of Jesus gained dignity, walked more erectly, defeated depression, and found inner peace and hope. Their oppressive environment no longer had the power to squash them emotionally or religiously. Jesus empowered them to be as fully human as they could be and, perhaps, more human than the oppressors.

Attacking our enemies is also vindictive; it is revenge. I think of a childish argument I was involved in as a child. We were playing football and the other team was beating up on us pretty badly. Our quarterback (he owned the ball) got frustrated and wanted to change some rules to benefit us. When the other team would not agree, he grabbed his ball and went home, calling over his shoulder, "Then, you can't play. It's my ball." Well, when we can't strike out at our enemies effectively, we pretend that we own God, after all, we are the chosen or the elect or the saved. We can act like we own the ball and use God to punish our enemies. This is the message of the Apocalypse, the Book of Revelation.

Jesus would not use his father to punish those who did not agree with him or even punish the enemy of his people, Rome. I don't know whether or not he actually preached to turn the other cheek, but I can clearly hear him saying it. He was a man of peace, not war. Most Jewish messiahs led small rebellious groups hoping to violently send the Roman occupiers back to Rome. Jesus chastised Peter for raising a sword.

———•◦•———

The sacraments, for Jesus, centered on people and offered them the Kingdom of God. Sacraments should echo the values of Jesus rather than the values of institutional churches. This will make the sacraments dynamic rather than static. Below I briefly summarize what I believe are sacraments and why. Following this are those acts that fall a bit short of sacred, but are important enough to be recognized.

Baptism: This is a welcoming ritual based on people of faith who with joy and commitment welcome others into their midst. We tend to think of baptism as the individual joining the group, but it is more of a welcoming ceremony where people of faith not only welcome the baptized but also commit themselves to participating in the life of the newly baptized. There is immediate and ongoing interaction between them; they become one. All of this is done in the name of God and in the spirit of Jesus.

Communion: This remembers Jesus who kept his faith and commitment strong enough to face death rather than turn away from friends and followers. Christians share this meal together as they literally internalize their faith and openly share it with each other without any barriers such as social status, ethnicity, or age. This demands not only faith in God but that we trust in those who share this great meal with each other.

Marriage: This is the ultimate human relationship that needs to be elevated within the Christian community far beyond what it is today. Protestants generally do not recognize this as a sacrament. Roman Catholics do, but treat it as far less than sacred with their liberal annulment policy. When we begin to see marriage as something truly holy, then the tendency to see it as a sentence to be endured that can be ended at will is transformed into something far deeper and more enduring. Couples link spiritually and extend their physical bond to include the presence of God within, and this adds a whole new dimension. Divorce would be radically reduced, although it would and should not disappear, for not all marriages have a genuine spiritual base.

Ordination: As a function of the church, it is not sacramental, but as a function of ministry, it is very close. We need to elevate those who minister to others whether they are ordained or not. Mother Theresa was not less holy than Pope John Paul II. A ministry of the laity is equally as valuable as the ministry of the ordained. We tend to confuse the laying on of hands with the consecration of the heart and minds of dedicated people.

The Last Rites: This offers consolation to a seriously ill person and his loved ones, but this does not make it a sacrament. The application of oil to the orifices of the body is interesting but it moves far too close to superstition.

Confession: Confession is nearly universal in the Christian movement, only how confession is managed is debated between denominations. Is it managed by the church through a priest or direct communication to God in prayer? My tradition opts for the latter. However, the first is far more meaningful because to talk to a priest, one has to seriously think about how he has sinned and speak it out loud so that someone else can clearly understand it, which, in turn, makes it clearer to themself. Absolution is quite different. Can someone truly say a prayer, make the sign of the cross, and forgive someone of their sins or however absolution is applied. This appears very close to magic, pulling sin from someone is like pulling a rabbit out of a hat.

Sin is a human condition. Sin will be dealt with more thoroughly in a later chapter; suffice it to say that sin does exist. Jesus trusted his followers and through them, all humans. This does not mean he was blind to sin. Both governments and religious institutions exploited and wrongly used his people. Tyrants ruled from the Herods to the Caesars. Wars kill hundreds of thousands and wound far more. Starvation takes life from many, and human nature has its dark and dangerous side. Evil appears to penetrate just about everything from the innocent child pulling the legs off an insect to the mass executions of political and cultural enemies. Confession and absolution distract us from the larger and genuine sins we should struggle against rather than concentrate on the inane sins of day-to-day living. We feel personally forgiven, while injustice remains around us.

The issue of what the Sacraments should or could do for believers needs to be more adequately addressed. Because ordination is a function of the church and has very little impact on ordinary people, we should inquire into what the sacramental impact is on people, rather than define sacraments as those church functions ordained by holy Scripture or religious tradition.

Sacraments should be sacred to us, the faithful and rather ordinary people. An infant being baptized is, for the most part, unaware of the holiness of the moment and is more concerned with getting wet with water too cold. In contrast, when I personally receive communion, I feel centuries melt away and the wonder of the presence of Jesus, the Christ, fills me. My complaint is that the actual reception of bread and "wine" is too short lived. In church we seldom have the luxury to remain on our knees and meditate and let the emotions of our spiritual life expand to fill our minds, spirits, and bodies or to share faith and love with those to our right and left. For me holiness is present; it reaches from the ancient past and grabs hold of the immediate present to transform me in ways that are a mystery.

Moving from this personal experience to acting on it becomes the genuine reward of our embrace of the holy. Do we rise from the table to follow the Master, to find the same understanding and forgiveness that Jesus himself gave to all? Or, do we rise from the table having had a profound sacredness that soon flitters away like a butterfly getting lost among the leaves? What makes a sacrament sacred is how we internalize and react to it. It is not how well the priest or minister leads us in the service. It is not the pronouncement of a church council. It is not the tradition of the church. It is not a presence in the Bible. It is us!

The ideal sacrament is when we encounter the holy and change takes place, however subtle it may be, and the change makes a difference in our living. There is no way to properly evaluate or test a sacramental event, an encounter with the holy, for it is seldom seen by another and can easily be confused with a psychological aberration. Visions that instruct one to do harm in the name of God are never holy, but are psychological or even psychotic. Simple things can push the adrenalin around in our bodies causing "highs" — high school graduation, meeting a celebrity, receiving a special award, winning at racquet ball, beating a chess master, seeing something spectacular, watching a sporting event you care deeply about and being victorious, seeing your child for the very first time, and so forth. The list is nearly endless.

There appears little difference between these "highs" and meeting God at a revival, in communion, visiting with a truly holy person, a saint, or sharing a healing of an illness thought to be terminal. This is about as subjective as we humans can be. Yet, because we cannot absolutely pinpoint feelings does not disqualify them. What is most truly holy is what we experience as holy; it creeps into our spirits and transforms and uplifts us; it makes a difference to us long after the immediate excitement passes.

This blurs the distinction between reality and spirituality. It allows for error, but it also lifts us above the mundane, the prisons of our bodies, and the imprisonment of rigid cultural values. The sacred frees us to be more completely human and moves us into the Kingdom of God.

Chapter Nine
BAD THINGS, SIN AND EVIL

The room was too bright, and Ralph too quiet. His eyes were closed, his breathing shallow and labored. Ralph's physician had called his wife and me, the family minister, aside and explained that death was imminent, probably only minutes or hours away, at best. His wife's pain was obvious, even though she had known months ago that Ralph's death was not far away. Sclerosis of the liver from a lifetime of drinking was proving itself far more powerful than Ralph's will to live or his family's love.

Now, I was alone with him, relieving the family of sitting and watching. There was nothing I could do. Later, I learned that my words of frustration, "I feel so helpless," had offered comfort and compassion. I had expressed my own frustration; my frustration echoed the family's own frustration and fearfully unspoken despair. In a strange way, I had given them permission to openly express their own frustration and anger.

This scene expressed itself to me as evil. Ralph had broken his body by drinking; nature passed a death sentence. The family, especially his wife, was scarred by loss and fear of the future. Some may say that Ralph had sinned, and his body had also sinned. But, neither Ralph nor his family deserved the pain they had received — Ralph's physical pain and their agony of grief, loneliness, and fear.

At this point in my life, my confrontation with death had been broader than I wanted. My father had died suddenly; I was called when parents had been killed together in an automobile accident, and when a man had shot himself in the head, lived to walk upstairs to his kitchen table to write a final note and went back to the basement to fire his second shot, killing him. A grandson had died after a mere six months of life losing his struggle to live; a high school student was killed on his motorcycle, and an eight-year old was chewed to death by his father's tractor.

All of these were tragic, appeared unfair, and stirred in my heart and head the problem of evil and sin. These are not necessarily the same thing. Evil is like a force outside of human control, the power of a tornado lifting a house from its foundation, a tidal wave spewing death on a shoreline, lightening felling a tree on a golfer caught unawares, and a forest fire swallowing acres of trees, animals, and people. These are natural evils striking out wantonly and without considering the righteousness or lack of it in living creatures.

There's a human side of evil like insanity pushing someone to kill his family, greed adding wealth while taking from those, perhaps, more "worthy" but less prosperous, a drunken driver hitting someone causing her to spend the rest of her life in a wheelchair, a bomb slaying an eighteen-year-old soldier before his life truly got started, or a terrorist stealing life by destroying a populated building.

In each of these cases, it is almost like a power unseen and unknown interfered in human life to maim and kill. When we say that someone is evil, we suggest possession by an evil power or influence that has taken over mind and body. This could be the meaning of disease — evil overpowering our bodies with cancer or stilling the heart, diabetes blinding eyes and cutting off legs, or a stroke drowning and starving a brain.

Sin, in contrast, is an intentional act or condition depending on the definition used. Many argue that sin is alienation from God, but this is a condition, not an act. Is evil, cancer for example, a sign of alienation from God? This could be argued either way, depending on the individual person. However, this also destroys the argument. Alienation from God cannot be a sign of disease when many victims are truly good people while others spew evil and die of old age while sleeping. Further, because most churches and religions have some form of confession, a faithful person cannot confess about the sin of diabetes or heart disease. Some may believe that illness shows that someone is a "bad" person, even when hidden from our eyes. This belief, it seems to me, shows only that we humans must have an explanation for everything. It is Adam and Eve eating from forbidden fruit of the tree of knowledge; it is playing god, the all knowing. When we realize that we cannot know all things and recognize that some things are mysterious and others irrational, we will begin to deal more effectively with evil and sin.

Look at a common summer occurrence, a thunderstorm. Science has come a long way explaining the lightening and thunder and the damaging downpours of rain. Science has not explained why a thunderstorm is part of our earth, why it can be destructive, or whether there is some earthly biological or physical need that these storms fulfill. We know what causes thunderstorms, but not why. Medicine still searches for a cure for cancer, but cancer demonically turns our physiological defenses into attackers that destroy us. This is both illogical and irrational.

Bad things are real; they happen. Nature is not evil. Evil is a human concept, a theological concept. Humans attach moral and ethical attributes to a physical world that is amoral and knows or cares nothing about ethics. What we now know about the world, the physical and the biological, is that, as complex as it is, it has no values. Even Darwin's "survival of the fittest" has no more value than a large boulder crushing a small stone. We cannot blame the world for what we perceive to be evil.

It seems apparent to me that human beings must find a reason for most everything, so we apply humanly constructed values to things and creatures. A modern example of this is the belief that only a great mind could have created the world and its inhabitants, or, the universe. Perhaps, the first step towards understanding is to realize that we humans are not the center of any universe or of any world. As large as our egos are, we are only the center of the world within our immediate experience.

Wake up, Christians, and find genuine humility. Not the humility that is subservient, but the Jesus kind of humility where we understand that we are not gods walking in a human mask, but people who are unembarrassed to walk among the poor and diseased, to chat with the ugly and unwanted, to yield to a tortuous death rather than strike against a fellow human being. Jesus, as the Gospel records, shouted in despair and anger, "My God, my God, why have you forsaken me" and left the unspoken words about pain and torture in his heart and head. Jesus did not play God. Later, his followers elevated him to godlike status, but Jesus never did this for himself. Even in the most spiritual of Gospels and the least likely to reveal anything about the humanity of Jesus, John's Gospel, Jesus took credit for nothing, always giving the credit to his Father.

To walk in the Master's footsteps is to become like a servant. Even with genuine humility can Christians truly better understand evil and sin? An over simplified way of speaking of evil and sin is to admit that we do not understand them. Christians who try their best to emulate Jesus can look directly at evil without trying to understand it. Jesus could struggle against evil without questioning its reason. It is when we admit that we do not understand that we begin to understand.

Evil is present and it is genuine. It destroys tiny children and topples huge trees; it rips towns apart and throws lightning's deadly bolts; it makes the malevolent and greedy rich while starving the needy and poor. Evil is relentless, acting every day, year, and century. It sends meteors hurtling through our atmosphere to crash on someone's home or a tiny village; it blows hurricane winds to flatten a forest; it turns a human body cancerously against itself; it nurtures rage until one nation attacks another.

This evil is dispassionate; there is no human face behind it. No devil's pitchfork prods it alive; no evil thought turns it on and off. There is no passion inspiring the evil. The one possible exception is war where passion stirs feelings and hatred replaces tolerance. We hated "Japs" during World War II and now the term "towel-heads," reflects a hatred for Middle Easterners. Even this is not stimulated by a demonic force, as much as we would like it to be. The search for a demonic force is a search for an understandable reason behind everything and repeats the mistake of Adam and Eve in the Garden. They sought to have the full knowledge of good and evil, that is, they tried to know all and become godlike themselves. This is a purely human quest in spite of the reality that we would prefer to blame someone else. Genesis blamed the snake, a human story trying to explain a human event from the perspective of faith. Even in faith, we humans like to cast blame elsewhere on evil spirits and demonic forces rather than take responsibility ourselves.

Lest we feel too badly about this, remember that Jesus did exactly the same. On the cross Jesus shouted, "Father, why have you forsaken me." Or, the evening before the cross, the unwitnessed prayer, "Let this cup pass, but not my will, but yours." Even the strongest among us falters before fear that stirs an unwillingness to look carefully at ourselves. Blame luck, treachery, or prejudice. Blame everyone and everything but ourselves.

At the same time, there are the poor of the world. Few of them, a Mother Theresa notwithstanding, seek poverty. Instead, they were born to impoverished parents, with the wrong skin color, or in a starving part of the world.

The problem of evil is extraordinarily complex. There simply is no easy answer. We may want to blame an amorphous demonic person such as the Devil, but that is simply a human reduction of complexity into understandable simplicity. The difficulty is that evil is not reducible to human understanding and simple formulas. Evil just is. It appears human-like from time-to-time like a beak-nosed witch and appears cold and without life at other times like a bank, an institution, foreclosing on a lapsing mortgage. Sometimes it appears personal and other times impersonal and distant.

The first thing to understand is that we cannot understand. We can tell stories that enlighten us somewhat, but they will never provide a clear and definitive answer. Jesus understood this, even when he lapsed occasionally (he was human, after all, and not a god walking in the disguise of human skin). To deal with evil, we look for the patterns of how

Jesus dealt with it. We may find our clearest answers in stories about Jesus and stories by Jesus.

Two parables come to mind when talking about how Jesus viewed evil. The first is the parable of the vineyard owner who needed some day workers and sought them in the town square, or its equivalent, and returned several times during the day for more workers. The last visit to hire workers was late in the day, so that those hired last had a very short work day. Work ceased when the sun faded and work became too difficult. This was all rather ordinary and expected during harvest. But, when the workers were paid, the last hired were paid first and the first hired paid last, the vineyard owner paid the last hired a full day's pay.

This was not fair because the first hired expected more money, at least a bonus for a full day in the heat and sun. A confusing part of this parable is that the first hired were paid the same as those who had worked barely an hour or so. By any economic formula, this is simply not fair. Each should have been paid proportionately for the time worked. Today, we pay by the hour, so it is easier to measure. In the parable the first ones hired complained. If they had been unionized, they would have probably threatened a strike, but unions, of course, did not exist. All the workers could do was vigorously complain about the unfairness of the situation.

Notice that it was not so much that they wanted the last hired paid less, they wanted themselves to be paid more. When the first hired questioned the vineyard owner, he explained that it was his money and he could do with it what he wanted. They had no right to complain. He had paid them a fair wage for a day's work.

Now, this may not sound like a parable about evil, but whenever cultural or economic values are turned upside down and reversed from the norm, unfairness becomes apparent and justice bypassed, evil may be present.

The question that those who first heard this parable must have puzzled over is the same question we do now, why was justice bypassed and inequity championed. True, parables are intended to challenge the ordinary and question accepted values, but still we like to probe its meaning as best we can. We can do this as long as we recognize that our interpretation is not the only interpretation, just one among many, as many, perhaps, as all those who read the parable.

Bypassing justice and championing inequity gives us an interesting perspective because we must deal with the unexpected victory of injustice and inequity. We cannot rise up and stone the owner as a man of evil; we cannot offer an easy answer or symbolize the vineyard owner as God who certainly can do what he wants with what he has; and we can praise the owner for giving more to the last because they needed a full days pay as much as the first hired. We can do all these things by how we interpret the parable, but few would agree with any of these interpretations. We all must deal with the unexpected mystery of the twisted ending of the story.

Jesus dealt with evil; he did not avoid it. Neither did he glorify it and make it appear glamorous nor vilify it and make it ugly. Jesus lived with evil daily as he walked among the poor and powerless, the sickly and weak, and the unloved and unrespected. The political and economic systems generally doled out pain. Jesus submitted to this evil when he was condemned as a common criminal, a dreg of society, and executed in the most painful and humiliating way. Rome executed him, Jesus yielded to it, and God permitted it. All three participated in this evil, but are all three evil? Even Rome, a large and successful empire has been named by history as one of the great eras in world events. For twenty centuries, the Roman Catholic Church adopted Rome's language, Latin, the language of the nation that executed Jesus, as its own holy language.

Who can understand these mysteries? No one I know.

Then, there was the young lad who, as many teens are wont to do, could not wait for his time. He wanted his share of the family wealth immediately so he could seek his own fortune. His youthfulness did not serve him well, for shortly he wasted all his wealth and became destitute in a foreign land, reduced to eating with the pigs, unwanted and unclean animals to the Jews of his day.

He had acted foolishly, now it was time to use his brain and think of a way out. Feeling powerless, he calculated that his best chance was to return home to his father's and older brother's wealth, maybe no longer as an equal member of the family, as a son and brother, but as a servant. Anything was better than his starving humiliation. He wanted to make certain that he would at least have an opportunity to live at home where food was plentiful and housing warm and cozy, so he carefully worked out a speech intended to sell his father on the idea that his youthfully foolish ways were behind him, that he would live differently, that he would learn patience and hard work, that he did not expect to return to the status of a favored son. He was willing to work for his food and shelter among the lowliest of his father's servants.

Not only did he carefully word his speech to evoke a positive response, the foolish young man memorized it, so he would neither verbally stumble nor show himself unrepentant. This kind of preparation was not truly the sign of a penitent man, but of a calculating confidence artist using charm and wit to get what he wanted.

Most know what happened to the so-called Prodigal Son. Before he could speak his thoughtful and well-rehearsed speech, his father wrapped his long lost son in his arms, welcomed him, and had the fatted-calf slain for a festive meal of thanksgiving. His older brother did not share his father's joy, but believed he had been slighted for his faithful, long-lasting, and tedious service to his father. The run-away brother was being feasted, not the diligent and faithful son.

This touches on sin, which we will consider soon in this chapter. But one of the many, many interpretations of the parable suggests an interesting configuration of personalities and situations. The younger son is greedy and unrepentant, only returning home when there are few, if any, alternatives. The world he had fled his home for was completely hostile to him, forcing him to violate the religious teachings he had lived with all his life. If this was not hell, it was certainly a hellish experience.

The father, in contrast, appears to have no harsh feelings that would erode his affection and caring for his young son. He yielded to the unfair request to break up his estate and give the young son one third of the holdings. What did he have to sell to make this possible, for the son could not take dirt or unharvested or even harvested crops along with him? Who knows, but we can assume that a third of all he owned was not trifling. Just the sight of his son returning excited him. Other fathers would have disowned him for walking away from his family responsibilities into a land antagonistic to their faith and traditions. But the father opened his arms, pulled his son to him, and hugged him mightily.

The older son is another contrast, closer in age to the younger son than the father. The older son's speech toward the end of the parable strongly suggests that he remained back on the farm so he would receive his "just reward." He would be the only heir, the one who would receive all. Behind this was guarded jealousy that the wayward son was welcomed back as if he had never done anything wrong. He not only did not welcome his brother back, but turned his back by refusing to participate in the celebration.

How could these two boys have the same father? The father is so forgiving, welcoming, and filled with generous love; the boys selfish and with an edge of conniving. It is almost as if the good father begat two bad seeds. Good produced evil. This is not what we usually want to hear. We want good news unshadowed by darkness. This story, as usual with the parables of Jesus, we try to understand but it strains our minds and drains our spirits.

Evil takes our emotions and shakes them until they spill out slopping on the floor, challenges our understanding of justice, questions our faith, punishes our bodies, and takes over our lives. Evil is illogical. It makes no sense.

The only positive thing about evil is that it forces us to feel and to think. Few can see the results of evil and not shed a tear, even when the tear is dry. Few can see the results of evil and not question it as our minds spin in confusion.

When bad things happen some turn from God, others to God. There is no uniform response except that our hearts weep and our minds search for reason in the midst of insanity. The foundations of our lives can be shattered or strengthened. Evil can radically change us and open us to new visions and hopes, new insights and dreams, new beliefs and faith. We just have to be open to not playing god by trying to have the answers to all things and to see ourselves, those around us, and the world with new eyes unclouded by past prejudices and values.

A cousin of evil is sin. Theologians (sin is a religious word) have defined sin in many ways. Most call it alienation from God, and this is nearly universal, for all have sinned and fall short of the glory of God. We are all separated from God, if taken literally, and since many take the Bible literally, why not this? Some distinguish between sin and Sin, i.e. a sinful act as opposed to a Sinful person. Others use the story of Adam and Eve as the way to define sin, disobedience and trying to be god-like. Still others consider the acts of Adam and Eve as humanity's original sin that is inherited and passed from generation to generation.

This appears to me to be philosophizing or theologizing a bit too much. Sin, as I reflect upon the life of Jesus, is more fundamental. It is an alienation of some sort between a person and another or others. Getting angry and smacking your fist through the wall, breaking the wall and your hand, is not a sin; it is stupidly loosing self control. A fit of anger may purge bad thoughts and feelings from us. Jesus jeopardized himself when he went on extended fasts or stopped Peter's sword and allowed himself to be arrested, but did not sin. Rather, he gave his life and words and work to and for others. This set him aside from others; this made him, as the church now claims, sin free. But he did not do everything perfect, for this would completely remove his humanity and make his earthly life a sham.

Jesus lost himself in others. He told numerous stories to intrigue and entrance, healed the wounded of body and spirit, defended the weak and powerless, and loved the unlovable and loveless. The ego of Jesus was reflected in the faces of the poor and injured, the foolish rich and the generous widow, the forgotten prisoner and the dirty-faced child. Jesus touched others to transform them, to agitate their minds, and to open new and unforeseen possibilities for them.

To commit a human sin is to do the opposite of Jesus, to neglect our neighbors, steal from a friend, strike an enemy, ignore someone ill, or lie to a child. To sin is to hurt another human being physically, emotionally, or spiritually. Hurting another need not be an intentional act; it can be thoughtless, careless, or neglectful. Sin is magnified when we gain from injuring another.

This leaves a major question open: is sin an act against God? Sin is a religious word, not a secular word. To say that one sins reflects an act against or violates a rule of God. To say that one committed a crime reflects an act against or a violation of a rule of society. Again, when we look at the life of Jesus, we get strong clues to our question. Jesus offered the Kingdom of God to the people around him, usually the poor and powerless, the weak and the sick, the forgotten and neglected, and the broken and wicked. Although he prayed frequently and went off alone to meditate, he spent his working and leisure time with people. He appeared to care little for himself, at least as the Gospels portray him. He had no fine clothing and hugged those believed to have contagious diseases. He allowed himself to be arrested and gave flip answers to his judges at his trial before the Sanhedrin the evening before the crucifixion ("You say that I am.").

Except for prayer, there is nearly nothing that Jesus did for God, the Father. Indeed, what could he do for God, the Father, the wonder who lives within and outside us, who gives us the spark of life and intelligence when other beings are relatively thoughtless? There is nothing that Jesus or any of us can do for God other than honor him.

Jesus honored God by serving people, human beings who carry within them the image of God. This is how Jesus honored his Father by serving His people nobly and well, by giving all he had in the effort to make things better and to give them the Kingdom of God.

We must do the same. Not to serve others is to sin against God. Sin is not necessarily evil, but, more significantly, not doing enough for God by serving our fellow human beings. It can be an aggressive act against people or a passive act of not doing enough. In either case, sin abuses God by abusing her people.

Chapter Ten
THE CURSE AND LIBERATION OF RELIGION

For several months I sat in a class on Hinduism's *The Bagavad Gita*. About twenty Hindu faithful sat on the floor with crossed legs, I perched on a chair or sofa with six or seven others while the leader, a well-informed guru in her own right, analyzed a passage of the *Gita*, verse-by-verse and word-for-word. The analysis was thorough and included both the Hindi and English versions of the text. The experience was similar to a Christian Bible study group searching every word and phrase for meaning, an exhaustive exegesis. The similarity did not end there, for the same surety of thought and doctrine was present in both environments. Each group, Hindu and Christian, knew their own interpretation was correct and all others, at worst, wrong, and, at best, misguided.

This surety that their version of faith is the one true holy revelation appears pervasive throughout human religions. This creates different groupings within the same faith such as Christianity with its huge number of denominations. Being sure that one is absolutely correct divides and creates hostility between different religions. Christians sent missionaries across the globe to convert the "heathen" to their version of the truth even though the different cultures already had their own understanding of truth. Indeed, what does heathen mean? My understanding is that heathen are those who believe in a god or gods of lesser quality than the God of Christianity. The term heathen was born as Christianity had its greatest spurt of growth.

Logically, all the different religions that claim the ultimate truth cannot each be correct. If there is only one ultimate Truth, all other pretenders to Truth must be either delusional or misstating the Truth.

As a lowly Christian, I confess that the Truth is something that I only hear about. Sermons have been preached about it throughout my lifetime. Televangelists condemn as evil those believers who disagree with the televangelist's version of the truth. Some religious fanatics willingly perform suicidal missions of terror against others, especially incorrect believers and non-believers. Their grasp of truth is so convincing to them that they consciously walk into violent death in order to gain eternal salvation.

Indeed, a strong conviction that a person or group of persons (religion or denomination) hold the unique and only Truth can be as destructive as it is supposedly creative. When people war against each other over interpretations of Truth, then those perspectives of Truth may be false. The idea that we hold "holy" wars over scriptural interpretation is a genuine contradiction. Indeed, holy and war exclude each other. A loving God cannot condone and support wars that kill and wreak devastation, usually against both sides.

Earlier in this book, I wrestled with the idea of Truth as an understanding held by a specific group or category of people concerning the meaning of life. As such, it can include the great mythologies of history, be mixed with faith and science, help make sense of a world that appears psychotic, or lend understanding to the searching and confused. By this view, Truth is relative, not absolute.

For the most part, however, world religions see Truth with a capital "T" as absolute. It is not a relative truth related to the era, environment, religion, or philosophy. It is absolute and timeless. Truth can be verified by religious authorities such as the Bible for Christians and Jews, the *Bagavad Gita* for some Hindus and the Qur'an for Muslims. The authority can be more personal such as a minister's or priest's sermon artfully and regularly repeating it like a mantra. As a Christian, I have heard countless times, "The Bible says...." In other words, if it is in the Bible it is incontrovertible. Often, it goes a bit further and becomes an interpretation of the Bible or Scripture. No longer is it what the Bible says, but it is what the interpreted Bible means. There is irony here, because any understanding of the Bible is interpretation. It is the same for any holy scriptures. Merely reading a passage of Scripture requires that we pass it through our minds cluttered with memories and biases, Sunday school classes, Bible studies, Sunday sermons, religious tracts, family traditions, and friendly discussions.

The absolute and incontrovertible aspect of Truth causes friction, prejudice, hatred, and destruction. The question of Truth is, perhaps, more critical today than in any past age. Holy Jihad attacks today's world like the Christian Crusades and Spanish Inquisition attacked an earlier age. Any group that believes it holds the absolute Truth can also believe that this Truth needs to prevail over all other truths. All other truths must be destroyed. We have seen this attitude in the past, and it dominates even today.

Believing you hold the absolute Truth means that those who believe differently are lesser beings, which births prejudice. Some Americans are severely prejudiced against Muslim "towel-heads" and Jews and sinners (those who disagree with those who really know the absolute Truth) of all kinds. This adds another dimension of hatred against people who are different in color, ethnicity, language, traditions, or perceptions of Truth. This is a curse of religion, believing that one way is the only way, that there is only one Truth held by the "elect."

I believe there is an answer to this problem for Christians: Jesus of Nazareth. To understand this, we must learn to grab hold of another thoughtful approach to the fundamentals of the Christian faith. I speak of the Christian faith because it is my own. Let others address their own questions concerning their own religions. They are better equipped.

The first thing to notice about Jesus is that he simply did not care who a person was for Jesus to love him or her. Jesus associated with sinners and Roman centurions, tax gatherers and lepers, rich young men and impoverished widows. This cannot be extended too far for he lived in rural Israel for most of his life. His experiences in the large cities were limited, twice in Jerusalem according to the accounts in the Gospels. The point is still valid. Jesus did not filter his experiences with people because of ethnic, religious, economic, social, or political reasons. He dealt with people as they were, not as he might have wanted them to be.

As pointed out earlier, he had a deep respect for people, even those on the lower socio-economic strata. Jesus respected the poor and ignorant, the outcasts and the aliens, the powerless and the powerful. This is a core difference between Jesus and the later movement named for him, Christianity. Later Christians became preoccupied with sin, sinning, and sinners. Sin worried them because they believed themselves powerless before it. Sin so overwhelmed them that they believed that only the deadly sacrifice of Jesus on the Cross could overcome it. This is ironic. When the Cross removed sin with forgiveness and sacrifice, the preoccupation with sin should have vanished. The Cross should have erased sin as a concern. What actually happened was that sin became more and more of a concern. Sin led to a denial of salvation.

Paul wrote quite a bit about this subject suggesting that faith led to forgiveness and brought the believer under the umbrella of the Cross and the promise of salvation as well as a place with Christ in eternity. This thinking continued in the early Christian community climaxing in the New Testament with the Apocalypse, the Book of Revelation. Here, life on earth is portrayed as totally evil and corrupt requiring a cleansing in a holy war against Evil. God would triumph in this confrontation and the saved would live in bliss with Christ. The enemies would be cast into fire and brimstone.

Coupled to this is the exclusiveness of those saved from eternal damnation. Many became elitists. Those who were saved were better off, healthier and wealthier, than the unsaved. An interesting symbol of this elevation is the parallel between the secular royalty and the royal robes of the Pope, Cardinals, Bishops, and parish clergy. The robes became more and more lush, colorfully setting aside and elevating the clergy to a special status. The clergy were, of course, saved, spiritually superior and became the royalty among the religious.

My faith says something quite different. Jesus loved people, even the corrupt and evil. His ministry cast out the demons within his people, did not kill or permanently torture them in a Hell of fire and brimstone. Jesus was a man of peace, not war. Somewhere our fear of damnation and evil twisted the love of Jesus into vengeance — vengeance strong enough to torture and kill enemies. Certainly, the early Christians were beleaguered and had many enemies who wanted to destroy them simply because they were Christian, but the way of Jesus turned the other cheek, responded to hate with love, lifted up those who were down, and he risked himself so others need not risk themselves. Vengeance is a strange inversion of the teachings and model of Jesus.

We eternally search for life everlasting, life with Christ forever. Christian theology added to the teachings and model of Jesus a threat of eternal damnation to those who had no faith. Jesus in contrast embraced both enemy and friend, kissed the ugly and the beautiful, invited the disreputable and the reputable to join with him, and dined with the betrayers of the people and his closest disciples. There is no evidence that Jesus of Nazareth ever wanted the worst harmed or destruction for anyone, friend or foe.

Some may argue that sinners chose eternal damnation, frequently a conscious choice. Jesus disregarded this and warmly welcomed those without the ability to resist temptation or refrain from evil thoughts as well as those with pure intentions and the strength to resist evil. Jesus warmly received everyone.

This is the liberation of Christianity. We are free from the weaknesses of fragile humanity, not because we are stronger than others, but because we know we are loved. Jesus showed no boundaries in his love and respect for human beings.

We can truly find comfort in the love of Jesus. We do not have to prove ourselves to Jesus. Instead, we celebrate his love. We are loved in spite of mistakes and faults; we are saved in spite of who we are because the love of Jesus is more powerful than our human weaknesses and fallacies and wrong thinking.

This does not create an aristocracy of the Truth that makes all those who understand that we are loved unconditionally elevated into spiritual aristocrats. This cannot be; for the moment we feel superior we ignore his love and embrace self-love. No longer do we have to prove ourselves worthy, for God's love makes us worthy. We are loved and we are safe in the Kingdom of God. People who are secure within themselves seldom have to prove themselves to others. They do not feel superior to others for love is for all, those aware of it and those not. When a person experiences the love of God in spite of his human impulses such as greed and lust, she or he no longer has to prove self worth. Thoroughly loved people tend to want to share love, not show their superiority over others. Truly confident people do not need to compete to prove themselves. Truly confident Christians do not need to prove that their understanding of faith is better than another's. It no longer has to be.

The Bible is not the exclusive revelation of Truth. Although it serves Jews and Christians (different versions, of course) extremely well, it addresses minds and spirits in tune with the melodies of their religious and cultural backgrounds. The *Bagavad Gita* does the same for those whose background includes primarily Indian culture, philosophies, and religions. The study group I participated in on the *Gita* did not convert me to Hinduism, but I could see and feel the faith around me radiate throughout the room feeding itself with fervor and peace, strange opposites that easily unify in faith.

There is no way that I can say that my Christian and biblical understanding of faith is superior or inferior. Christianity speaks to me about the love of God revealed in Jesus. Hinduism speaks just as strongly to my Hindu friends with equal love. Whose faith is better? Neither, because each speaks with meaning to its own faithful. Each speaks the Truth that makes sense for its own people.

My spiritual pride would be flattered if the Bible is Truer than the *Gita*, but this is pride that has no genuine place in my search for faith and understanding. Our human pride should not be an ingredient in our search for Truth. On the other hand, recognizing that another is neither inferior nor superior to me twists pride into the right kind of humility.

The corollary is that Hindus may hold that the position that the *Gita* is Truer than the Bible. Indeed, India banned Christian missionaries many years ago from doing any evangelistic work in India because it conflicted with the nation's Hindu history. Also, the missionaries taught that Hinduism was a pagan religion. India found this insulting and suggested that the Christian missionaries were less than honest.

Let us talk some God-talk. When we talk about God, we talk about the profoundly unknown. The use of some of the characteristics of God as spelled out in most religions and, most certainly in Christianity, elevates God well beyond human knowledge or capabilities. God is called omniscient, knows all things. In the world that we know, the universe is endless; God's knowledge is also endless. That is a huge statement that challenges our limited imaginations.

God is omnipotent, all powerful. Using an anthropomorphic image, God has the ability to crush the world between his or her fingers or snap the earth with a finger and send it across the universe to a galaxy we may not know exists. Of course, I need human images to talk about God because I have no heavenly images that work.

God is omnipresent, is everywhere at the same time. God lives in the earth's sun and, at the same time, is deep within a black hole, shares space with me in my middle-class home and shares space in the shack of a starving African family. God also shares space within our being, although I admit I know not what that precisely means. Far too many try to isolate this aspect of our spiritual existence into a specific location, the head, the heart, or even the bowels, an ancient biblical image. So I toss my rational mind aside and free my emotional side to feel those ineffable sensations that stir within.

Omniscience, omnipotence, omnipresence, and those feelings[3] within stir and move us and are, also, three characteristics we humans attribute to God making him far more powerful in all ways than anything we know about or experience.

Why is it that we often limit God to our own personal beliefs and prejudices? This restriction is unholy, for it tries to restrict the unrestrictable. We humans continually perpetrate religious thoughts that suit our human thoughts and wants. Like the Adam and Eve myth, we aspire to be like God, that is, we make God into our own image and, by defining God to suit our own beliefs and we elevate ourselves as the "Chosen," as the elite among the inhabitants of the earth. Those who share our beliefs and lifestyles are the "saved." The "unbelievers" or "wrong believers" are condemned. Everyone else is wrong.

Yet, the logic of faith strongly denies this. God is so powerful and so filled with love that she reaches to embrace us all, not a select few. God speaks in whatever voice he chooses, reveals himself with whatever face she chooses, and embraces all, as did Jesus, with love, a love that surpasses anything we can understand. Even the greatest theologians, the greatest minds of all living faiths, cannot grasp the knowledge, mystery, and wonder of God.

---

[3] There is much danger here, for our internal feelings can mask prejudices, hatred, insanity, and total irrationality. Not all that we feel within comes from God. It can also come from the worst that is in us.

Who really killed Jesus of Nazareth, his Jewish opponents? His Roman conquerors? His greedy merchants? His opponents who vied against his followers? None of these, and all of these. He was crucified by those who wanted to control religious thought to fit specific preexisting religious tenets, also a political goal. He has been crucified over and over again by Christians who believe that only their way is correct, by those who restrict the mind of God to a specific and definite value system, and by those who would pretend to be gods because their way is the only way and their knowledge the only Truth.

Holy peace in the world can only be found when we set human minds and hearts free to rise to meet a God of many faces and many cultures. It is not God who changes faces and becomes a god that meets the criteria of the various religious expressions. God reveals himself to people in such a way that they can fully and completely relate to her. A person in rural India cannot meet and understand a God revealed in Jesus, a peasant dressed in poor robes. An Indian peasant meets and understands God through the images and world setting he knows and understands. An aboriginal woman in the heart of remote Australia cannot relate to a God robed richly when they wear skins for clothing and know nearly nothing about valued jewels.

We dare not limit God to a single or even a few human cultures. God may seek to reach humans in poignant ways, but He uses many ways for many people. Any other view is egoistic and extraordinarily vain.

Look at it a bit differently. From the very conservative Christian view, if only those who know and accept God in Christ can know salvation, then huge segments of humanity are doomed to die in Hell. Mohandas Gandhi was not a Christian but he was one of the finest human beings in history. He birthed a nation, sacrificed himself repeatedly to seek justice for his people, lived in complete humility, and truly lived for others rather than for himself. Did the God of Jesus of Nazareth condemn this man to eternal punishment? Hardly! To suggest this and similar acts is to paint a picture of God that is more monster than lover, more vicious than compassionate, and has internal contradictions that make him a Dr. Jeckel and Mr. Hyde.

We do not truly have the mind of God, as Paul argues, but within the limitations of our fallible human minds, we can make conclusions that make sense to our religious sensibilities. One is that God is good. He is not, as the Deists once claimed, like a clock maker who builds the clock and, once it runs properly, leaves it alone, never to deal with it again. As creator of billions of planets, which began as minerals, water, air, and rock and their derivatives, he set them free to become. Most of them remained mineral in content, but at least one of them balanced these ingredients so carefully that the proverbial finger of God let life rise from lifelessness.

As life developed, one species that we know of, humans, developed minds that think and have feelings and sensitivities. Thinking opened new possibilities as intellectual and physical skills and wonder grew so that rational thought happened. In spite of this, strangely, humans are not rational beings. Tied closely to our thinking is our feeling. Feelings dominate. Feelings can warp thinking. One woman, about to birth a baby girl was wrestling with a name. Elizabeth was the name preferred by her husband and her parents. The woman became rigid in her opposition to the name. She had known a child years before who had teased her unmercifully. The name was tied too closely to that memory, so it could not be used. She did agree to name her child "Lisbeth." Emotion overwhelmed logic and the closeness of the two names belied her opposition. There is little logic here, but lots of emotion.

Prejudice and bigotry are common examples of feelings overcoming rational thought. A friend was so angered by racism that he became bigoted against racist people and could not deal with them at any level.

Romantic love is the other universal example of feelings overcoming thinking. Love blinds reason. Incompatible people often marry because they fall in love (or lust). A bright woman falls for a manly laborer only to find that, as the relationship matures, there is very little to talk about and share. Each lives in a world that excludes the other. One prefers watching a football game guzzling a six-pack of beer while the other prefers watching "Masterpiece Theater" sipping white wine.

Seldom do couples like this rationally work out their problems and separate amicably. Instead, their separations become bitter and ugly. Love becomes hate. Emotions overcome all.

Nations war against other nations because they cannot work through problems using rational thought, compromise, and diplomacy. War is irrational at best and organized murder at worst.

Our religious experiences emanate from our feelings, from our emotions, from that part of us that reacts to tenderness and harshness, love and hate, gentleness and anger. We think, but we think religiously with our hearts and sensibilities exposed. If all of our rational thought could be fully harnessed and protected against our feelings, we still could not talk about God properly. It is only when our feelings (hearts) become part of our thoughts that God-talk becomes genuine.

It is at this juncture that people of faith make what I consider a fatal mistake. We feel God in our hearts and try to God-talk rationally. A difficulty is that our feelings tend to overwhelm us; we become egoistic and reflect an understanding of God that comes from our feelings. When we think of God we think of him while our feelings stir simultaneously. We may be at peace, or face an impending crisis, have a headache, a fight with our closest friend, just received a promotion at work, read the obituary of a neighbor, watched our favorite sports team get trounced, or clung tightly to our lover. We do not talk to God with a head emotionally empty. This never happens. Even when we sleep, we dream.

From our emotional being emanates religious bias. Our way of believing has to be the only correct way to believe, or what hope is there? Other religious beliefs are wrong. Ours must be right. Our feelings take over, and any threat to our salvation must be dismissed as wrong, heretical, and pagan. Ours is the way, the only way.

Respect for other ways cannot truly exist side-by-side with our faith. Other religions must be dismissed. Of course, this disrespects God by limiting his power to fit within the box we humans have constructed. Think about it, God can only show himself to humans in a form that is compatible with a specific religious or ethnic framework from Christian fundamentalism to Islamic radicalism to Hindu mythology to aboriginal animism. This lists four expressions of the divine within present human experience. Each of them makes exclusive claim to the absolute Truth.

The time has arrived for people of faith, all faiths, to let God express Herself as She wishes, not what suits the biases of any particular group or individual. Jesus leads the way, as I understand him. Jesus accepted everyone within the world he lived. He rejected no one. Some rejected him; else they would not have executed him as a criminal. Jesus accepted and respected all those he knew, Roman centurions, widows, wealthy tax-gathers, dirt-smudged children, harlots, argumentative lawyers, and ambitious and cocky disciples. It is true that Jesus spent most of his life in the rural countryside, so he had not met many foreigners or people of other religions. Buddhist monks did not walk the rural roads of ancient Israel; Hindu priests did not worship there, and Islam had not yet been born.

Jesus would not have necessarily agreed with them, but he would have respected them for their faith and commitment. He would not have condemned them. Jesus would have walked beside them, learning and teaching, absorbing and sharing, joining them as they joined him. His life or ministry would not have changed, for he had found a way that was particularly his own and had developed within him as he traveled through his life. As it is said, "Go and do likewise."

Chapter Eleven
LIVING A GOOD LIFE IN A PEACEFUL WORLD

There is a gap in this book that needs filling. If, as I propose, the heart of the Christian faith is following a Jesus who loves and respects people where they live, their status in life, as well as the potential for evil lying within, why should anyone live a good life; we already have received the love we crave so much? Does this not remove the incentive to do good, live a clean life, and show dedication to God?

Indeed, our competitive culture is based on reward and punishment. If we perform well on the job, we receive a raise; do poorly and no raise or lose the job. Compete well in sports and win, compete poorly and lose. Live a good life and be rewarded with eternal life, be saved; live a life of evil and go to Hell. This appears to be the rule of living in the modern and the ancient world.

This general rule holds until we consider economics and war. A poor person may live an extremely good life and still remain poor. A wealthy merchant may be contemptuously evil and remain wealthy and gain even more wealth. Wars are not based on justice or good living or being on the side of good. Wars are won by who has the biggest gun, the largest army, or the sneakiest attack. The good guys are usually the ones who win, but not always.

For Christians, the Bible is contradictory and ambiguous on this. David killed the husband of Bathsheba in order to have her. He lived as a king and died without severe punishment. Jesus of Nazareth lived the superior life filled with love and compassion, but society hung him on a cross to die in agony as a criminal.

To wade through this sea of confusion on how we should behave and what motivates us to be the kind of people we are, look to Jesus. Jesus led a life of high risk. He befriended those outside the societal, religious, and political elite. Some were laboring fishermen, poor widows, those with scarred and ugly faces, village outcasts, betrayers of the people such as tax gatherers, and the list goes on. His reward for all this was an ignominious arrest, condemnation, and death. To best understand this we need to look at and seek to find the source of Jesus' motivation.

Jesus was secure. He knew he was a favored son of God. He did not have to work to gain that spiritual status. It was already his. In modern conservative thought, Jesus was saved (had a relationship with God) and knew it. Jesus was not weighed down with the baggage of seeking salvation, of needing to live a life that would reward him with eternal life. Instead, he was free to act and interact with others without regard to himself.

This is a significant difference. Those who live "holy" lives in order to gain eternal life are not truly holy for they are motivated by self-concern. These "spiritual" people do good deeds to be favored by God, to reach the ultimate goal. Jesus looked at a needy person and saw a needy person, not an opportunity to do good things. Jesus was motivated by the needs of others, not his own need.

"Are you saved?" is a frequent question by evangelical Christians. Ultimately, this question reaches into our human psyche and our need to take care of ourselves. The revival preacher's attempt to convict his or her listeners of sin, convince them that they are filled with sin and evil, and that the only way to free themselves and to find eternal life is to confess their weakness, seek forgiveness, and be saved to live with God forever. These sound noble enough and they are certainly not evil, but they are totally self-serving. In a convoluted way, seeking salvation is more accurately running away from Hell. The threat of Hell is often more daunting than an invitation to Heaven is alluring.

Looking again at Jesus reveals doing good with neither daunting Hell nor alluring Heaven to motivate him, and this may appear emotionless. It is not. When Jesus healed the demoniac, Jesus felt the spiritual and psychological pain of the demoniac. He did not look at the man dispassionately, but with warmth, concern, and love. Jesus must have been elated by the experience as the demonic pigs symbolically jumped into the chasm and freed the man from the inner pain that wracked him. Jesus felt the joy of the man, not the joy of his power to heal.

There is a significant difference between the way of Jesus and the way of the Christian teachings beginning with the writings of Paul. Paul focused on personal salvation and the gifts of the Spirit. Even in the writings that do not specifically mention either, they are strongly implied. Salvation is gaining eternal life, or as Jesus stressed earlier, the Kingdom of God. This is a reward and punishment motif. The object of faith is to win God's approval which is gained, ironically, by faith. James would later amend this to include good works as a necessary prerequisite for salvation. In either case, Paul or James, the object is a significant reward for the believer. Faith or works leads to the ultimate payoff.

The other side of this theological coin is the gifts of the Spirit that Paul talks extensively about in his first letter to the church at Corinth. Gifts are skill sets that come from a faithful and spiritual life. The gifts include such things as healing and prophesizing, speaking in tongues and preaching. Again, gifts are a reward of faith that blesses a few with special talents others do not have. It establishes a spiritual hierarchy that stresses significant personal achievement. This focuses the results of faith on personal and individual gain, even though this gain may benefit others such as healing. It is noteworthy that Jesus never offered anyone the gifts of the Spirit. Indeed, it is contrary to his ministry, to set anyone aside as special, to set them apart from ordinary people, causes them to feel superior. Jesus never showed the gifts of the Spirit. He never spoke in tongues, for example. He wanted to remain as close and as intimate with those who heard him as he could. Gifts could have created a barrier.

During the ministry of Jesus, these gifts that Paul wrote about do not appear as spiritual gains for Jesus. There were rewards for Jesus, if they can be called this, for the crowds following him grew and the stories about him created legends about him even as he lived. But look at his life as best we know it. When he preached, lawyers challenged him strongly enough that it precipitated a movement to kill him. When he healed, the Pharisees mumbled against him. As the crowds that followed him grew, he needed, from time-to-time, to isolate himself. The response to him tended to be more negative than positive, although this is hard to measure, for the Gospels tend to favor positive images of Jesus. There are clues, such as the crowds choosing Barabbas instead of Jesus just before his crucifixion. Other clues are more logical than evidential. There is little about him in the secular histories written around or during his day. No crowds protested his execution. No one came to his defense. His closest associates fled in fear of their lives.

Jesus lived in a hostile environment. Some of his fellow Jews wondered about him because he taught things that contradicted their historic understanding of Judaism and, more significantly, because he challenged the contemporary religious power structures of the Jews under a non-Jewish king and the foreign influence of Rome.

Then there was the opposition of Rome that tried to control any movement that might result in civil unrest or insurrection. The Maccabean revolt was only a few generations earlier. Rome wanted peace in the territory they had conquered. Unrest made it more difficult to rule and far harder to collect taxes, a source of wealth for the Empire.

Jesus as a wandering preacher was not completely unique. There were other itinerant preachers including his mentor, John the Baptist. There were also magicians and political revolutionaries, as well as the Pharisees, who constantly struggled against the more politically powerful Sadducees. But the approach of Jesus was unique. Although he did not invent parables as a form, he transformed them into stories usually without direct moral lessons, but that morally, spiritually, and intellectually stimulated people while provoking thought and self evaluation. The stories respected the people rather than condemned or chastised them as did the Baptizer. They were not intended to inspire awe from the listeners as did the magicians with their illusions that elicited widened eyes and "oohs" and "aahs." Jesus' stories did not talk down to people as the superior priests often felt compelled to do in communities with mostly uneducated country folk.

Jesus assumed intelligent and spiritual alertness in spite of the reality of little or no education in his audiences. He believed that the people he spoke to could think logically and question illogic; they could discern between justice and injustice; they could hear the silent voice of God speaking to them by way of the voice of Jesus as well as within their own hearts and minds. Jesus accepted people as his equals, not as inferior beings.

His motivation for his ministry was for those people he addressed and those he met. None of them could reward him, but they could stimulate him. He gained no wealth, but was never truly poor. He had no home, but found shelter and succor wherever he walked.

One of the key differences between Jesus and others is that he was truly satisfied with himself. His relationship to the Father was secure and unbreakable; he knew where he was religiously and spiritually; Jesus understood his intellectual capacity; he knew that no matter what happened to him, who confronted him, or who became an enemy, he could deal with them without any exterior or interior changes. Jesus lived with the most freedom there is, he was completely satisfied with himself. There was no one he had to prove himself to including himself. His parents may have laid a foundation in him, and the foundation was so solid that he no longer had to prove himself to them or anyone else.

As he walked along the roads of his day, he did not have to satisfy a boss or supervisor who looked with critical scrutiny upon his work. His preaching and storytelling were never designed to satisfy people. To the contrary, Jesus wanted to stir them, make them think and reconsider everything in their lives.

Most important, Jesus never played it safe. His lifestyle was risky and dangerous. He dared to challenge authority and established faith. He dared to question the meaning of justice and to associate with the powerless rather than the powerful. Name dropping for him would have been a waste of time. "I met a beggar the other day" did not add to his image as someone with authority, compassion, and love.

Jesus is the one to emulate and follow. He never did anything to win his Father's love, he already had it. He did nothing to make everyone in his audiences happy; for contentious questioners were with him everywhere he went.

Jesus lived a good life, a moral and useful life because he was secure in himself and it was the way he wanted to live. Ah, when the rest of us mere mortals can follow him as our guide, then we will live ethically and morally because we want to, not to win ourselves a place in Heaven.

Jesus was motivated by doing what he did. He did not need praise from others, only an opportunity to tell his stories, embrace the people, love his enemies, and restore wholeness to the broken and ill. He was motivated because he was the Son of God, a special person who had an intimate relationship with his God.

When Christians do good it is not to get something, but to celebrate the Kingdom of God that Jesus has given us. We are the sons and daughters of God. When we respond to the message of Jesus we come that much closer to God because we can move away from total egoism, from total concentration on ourselves and our future. Jesus gave us the Kingdom of God. The future is now. To use more conservative language, we are saved. We respond to what is ours, what is in us, the God within and the loving message of Jesus that welcomes us to the Kingdom of God.

We do not do good to gain the Kingdom, we already have it. We do good in order to celebrate, to offer thanksgiving, and to recognize our potential as the sons and daughters of God. This frees us to become.

The Christian life does not respond to threats of Hell, but lives free and without threat or fear of threat. The Christian life is the ultimate life because it wins nothing for us, but is a free choice from grateful hearts.

The Christian life is also a mature life. This means that when a person can get beyond some of our more primitive human tendencies such as greed, jealousy, self-centeredness, and an oversized need to be accepted by all, then the more mature capabilities of humanity can rise to the surface and dominate. When we truly learn to share with others even to the point of risking ourselves, when we have enough self-confidence to celebrate the success of others, when we realize that we can only find true inner meaning and peace as we let others in, and when we can respect ourselves enough that we no longer crave to be popular, then we can truly begin to follow the path of Jesus of Nazareth and truly be Christian. Our faith must mature and we must always strive to remain mature. Children seek recognition; adults seek to serve.

To live a good and Christian life we live to benefit others within our capabilities. This is not a spectacular life for none of us can be God. We cannot do good for everyone. Some will resist our efforts to do good and this may truly be best for them. In America we learned much from the civil rights movement where paternalistic whites had to learn some bitter lessons that blacks could indeed take care of themselves. They were capable of leadership and generating creative ideas. They did not need to lean on the wealthier and better educated whites. Indeed, blacks needed to win the white majority over to be sensitive to the genuine needs and situations of blacks in our culture, but black Americans were not children needing leadership from white adults. Blacks already were fully mature adults.

I have sketched an ideal overview, but the ideal has to be translated into everyday events and the contentious issues that confront our society and our world. In many of the issues we face today there is simply no easy black or white answer, but vast areas of gray. But most of the arguments are crafted so that the answers appear to be black and white. Below, I offer a two representative ethical and moral issues we face today looking at all sides of an issue is the right thing to do. Following them I will be more direct in confronting some of these issues.

ABORTION

PRO-LIFE
Life is sacred

The essence of human life is sacred. The germinated seed lives. Projecting the quality of life is not as important as human life itself. This becomes more critical when we consider the thinking of Albert Schweitzer, who considered all life sacred, from the pesky gnats to homo sapiens. One is not more valuable that the other.

Birth guarantees love. Babies are special and will receive continuing love and support.

The life of the baby is paramount, especially when compared to a woman having an abortion without a desperate life-threatening need and sometimes this is not considered, only the fetus.

PRO-CHOICE
Quality of life is sacred

Is life, from a human perspective, sacred or is the quality of life sacred? Are the lives of saints and sinners equally sacred? Mother Theresa and Adolf Hitler were not equal. All are not equal. Neither are newly born children. A child born in extreme poverty will not have an equal opportunity for happiness and success as an upper- or middle-class child.

Birth does not guarantee love. An unwanted child can be permanently scarred by a lack of genuine and supportive love.

Birth is a natural process involving a woman's body, which she has, or should have control over. It is not a concern of a society to monitor or interfere with any individual woman's (or man's) body.

Abortion is immoral, sinful, and criminal. It must be eradicated completely.	Abortion has been a reality of life for many, many centuries, if not the entirety of human societies. A difference is that legalizing abortion has made it available safely and affordably for those in the lower income brackets. Making it illegal will not eliminate abortion; it will only make it unavailable to those with little or no financial resources. It becomes discrimination against the poor and remains a benefit for the well-to-do.

To bring Jesus into this argument is difficult. The times were quite different. Infant mortality was extremely high and sterile birthing conditions did not exist. Laws did not cover this kind of issue. Also, since infant deaths were so common, abortions probably could not have been detected. Modern medical methods did not exist so abortions would have been extremely risky. There are some clues, however.

Jesus believed in people and trusted them more than we tend to do today. He lacked both ancient and modern cynicism. Somehow, he was able to discern intelligence and sensitivity others could not. The law and some of the religious convictions of that day denied the intelligence and sensitivity of ordinary people. Those who wielded power ruled and they denied much to peasants. Jesus resisted this kind of control by giving personal control back to the powerless. Jesus would have allowed people to make their own decisions without adding the burden of law that blurred distinctions and strongly favored the rich and powerful while denying equality to all others. He would have resisted making unfair law and would have supported teaching ethics, morals, and other decision-making techniques.

Jesus spent his ministry working with those at the bottom of the social, religious, economic, and political strata. He opened his mind and heart to all. As we work through the New Testament Gospels, we clearly see Jesus preferred to bring dignity to the undignified, knowledge to the ignorant, wisdom to the thoughtless, and spirituality to those who felt overwhelmed by life. Jesus would have struggled against allowing the well-to-do privileges denied the poor.

On the other side of the issue, life was precarious and dangerous, especially for the young. They needed more protection than adults. Abortion at will would have not been within his thinking, at least not without exceptional reasons. But, he would have wanted love and responsibility to be the keys to parenting.

HEALTH CARE

Personal, Private Health Insurance

Health is a personal and private matter and not to be meddled with by big government.

The rapid rise in premiums has forced businesses to share expenses.

Insurance is personal and should be paid by the individuals, not be a corporate benefit.

Insurance should remain in the private sector rather than with any governmental involvement and managed by insurance companies.

Universal Health Care

We are social beings and should take responsibility for each other.

The cost of ill and damaged human beings is far more costly than denying care.

This becomes one way to improve economically. People are our primary resource and they need health protection to perform properly in the workplace.

This demands premiums paid by all, but some jobs cannot help and some people cannot pay; they have little, if any, money. So, additional financial aid is needed.

Jesus was a healer. One of the more useless arguments in religious history is the face-off between those who argue that Jesus miraculously healed the sick as cited in the Gospels and those who argue that he healed those with psychosomatic illnesses. Jesus embraced, touched, spoke to, spit on dirt to give sight to blind eyes, and in other ways made people well. How he did it is of little importance unless one takes everything in the Gospels as the literal truth or, on the other hand, as fantasy.

The most important point is who Jesus encountered in the healing stories. Did he reject the elite? Or did he heal all regardless of social, political, and religious status? Jesus did not discriminate. He chose to love and assist all.

These representative cases cited above have been terribly sketchy. They represent one way to view issues in a more Jesus-centered way.

There are two other issues that can be confronted more directly: war and the death penalty. Both of these deal with killing human beings in ways that are sanctioned culturally and legally.

The Book of Revelation, the final book in the New Testament, portrays a Christ who has not yet conquered evil and foresees a coming battle, Armageddon, where the armies of Christ (good) will engage the Devil (evil) in a final conflict. The winner will live in eternal bliss while the loser will be cast into the fires of brimstone to suffer eternally. This suggests a couple of things: only war can settle the differences between good and evil, and one must be the complete victor; the loser dies painfully. In this conflict love and compassion do not exist.

The life of Jesus does not reflect this. The life of Jesus, as seen through his words when separated from the editorial changes made by the church, reflect much love and compassion, forgiveness and understanding. The Gospels, as a whole, more accurately reflect this as well. Jesus never physically attacked anyone for any reason including to kill or maim. Indeed, he stilled the hand of Peter when he raised a sword to the Roman soldiers as they sought to arrest Jesus. This episode is interesting because nowhere else is a weapon suggested for Jesus or the Twelve. They walk the countryside weaponless.

Read the accounts of the upper room when Jesus exposed a betrayer then sent him on his way without a harsh word. Jesus took the demoniac and pulled the evil out of him, but did not kill the demoniac, although the evilly possessed swine ran over the edge of a cliff. Even the significance of Jesus chasing the merchants from the temple is found when he challenged some Jewish customs and did not reflect violence against human beings. At this particular point in Jewish history, the people brought animal sacrifices to the temple. The kind and size of animal varied with the wealth of the person. The merchants sold sacrificial animals and changed money to complete the sales.

When Jesus met outcasts, he embraced them; he defended the poor widow; offered the centurion a place with him; and brought Lazarus back from the dead. There are no scenes where he promoted injuring or killing the worst of his enemies. Jesus more readily accepted his own death rather than inflicting death upon another.

War intentionally imposes death and devastation on as many of the enemy as necessary to win. There is a flip side to this as well. The winning side experiences death and devastation; it's just not as costly as it is for the loser. Jesus never supported any activity that caused death and devastation.

In reality, however, the "good guys" frequently do not initiate a war, but have it imposed on them by invasion or other intolerable acts. Does this render the peace as Jesus would support it meaningless and impractical? We must live in the real world, do we not? Following the ideals of Jesus would be great if everyone lived by those ideals, too. There are greedy and psychotic world leaders who would follow the ideals of no one no matter who promoted them.

This presents a problem, one that Jesus never faced. There were no significant wars that he participated in personally. His world, from what we know, was more deeply involved in one-on-one relationships. Although he did preach, for the most part these were before tiny audiences. He lived his life for people to the point of accepting his own death rather than violate the principles and faith he believed in and taught. Because he could draw a crowd and gather a following, Rome considered him a threat to their rule and political stability. They executed him, and he did not resist.

This leaves me with no clear guidelines except my faith as I experience and interpret it from the Jesus I have met in my life. Hence, there is no such thing as a just war. Wars kill and seldom settle arguments or conflicts. Both sides are punished, right or wrong. Having said this, there are necessary wars. Hitler attacked the world. The communist influence attacked South Korea. Genocide in Europe and Africa killed millions.

Homosexually threatens to split nations and churches. My own denomination appears ambivalent about it, yielding to public opinion rather than looking to the activities and teachings of Jesus. Officially, a church, for example, only can deal with the gay and lesbian issues when it impacts the clergy, those set aside by the church for ministry. Unofficially, churches can label people or behavior as abhorrent or distasteful. Are homosexuals sinful and evil on the basis of their sexual orientation is a question that plagues our society and others. This issue needs to be divided into two: are gay and lesbian orientations or activities sinful? And are sexual acts that involve violence sinful? The first is rather straightforward while the second finds its core in a belief that homosexuality breeds sexual assaults, especially against the young. Let's deal with the second first.

Violence is wrong. Any act that forces itself unwillingly upon a person is wrong whether it is physical, psychological, or spiritual. Society tends to find physical violence worse than emotional violence. Someone who sits in a wheelchair for a lifetime is easily seen and easy to sympathize with. Emotional damage is unseen and seldom draws our sympathy. A child raised by lazy and apathetic parents frequently is also lazy and apathetic. As the child grows, people find little sympathy for that young person and blame all the misfortune that follows this kind of behavior on the young person. There is no attempt to understand a broken spirit and even less of an attempt to deal with or heal the broken spirit.

The physically crippled receive sympathy. The emotionally crippled receive contempt and wrath. This tendency fails to appreciate the depth and complexity of human beings. Those who sexually abuse another, either physically or emotionally are wrong. It makes no difference whether they are heterosexuals or homosexuals. Violence is wrong. As the father of three daughters and one son, I was far more fearful of a heterosexual raping my daughters than of a homosexual seducing my son. (Notice that this statement reflects a prejudice I wrongly had that understood physical violence as worse than emotional. However, in rape physical and emotional violence are linked into one act.)

I have always wondered why our culture assumed that a gay or lesbian person would seduce children and young people, or even rape them. The reality is that there is no difference between violent deviant behavior in homosexuals and heterosexuals. Each produces its sexually perverted personalities. More significant is the reality that most people of all sexual orientations keep their activity at home and private. Homosexuals are filled with the same warm feelings of love and healthy intimacy in their relationships as heterosexuals.

My personal encounters with gays and lesbians have been limited, but when they have occurred, I have neither felt threatened, nor anticipated a threat. Indeed, most of these encounters have been positive experiences where healthy, sensitive, and thoughtful conversations happened. What a terrible shame that bigotry and prejudice have kept some in the closet.

There appears to be scientific evidence that homosexuality may have either genetic or congenital origins. This makes it part of the natural development of some human beings. To me it makes no difference. Gays and lesbians are simply human beings who have a different perspective on life than others. This is okay. There is nothing wrong with this.

I simply cannot picture the Jesus I know caring, one way or the other, unless it hurts another. Jesus obviously loved so many people who were far out of the mainstream that adding another dimension would make no difference to him. Indeed, if the culture of his day found homosexuality as objectionable as this age does, then Jesus would have embraced them because they needed his love and understanding; there would have been so little of it around.

This chapter could easily become a book in itself. So, let me write about one more issue for which Jesus is completely relevant — capital punishment. The whole penal system, including its most severe punishment, was developed as a deterrent to crime. The word "penal" comes from "penitent," being truly sorry for what one did, a religious term, and part of the preparation for forgiveness in traditional thought. The confessional of Roman Catholics enforce penitence. Punishment is mixed with and a part of deterrence and penitence. Hence the severity of court sentences varies depending on the crimes.

Admittedly, there are people in our world whom we cannot rehabilitate. We do not understand them, and the few we do understand, we do not know how to cure them. This said, there is no justification for killing another human being. The law justifies it for self-defense, but little else. Euthanasia is outlawed. In short, the laws of our country outlaw killing of our fellow human beings. Yet, the law, contradicting itself, imposes the death penalty for certain crimes. The death penalty kills; no matter how many arguments for it, it kills. It may or may not punish. For some, it may release them from a painful life, even though most still fear death. Living in prison may be more painful than escaping it in death.

In a political campaign, the death penalty became a contentious issue. One candidate, for example, aired several advertisements with family members of those murdered, which said that they could not trust the opposing candidate because he may not impose the death penalty. This is not justice but vengeance. You killed my brother, so let us kill you. Vengeance should have no part in the justice system.

Jesus, to the contrary, loved life and loved people. He did not choose to kill to free a soul so that it could rise to heaven. No, he healed the dregs of society, he embraced the lepers and insane, the impoverished and well-to-do, the ugly and unwanted. Indeed, the laws of the day sent Jesus to the ugliest and most horrible form of the Roman death penalty. Jesus personally experienced the unjustness of societal vengeance. Certainly, Jesus was not a criminal, but many of those we execute today are, but in either case killing them is wrong. Death does not rehabilitate, it is simple vengeance.

Jesus was innocent of the charge against him of insurrection, and so are some of those on today's death row innocent. Modern science has demonstrated this through DNA testing. We dare not risk killing an innocent person to satisfy our vengeance. The ancient Romans did this to Jesus, and they were wrong, very wrong.

Chapter Twelve
PRAYER, HOLY TALK

Prayer is the heart of faith. It is the primary connection between people of faith and their God in all religions. Hindus pray before ornate statues. Muslims face toward Mecca and kneel nearly prostrate as they pray. Christians are somewhat confused, for some believe primarily in ritualistic prayer, those that are written and recited, while many others believe in extemporaneous prayers. Native Americans frequently use dance and chanting as their way to pray. The ways to pray vary, but the results are frequently the same, those praying feel connected to God.

This is the heart of prayer, being connected. In a world with massively confused values, with war negating struggles for peace, with bigotry vying with love and respect, with the have-nots losing to the haves, people can feel isolated in their confusion. We can question the value of life by consciously or unconsciously supporting too much inequity and injustice and with world leaders arguing over the price of oil and who should control nuclear energy, which causes isolation and a sense of powerlessness grows. Prayer becomes our faithful voices crying for righteousness. We need to connect to hope, to find a source of hope and strength, to relate to the power of God. The power of God stirs the God within and empowers us to find meaning in life. We find ourselves as we relate to God.

Prayer is relational. How we pray may be more closely tied to culture and tradition than to connecting with a specific religion. Different ways to pray predominate in different societies and within various groups within these societies. Ritual and chanting appear to be nearly universal forms of prayer.

Ritual prayer is frequently encountered in organized religion. Within the Roman Catholic Mass there are many, many prayers, some are memorized by the worshippers, some are carefully recited by the priest, and still others are sung and chanted. There is variety, but there also tends to be repetition. The Our Father and the Hail Mary do not vary while many prayers are adjusted for the seasons and special celebrations.

Repetition is critical to prayer. We humans tend to prefer variety and creativity; however, we still rely on repetition and sameness. Even extemporaneous prayer tends to be formulaic. Prayer is more than mouthing words, it also comforts. To use an analogy, few would enjoy retreating to their homes after a day's work if the furniture and ambiance differed each evening. Familiarity is necessary for comfort. We like to live in an atmosphere that is the same and comfortably familiar. We want the comfortable chair and the worn slippers that fit so well. We want to greet the same faces of our spouses and children; we want to relax and know that even our bad habits are acceptable in the familiar and comfortable world of our home.

Prayer is similar. The redundancy of prayer soothes our spirits and souls. Familiar words make prayer an intimate experience that reassures and comforts us. We do not have to think about the familiar. Because we know what words are uttered, we relax and let it happen. We do not have to wander around the maze of complex thoughts, but submerge ourselves into the soothing and mindless milieu of the known and trusted. We free our minds to float free, uncontrolled, to encounter feelings and emotions usually kept hidden and under control. This helps us to encounter God without restrictive rational barriers.

There are times when we encounter nothing. God remains hidden. In spite of this, we still feel better as peace and comfort embrace us tenderly. Prayer has happened and we are slightly different, perhaps not enough for others to notice, but the silent divine embraces us in the midst of words spoken and recited and in the midst of receptive minds and hearts.

A close relative of ritual prayer is chanting. Most think of a chant as a tune that follows the basic musical rules of Gregorian chants. I would like to widen the definition a bit to include any prayer that uses rhythms. This broadens it to include mantras that use meaningless phrases such as those offered by Transcendental Meditation and recitations of biblical phrases; we use the one we know and connect with our religious orientation.

Gregorian chants elevate the spirit almost immediately with their beauty and rhythms. They establish a mood of holiness that has little intellectual content but much emotional. Chants tend to free our feelings and wash us in the sacred. Newer chants, the sounds of carillons in the afternoon, annoying to some but enchanting to others, join more traditional chants in the lives of many. Organ music mixed with the sights and scents of familiar church environments embrace memories and link us to religious experiences that lift us mystically. An old Gospel hymn floats into our hearts and warmly embraces us. A classical church hymn tingles our nerves and butterflies our stomachs.

The loud chanting from the minaret of a mosque calls Muslims to prayer by piercing their spirits with godly feelings. The singing and dancing of tribal Africans evoke awe and wonder transporting its people into a new world filled with spirits and marvels.

Intellectual content is frequently missing from a chant. Even carefully written prayers, after awhile, become familiar and comfortable. The careful thought put into them is lost as rhythm supplants thought and emotions crowd out logic. Prayer transforms ordinary day-by-day people into people at peace with themselves and the world if only for a moment. For many, prayer returns them to the mundane world refreshed and reinvigorated to take on life's challenges.

Meditation is a form of chanting. Popularized by Transcendental Meditation during the 1960s, it is as old as religion. Ancient mystics practiced it centuries ago. One Roman Catholic monk found the routine and repetitiveness of washing dishes so relaxing to the mind that it became a meditation fusing him with God. Hindus make it part of the daily routine, repeating a mantra until they slip into a trance, an altered state of consciousness, a meditative state. For them, the ideal is to move so deeply within that they experience a state of nothingness, no thoughts, no awareness, but complete union with God.

Most meditators do not reach the "nothingness" state, but find an equally valuable holy experience nevertheless. Their bodies and minds relax and peace settles over them. The experience takes over mind and body and, because they are related, each refreshes and renews the other. With a quiet mind and body, the God within is free to touch and embrace. A cautionary note here that applies to all forms of prayer, some confuse a genuine religious experience with psychological aberrancy. It is far too easy to confuse our own inner voices, compulsions, or the voices of illness with a voice from God. Those who hear voices in their heads tend to have delusions. Guidelines for distinguishing the difference tend to come from religions' holy writings. In these writings, the characteristics of the divine are spelled out with some clarity. If a voice from within does not conform to the divine characteristics, then the voice is not the voice of God, but something quite different. This is true of all prayer, not only meditation.

When there is confusion or lack of clarity in the holy writings, look in supporting documents. The voluminous writings of Jewish Rabbis over many centuries have created a biblical interpretive document of immense importance within their faith. Here is a source that helps erase the confusion of images of God in the Jewish Bible such as between a nurturing God and a vindictive God.

No person of faith should blindly obey an inner voice until the content of the voice has been verified to conform to established and valid teachings of that faith. The voice could be anger, hatred, or insanity speaking rather than God.

For the most part, however, listening to the voice of God within is more closely identified with holy relationships, usually between the praying individual and God. Seldom is this voice an instructional encounter, but rather a union where the distinction between the person and God becomes blurred and each becomes the other. Meditation is the commonest expression of this holy merging.

Meditation is a human-induced state within the context of faith. Faith induces greater faith so a meditator moves within and meets and merges with the God within. Without faith as the motivation, meditation is little more than self-hypnosis reaching inside the individual to meet an individual's memories, prejudices, and opinions. The experience may be peaceful and rewarding, but the content is weak and shallow. After all, encountering oneself seldom opens new paths to wisdom and holy experiences. It leads to the self in its fullness and in its weakness.

Prayer is communication with the divine. The communication can be finding and experiencing God much as one finds and experiences a friend. Words are unnecessary, but with a handshake or hug they embrace each other. This seeks a relationship with God as opposed to seeking something for oneself. This latter, however, is probably the most popular use. During World War II, there was a saying that there are no atheists in foxholes. The implication is that fear drives people to God because they do not want to get hurt or die.

People often say to an ill friend that they will pray for them. We feel good about praying for another and hope that God will intervene, so personal gain is a primary reason to pray. We also pray for athletic team victories and for the health and well-being of participants. A key prayer at worship services is for forgiveness so that we will be saved and the gates of Heaven opened to us. These are "selfish" prayers because the person praying pleas for something that will benefit her. To understand prayer we again look to Jesus for guidance.

The New Testament offers many strong illustrations of the prayers of Jesus. The Lord's Prayer is the most significant. In my mind, it is doubtful that Jesus himself initiated this prayer. This is more likely a prayer of the church picked up by Matthew and Luke (slightly different versions) for their Gospels. The final words of Jesus from the cross offer another series of prayers by the church. There are seven prayers in this series and there is no duplication, which is expected of words most likely to be original words of Jesus. Without going into a technical explanation for why I believe these prayers did not come from Jesus, suffice it to say, the prayers vary somewhat from the image of Jesus that his stories and words have revealed. Frequently, these prayers better echo the historical situations at the times the Gospels were written.

Jesus lived a life that served him poorly by most human standards. He focused more on others rather than himself. He was executed as a criminal without any evidence that he recanted or disavowed the charges. He accepted the ill-conceived judgments against him. If he were truly afraid of losing his life, he would have put up some kind of defense. He did not. Jesus prayed for others rather than himself.

Jesus offered the Kingdom of God to his people immediately. He did not make them a promise that, if they lived a faithful and correct life, they would receive the Kingdom at a future time in another life. Rather, he offered the Kingdom as an immediate reality to enable them to live a better, more fulfilling life. He did not offer his followers an "iffy" Kingdom, but a genuine Kingdom. They were offered an opportunity to live life in response to the gift they received, not in order to get it.

The Lord's Prayer prays for God to give them the Kingdom "…Thy Kingdom come, Thy will be done on earth as it is in Heaven." Notice that this refers to earth becoming like heaven, rather than leaving earth for heaven. Think about prayer as thus far presented in this chapter; it is a union with God now, not a future promise. Jesus did not ask his followers to wait until after they died to experience God or the Kingdom.

For himself, Jesus did not wait until after his crucifixion to experience God, his Father. Put more strongly, Jesus did not wait until he suffered to give others an experience of God, his Father. His initial encounter with God as presented in the Gospels was his baptism. This was not as a result of his faithfulness, but the event that initiated his faithfulness. Surely the accounts of this experience are the Gospel's writers attempt to express the inexpressible in terms that would make it more understandable to their readers, and it does this quite well while showing how Jesus began his ministry. He became the true son of God, not as a result of his faithfulness, but to inspire faith, to bring it alive, and to share it with others. The Kingdom of God became part of his life and then he began his ministry.

There is also a promise of Heaven for the future. Ah, Heaven, so there must also be Hell, the habitat of the Devil, Satan, Evil, Beelzebub, and assorted other characters that explain the bad things in the world. Heaven does not explain all the good things in the world. Rather, Heaven is understood as God's residence and, hopefully, our future residence. In the ancient world Heaven was located in the skies and Hell in the fiery earth's center. Today scientists tell us that the heavens are bitterly cold and the center of the earth is fiery. By scientific standards, both are uninhabitable.

We are not discussing science; we are discussing religion with a primary focus on Christianity. Heaven is a spiritual world of God and good, and Hell is a demonic world of Satan and evil. This is not a Jewish concept, but more closely aligned with Zoroastrianism that also birthed the dualism of body and spirit.

Zoroastrianism was religion, primarily in Persia, that worshipped, Mazda, the god of light, which separated the body and spirit and still lives as a minor religion in isolated parts of Asia.

Jesus had no place in his thought for such dualism of the world or of humans. His Jewish roots suggested that the world was fundamentally good; after all, it was created by God, the Creator. God would not create an evil world. Humans got a bit greedy and introduced evil with help from a snake. Later, Jesus gave the Kingdom to his followers during their lifetime. He risked giving the Kingdom to evil people. This is a huge risk that no one else in history would have taken. Jesus did not discriminate among his followers. He never said that a slave or freeman

could not be his follower, that a Sadducee or a Pharisee[4] could not, that
a Roman Centurion could not, or that Herod could not. He welcomed
everyone. An evil person could become a follower with the intent of dis-
crediting Jesus and his inner circle, the Twelve. Indeed, one from the inner
circle did betray him. Nevertheless, Jesus gave the Kingdom to everyone.

Jesus did not always follow the religious language of his day but the
generations that followed added words that made him appear to use the
language of later generations. Rather, Jesus brought his own unique
lifestyle, religious thinking, and human interaction to his world. One of
the reasons that Rome decided to execute him was simply that he did not
follow the behavior patterns of the various cultures in that part of the
world. Specifically, he did not follow the general behaviors of either the
Pharisees or Sadducees. Jesus was different. He did not expel any from
following him if they were crippled, ugly, diseased, outcasts, lawyers, tax
gatherers, insane, or even sinful evildoers. His prayer patterns probably
diverged from the popular and conventional. Most of his prayers, as
recorded in the Gospels, were silent and alone. He took time from his
followers to isolate himself. There are subtle hints that he practiced
meditation while in the wilderness. If so, then prayer for Jesus was
establishing and reestablishing his relationship with his Father. These
periods of renewing his relationship with his Father kept him alive to his
ministry.

Let us return to the selfish side of prayer. For as long as I can remember, selfishness is frowned upon as wrong. Christians should be humble and
self-effacing. More and more, I am convinced that this is a misconception
of what it means to be Christian. There is little or no evidence that Jesus
was humble and self-effacing. To the contrary, he was willing to argue with

---

[4]The New Testament maligns the Pharisees. Historically, however, they were the "good guys." Pharisees were students of their faith, Judaism, and kept it assiduously. They protected their faith and, after
the fall of Jerusalem, became the core of Judaism, the Rabbi, the teacher. Their portrayal in the Gospels
helped feed the anti-Semitism that has existed from early in the Christian era until today. This is a
tragic misreading of the historical events during the times of Jesus and after.

his opponents, frequently angering them in the process. He did not belittle himself at any point. He walked among people to offer them the Kingdom of God, good stories, spiritual wisdom, healing, self-confidence, and love. He did not shy from angry officials or disgruntled religious leaders. His only sign of humility was that he saw his followers as equal to himself. Of course, he trusted his followers, their intellectual and spiritual talents, so even this form of humility was not very humble.

He did move away from people to renew himself and his relationship with God, so Jesus selfishly prayed for himself. He needed extra strength to face his enemies and still love them. He needed support to manage life in a hostile environment. He never hunched fearfully in a foxhole as in the World Wars, but he confronted verbal missiles hurled daily by his opponents. Responding to this was part of being human.

Prayer opens another topic — God within and God without. Some Christian Pentecostals pray loudly, with hands pointed to the heavens, and heads lifted high. These gestures relate to the idea that God lives in Heaven. This Heavenly God, also called the Creator, is outside our human bodies and appears to reside above. There is little reason to lift our arms in adoration for a God who lives on earth. Artists frequently portray this image of God above as an old bearded man sitting or standing on a billowy cloud. Portraying him as a human image totally puts God "out there."

This God is not one we attempt to have a warm personal relationship with. Rather, he is the creator of all that is, a builder of planets, soil and water, plants and animals. This God is remote and prayer is usually appeasement to fend off his wrath and to get his help with enemies, especially those whom we fear. Before discussing the God within, we need to reconcile the God without and the God within into a harmonious whole.

It would be interesting to use modern science to begin this discussion, because quantum physics offers some interesting possibilities. However, science is not a source that can be properly used to "prove" spiritual or religious ideas. To do this reduces religion to science and removes religion's independence. Science offers many answers, but not those of the human "heart" or spirit. Religion is beyond the scope of science, as it should be.

Begin with a logical contradiction. God is every where at the same instance that God is at one particular spot. Normally, we would say that God is everywhere and part of God is at one particular spot. This is like throwing a blanket on a bed so that it covers the entire bed. Part of the blanket covers a pillow, but not the entire blanket. When we speak of God we move beyond logic and accept that any specific part of the bed is covered by the entire blanket. In God-talk, God is everywhere and where God is, a specific spot, he is totally there. This is illogical; however, God is illogical by human intellectual standards. So God may be everywhere in the universe, but at the same time, the God within me is all of God. God is totally within each person.

Parallel to this is the power of God. God as Creator created the entire universe. This is extraordinary power. When a person prays for healing, the entirety of God is present within that person, so, to a God who created everything, God should be able to totally heal an individual of just about anything. Healing does not always take place. This disjuncture between what should be and what is suggests a couple of things. People do not control God. Sounds basic, but those who argue that to believe totally in Christ promises salvation think that their mindset (faith) can indeed control God. Because when one believes in God, God must respond, as promised, and save the believer. Hear the refrain of an evangelist at a revival, "Give yourself to God and be saved." When you give yourself to God, God is obligated to save you. Humans tend to translate their wants and desires into what God can and will do for us.

God is the ideal of human inventiveness. Intellectually we acknowledge that God is far beyond our imaginations, but this makes little difference. We tend to reverse the biblical injunction in Genesis 1 to make man (humanity) in the image of God. Rather, we make God into our image — an old bearded man enthroned on a cloud. Perhaps a better human image would be of the comic book superhero, Superman, who takes on human characteristics and expands on them. Our eye sight is excellent, but Superman has x-ray vision and can see far into the universe; gravity anchors us to the earth, but Superman can fly beyond earth's gravity; we need oxygen to breathe and live, Superman can fly to the moon without additional breathing apparatus or swim beneath the sea; we must wear protective gear against bullets, Superman repels bullets harmlessly off his skin. This is not God but human fantasy.

Human prayers call for God to do for us what we cannot do for ourselves. We cannot heal ourselves, but God can; we may face failure on a critical test (SATs), but we pray that God will bolster us to super achieve so that we will pass; we are frequently powerless against our mighty and powerful enemies, but God can vanquish even the strongest enemy. John, a Christian imprisoned by Rome on the Greek island of Patmos, wrote the Book of Revelation to show the power of God over Satan in a final conflict, the battle of Armageddon. Oppressed Christians could do nothing against the power of Rome, but God could successfully do battle against the mighty and viciously evil Rome. What the ancient people could not do for themselves and others under the oppressive thumb of Rome, God could and would.

To better understand this role of God, I again turn to Jesus. Jesus himself could not vanquish his enemies and even praying for help was not useful. He still was arrested, was tried, suffered and died at the hands of the Roman Empire. He did not ask God to do what he could not do against an enemy. Rather Jesus did what he could do. He loved his enemies even while they killed him. Jesus invited the centurion to be a follower. He told stories to engage foe and friend. Jesus, on his many trips to be alone, sought from his Father the strength and wisdom to deal with all that life thrust on him. Jesus did not ask that God swoop down from his heavenly perch and rescue him from danger, confrontation, and pain, physical and spiritual. He only asked for the strength to do what he had to do without striking back in despair or anger.

From the perspective of human logic, for God to intervene in human affairs, especially by request (prayer), denies our humanity and potential. There is little motivation to grow, mature, and become more fully human if we face no stress, never have to solve problems, never conquer adversity, never feel pain, and never agonize over difficult decisions. If we never confront difficulties, we cannot find within ourselves the deep satisfaction of finding solutions, of conquering pain and fear, and of converting a negative into a positive. It would certainly be easier if God would take over and make all the difficult decisions for us, leap all the barriers before us, heal the broken hearts, change failures into successes, and make all the right choices. If we avoid responsibility, unfortunately, we would not remain fully human and children of God; we would become less than we can be and children of emptiness.

Jesus gave the Kingdom to his followers. He did not solve all their problems, wipe out poverty, political and religious bigotry, fill empty stomachs, or strike down enemies. Rather, he gave them the Kingdom of God to strengthen their personalities, improve their character, restore their dignity in the middle of humiliating circumstances, and offer them possibilities in an atmosphere of hopelessness.

The God within fulfills the promise in Genesis 1, humans created in the image of God. When linked to the passages that write of the preeminence of humans as compared to the others who cohabitate the earth with us, plants and animals, the image of God within becomes another proof that humans appear superior to other creatures. This explains the domination of humans over our world, but misleads us when referring to the God within.

Humans generate many emotions within. Stomachs butterfly with nervousness, heads ache with stress, hearts beat to reflect our moods, unwanted thoughts thoughtlessly intrude, muscles jerk spastically, slowing breaths calm our thoughts, sad thoughts water our eyes, and happy thoughts put grins on our faces. An ancient question asks what is the relationship between soul and body.[5] An interesting question demands an answer. I believe they are inseparable. When we physically hurt, we feel anguish; when in a bad mood, we tend to have headaches; a long illness can initiate depression; extended physical exercise can create an emotional high; testing intellectual activity tires us; some phobias paralyze us; and a good spiritual experience invigorates us. These realities strongly suggest to me that the physical body and the spiritual body are one. Death does not free the spiritual body to move on into eternal life (Christian) or incarnate itself in another physical body (Hindu). The physical body and spiritual body cannot be separated. To talk of one is to talk of the other. The physical and the spiritual are intellectually separated so that we weak and relatively ignorant humans can discuss them with some clarity. Hurt feelings are not the same as a physical bruise in human understanding, but they both can hurt.

The God within embraces all of us, both our physical and spiritual beings. The same God is in me, a Christian, as is in someone who worships the sun. This makes us holy, not because we live better lives or have stronger beliefs, but because we are people. The God without is the God within. The difference is how we perceive the divine manifestations. The God without is the Creator and the one we seek when we want something. The God within is the God we experience in our daily living and during our spiritual highs

---

[5] I am not going to define soul, but the general understanding is probably as close to its true meaning as anything else. It is more of a philosophical/theological term than a scientific/biological one. Soul is interlinked to our minds and brains, i.e. the central nervous system and especially to that part of the brain that houses emotions and thoughts.

and lows. We encounter the God within when we chant and meditate.

Prayer is more than chanting and meditating, for it can and does mean a conscious encounter with God, the God within. We can think as we "talk" to God, for there is no better place to muse over serious issues that need resolving, to clear our heads from our biases and to free our minds from long-held opinions. Prayer is where we move beyond ourselves to discover greater wisdom and insight.

———————•·•·•———————

Those who pray for miracles usually misunderstand miracles. True miracles are not God's intervention into human history. Some have prayed for miraculous healing for the terminally ill, and find it. Others pray for the same thing and do not find it. The latter failure is frequently explained that God's wisdom is greater than ours, so getting what we want may not ultimately be the correct solution.

To look at it from the perspective of Jesus offers a different experience. As Jesus hung from the cross trying to breathe as his lungs were constricted by the pressure of his sagging body, pain and reflex panicked him. Stop breathing and we panic physically and gasp for air. This reaction is part of how our human bodies take care of themselves. In addition to reflexive panic, Jesus experienced great pain. Hanging from a cross causes pain, the chaffing of the ropes or the cutting of the hands causes excruciating pain. His body was suspended in an unnatural position and his body weight pulled his joints apart as if tortured on a rack.

Speaking was difficult if possible at all. The Gospels record of the final words of Jesus reflect emotional responses closely linked to pain, so, even when not spoken aloud, they echoed Jesus' need to be free from pain and panic. If he uttered such a prayer, it was most likely internally thought rather than vocally spoken. In any event, his pain was alleviated by death some time after being lifted from the ground. A physical miracle never occurred. But, even as he agonized over the torture, he never lost the battle. The Kingdom of God remained his as he was faithful to his life's role. Through it all, he remained true to his mission and ministry. He died in human dignity even though this situation was anything but dignified. His life took on meaning because he never quit on himself or God, his Father. The intimacy of his relationship with the God within brought victory from defeat. It was not a future victory, but immediate and genuine. Jesus was victorious in death.

Chapter Thirteen
THE RISEN LORD

As Jesus energetically trod the footpaths of the ancient world healing and offering the Kingdom of God to all who accepted it, he flirted with death. As long as people gathered around him and listened and responded to his words, his own death by the authorities threatened him. Jesus never hesitated to continue his ministry and never went underground to hide from the authorities. But he never sought death either. In his debates with authoritative figures like the lawyers and Sadducees (a group made up of aristocrats and priests), he never directly attacked, but let the subtleties of his ideas trap them. He did not have the venomous tongue of John the Baptist, but always remained peaceful. The Baptizer vigorously and loudly chased death, but Jesus gently used his tongue while inviting his enemies to join him and never verbally attacked them. The Romans killed him as a common criminal, an insurrectionist, a low-life enemy. He just did not seem to stay dead.

Christians proclaim Jesus as Lord, a proclamation of the Lord of Easter, the Jesus who died and rose from the dead, a promise for the afterlife. Christians have neglected the genuine Jesus in our drive for salvation, to live forever, and to gain the Kingdom of God as a future and permanent existence in glory. In our search for human immortality, we have neglected the teachings and life of Jesus of Nazareth, the human who showed us a different way to live and gave us the Kingdom of God for today, more a present reality than hope for the future. Nevertheless, there is in the life, ministry, pain, and death of Jesus a reality that reaches into the future and speaks to and inspires us now.

To better understand the meaning and power of the Risen Lord, the Lord we experience in life, we look again at Jesus of Nazareth, as best we can view him in the Gospels and other contemporary literature (scant amount of it) as well as the way the later church through the New Testament portrayed him. The New Testament offers conflicting stories and titles. An early title from his birth calls Jesus King of the Jews. This title was sarcastically conferred at his death, but is more clearly outlined during the birth stories of Matthew. Mathew cites the reason that Joseph, Mary, and Jesus fled Israel was because Herod the Great ordered all new born males slaughtered to prevent one of them from usurping his throne. "Kings" from the East, the Magi, sought Jesus to bestow royal gifts upon him.

In startling contrast, Luke portrays the holy family as peasants who traveled to Bethlehem, the city of David, for a census ordered by Rome. Mary rode on an ass, not as royalty, but as impoverished with so little clout that she and Joseph could only find cover in an animal stable. Mere sheep workers paid homage to the child; they had to walk in from the fields to see him, and brought no royal gifts.

Neither birth narrative matches historical evidence. For example, there was no census recorded in Roman historical sources, and it would have been too complex logistically to force people to return to their birth places. Far easier to count them where they lived. Also, no historical records suggest that Herod conducted a general execution of males less than two years of age during this time frame. This does echo the Old Testament story of the birth of Moses and the reaction of Pharaoh.

Other evidence reflects his peasant life style. The short interlude in Jerusalem at age twelve has Jesus proving himself through his wit, not his status. Indeed, his status was questionable as Luke told the story.

He walked the countryside as a peasant, not riding as wealth and royal status dictated. Only his entrance into Jerusalem for the final days of his life belies his royal stature and, then, it was on a donkey in contrast to Pontius Pilate entering on a war steed followed by Roman troops to safeguard the city during the Passover festival. Jesus' students who walked with him came from peasant-like backgrounds. None of them was ever identified as part of an important social, religious, or political family or class. All were working people.

Jesus moved frequently, never having a home or worshipping at a regular location or having a common place to meet friends. He slept on the ground or in another's bed. As he traveled, he never feasted, although he talked about it in his parables. Probably, he seldom chose what to eat, but ate what was laid before him by generous hosts.

Jesus had little money. He chose Judas Iscariot to manage the money for him and the Twelve, but it is doubtful that they accumulated very much of anything beyond their next meal or bed. Also, for the most part, his associates were also peasants. No one in a position of wealth or power numbered among his closest followers. Some almost did, but like the "rich young ruler," did not stay.

This rather ordinary person with an extraordinary spirit and intellect influenced his immediate world very little. His followers numbered in the hundreds and his direct influence appears more negative than positive. His Roman execution and the disfavor of the crowds when they chose Barabbas rather than Jesus during the events immediately before his crucifixion demonstrates this. He influenced his followers deeply, but after his death most joined the Jewish dispersion. His greatest influence happened later among the Gentile, non-Jews in lands ruled by Rome. This fame among Gentiles was the work of the evangelizing of Paul, a Jewish Pharisee and a Roman citizen.

This suggests two interesting questions: What inspired Jesus to work with the peasants and others during his earthly ministry? How did Jesus become the spiritual leader of his followers after his death to the present age? Both questions relate directly to how we experience the Risen Lord.

It is difficult to understand how difficult Jesus' life was. His family members, at best, were artisans and peasants. Peasants were not at the lowest economic scale, but close enough to make hunger a day-to-day issue, have fragile health, and have little community power. We know nothing about whether he had a personal mentor or other significant role models. There is so little evidence concerning his day-to-day living that all we can do is make some intelligent guesses while recognizing that the 21st Century is far, far different than the first.

At some time during early adulthood he followed John the Baptist. This indicates he was a seeker, a seeker for truth and spiritual wisdom. Raised a Jew and influenced by the Baptist, later rejecting John's position, Jesus moved on to offer an alternative to both Judaism and the teachings of John the Baptist. These are major shifts in thinking and believing, an intellectual and spiritual revolution. Although we have no idea of the time between his transformation from his alliance with the Baptist to adopting a more independent thought, we can suggest that it was not over an extended period of time, perhaps only a couple of years. What caused this transformation must have been profound and powerful. Something talked to the God within Jesus that set free the self-realization that he was a very unique person and that he had been called by God, his Father, to work with the people of his day in a very special way that differed significantly from his Jewish heritage and the later teachings of the Baptist. He was raised on the Jewish Torah, but felt free to violate the Sabbath laws, instead of stoning a harlot, he welcomed her into the family of discipleship, rather than supporting animal sacrificial rituals, he chased the merchants from the temple, and he criticized established customs and traditional leadership. The spiritual break from Judaism was clear, but it was not hostile. If anything, it was more practical; he only challenged Judaism when it interfered with his own processing of faith and custom; he confronted traditions only when they became barriers to justice for his people.

His break from John was less subtle because John was a strong, energetic, and a zealous spokesperson for his interpretation of life and faith. John's opinion of people was low. His sermon just before the baptism of Jesus was harsh, calling his audience some pretty ugly names like snakes. He promised them eternal punishment and said they were not worthy of salvation. Indeed, they were so bad that only baptism could wash their bodies and souls of the evil that permeated them. They were the worst kind of sinners.

Jesus submitted to this baptism for sin and evil to mark the beginning of his new message that stressed his respect for people, not disdain, that people were welcome in God's Kingdom, and that they were indeed worthy his love.

This turnaround of Jesus was monumental. He was inspired to initiate a new way to think religiously and a new perspective on whom and what people were and are. This demonstrated that Jesus, was unique in history, and that he formed a continuum in the growth of our human understanding of God, especially in that part of the world where he lived and ministered. In a strange way, what enabled Jesus to bring something new and refreshing to the world was not something new, but something quite old, a relationship with the mysterious divine. In the language of the New Testament, it was the relationship between the man Jesus and his Father and with their people. Jesus experienced his Father, not as the creator God out in the world, but as the inner parental spirit that nourished and enabled him to expose himself. Jesus let people draw so closely to him that they could wrench his heart, as did the betrayal of Judas, the braggadocio of Peter when he denied that he would betray Jesus just before the trial and then did so, or the squabbling between James and John over who should have the seat of honor next to Jesus.

The spirit within freed Jesus to risk himself for others, not in a heroic way by waving a sword in the face of an enemy or some other spectacular act, but by challenging the important values of life and living. He dared to trust others, even though some of them, perhaps too many, would reject him and the Kingdom he offered. As important, he did not ask for trust from others before he gave them his trust. He risked his life in order to give life. Jesus dared to give his best and asked for their best in return. Jesus dared to risk himself because he was secure in his faith and secure in his person. He was one with God, his Father. Within him was a spark of the divine, a divinity that leaped human and world boundaries.

The first glimpse of this was revealed in the first chapter of Genesis in the seven-day creation sequence when humans were made in the image of God. Some have suggested that this means that we physically reflect the form of God. This idea is too trivial to consider, although it serves well those who have created God in their human image, making God like man.

Rather, the divine embraces humanity in the most intimate way. By being a part of each of us divinity stretches across the generations of humans, across the centuries of history, across the gradual maturing of humans as beings aware of themselves and others. Humans became sensitive to their minds, spirits, and bodies. Sometimes, this confuses us for it is within human experience but beyond human understanding. A living spirit who embraces us all remains independent, reaches across time to embrace all generations, and exposes herself to all kinds, the good and bad, the intelligent and those not so intelligent, the physically healthy and unhealthy, the sensitive and insensitive, the handsome and ugly, and the sacred and profane. This spirit makes no rational sense.

Jesus experienced the physical and spiritual unity more intensely and clearly than others. His calling to ministry was neither casual nor flip but directed him to question the accepted and to challenge everything. Jesus looked in the faces of those who encountered him, friendly and unfriendly, and saw value and worth, the image of God resting within each. He reached out to them at their worst and at their best, although the Gospels strongly suggest that most were nearer their worst than their best.

He understood with great clarity that he was more than just a Jewish man, but united with God more strongly and spiritually than those around him. He was not a mere prophet with a great message but brought his followers the Kingdom of God. His followers were all who listened to his stories and sermons with serious interest. It certainly included the Twelve, but also all who heeded what he offered them and, also, may have included enemies as well as friends, those intending to destroy him as well as those who protected him.

He spoke, touched, and gave the Kingdom to all who received it. This power to act as a direct link to God was a quality more unique to him than anyone. Great prophets spoke words of wisdom and faith, but Jesus spoke and in his words was the full power of God. Later generations of Christians would call this power the Holy Spirit, an unseen power that transformed people. This Spirit of God was not special to Jesus or his age, but was the power of life that exudes from God throughout time. Jesus was the special expression that moved people, then and today.

This special quality of Jesus to confer God's Kingdom was a one-time event for Christians (the different ways that God expresses himself to other cultures and religions makes Jesus an event unique for Christians). The Gospels dramatize this event, the passage of God from older times into newer times in the baptism of Jesus by John. John represents the old or Old Testament, and Jesus the new or New Testament. The clouds opened and the finger of God, the Spirit, embraced Jesus and empowered him. The New Testament was born. Symbolically, John passed it on to Jesus, the old giving way to the new.

This special person, Jesus, was crucified and his human life ended, but he had passed on the Kingdom of God to others. This Kingdom intensifies the God within each person and expresses itself to the world as the Risen Lord who lived beyond death within the hearts and spirits of those who accept the Kingdom of God. John's Gospel expressed a similar thought when he wrote that the Word (Jesus) was from the beginning. The God of the old revealed himself in the one who offered new life and the Kingdom of God, Jesus of Nazareth.

When Jesus died as a criminal, by the standards of that day, and in disgrace, his followers fell back to their encounters with him which included, for many, their encounter with the Kingdom of God. This is far more than fond memories, for when they received the Kingdom of God within, the Kingdom became part of them, the God within was strengthened and empowered. God, Jesus, the Kingdom, and the renewed and reinvigorated followers became spiritually united, became one. This is not static any more than life is static. It is a dynamic relationship that inspires and transforms; it makes people feel new.

God, Jesus, and the Kingdom are not locked into an individual or a special group of people, but are a living entity that reaches across boundaries that humans cannot. This is the Risen Lord, the Lord of the Resurrection, and the Lord of the Christian spirit.

Jesus of Nazareth died on the Cross, but the Spirit that reached back to the beginning, the old, and that empowered Jesus to become the special dispenser of the Kingdom, the new, lives. This aspect of Jesus reaches through the ages to touch, from the beginning, the time Jesus walked and taught, to now. The Risen Lord lives today; those who accept and embrace the Kingdom of God are aware of this living presence available to all.

Life can be one of the most agonizing things. Depression overwhelms many, making day-to-day living extremely difficult. Cancer ravages human bodies, and sometimes its treatment is nearly as bad. Diabetes steals legs and eyes. War constantly rages somewhere and our country, the United States, tends to be involved in more than its share of them. With certainty we reduce and threaten to eliminate the natural resources of our planet. Poverty starves millions of earth's people. Tsunamis, tornadoes, and hurricanes kill and destroy. Sometimes life hardly seems worth living.

Then comes Easter, the season of hope, renewal, strength, and wisdom. Conquering death seems the most important thing. The afterlife is a veritable Eden of perfection and the absence of all that causes pain and devastation. So hope anticipates eternal life as the final and complete answer to all.

Easter is so much more than this. Jesus offered his followers the Kingdom of God during their lives rather than as a promise for the future. He saw a blind man and gave him sight, not a vision of future sight. He saw a leper and healed him; heard of a dying daughter and restored her life; and met a despised tax-gathered and welcomed him into his heart.

Jesus saw the Temple merchants abuse his people by taking money some could not afford and chased them from the Temple; he challenged a rich man to follow him; restored dignity to an impoverished widow; and offered the Kingdom of God to everyone.

Easter passes the Kingdom of God to everyone throughout all generations. Moderns who receive and accept the Kingdom of God may instantly or gradually change (sometimes awareness of the Kingdom comes slowly), they are converted or saved to a new way of living, not waiting for something to happen at a future time. The conversion or salvation is a spiritual empowerment that transforms living. A person feels more value in living. A cancer patient nearing the final stage of life finds despair changed so that quality and value of life is more appreciated in the time remaining and the patient no longer wastes much time brooding about the terrible disease that grips his body. An impoverished man finds dignity and value in spite of a lack of financial resources or the contempt that those better off heap upon him. A wealthy Hollywood performer discovers personal richness in serving to enrich the lives of others. A severely depressed woman finds her depression slowly evaporates as newly found meaning and appreciation for life replaces despair.

The Kingdom of God, resurrection, promotes quality and meaningful lives. It does not remove our humanness, we are still emotionally and spiritually frail beings, but the Kingdom offers us strength and reassurance; we are not overcome by our frailty. We develop inner resources fueled by the God and the Kingdom within. The power of the Risen Lord has made us new. The ultimate gift is life, not death.

An additional benefit of the Kingdom is the dissipation of the fear of death. Many are so preoccupied with entry into the eternalness of Heaven because the idea that we die is unacceptable. They get the "Adam and Eve" syndrome. The Adam and Eve myth is about the human inclination to have the knowledge of God and, with this knowledge, comes power. To gain eternal life is to gain an attribute of God. Our human conceit already suggests that we are the only truly intelligent beings anywhere. We are, therefore, closer to being like God than any other creature. Similarly, God is eternal, so as near Godlike as we are, we should also be eternal.

The idea of death is repulsive. Death appears to negate life. We live a full life; we love and receive love; we earn an income and build toward retirement, not death; we contribute, however little, to make life better, not elevate death; we parent children to add to life, not death; and so it goes. Death makes no sense, except for those suffering without hope for cure. Well, we do, from time-to-time, impose death on others like those whom we think do not deserve to live such as criminals and hardened killers. We wage war against our enemies, provoked and unprovoked. But death is intended only for the "bad guys," not us, the good guys. Execution is the worst of society's punishment for evil acts.

We find every way we can to avoid or deny death. Death happens; it is part of the cycle of life. Yet death stares us in the face as the elderly pass away; grandparents die as do fathers and mothers. Accident and disease snatch young friends long before they are ready. Sometimes we personally face death only to have it run away as modern medicine cures and protects us from death.

Easter conquers death, we are told, yet the saintly ones die, sometimes horribly and, more frequently, most slip gently into death as we sleep or are heavily sedated. Death is the ultimate enemy. The so-called grim reaper follows us all with his scythe poised to cut us down.

Again, look to the model of Jesus to grasp an understanding that makes sense for living and for faith. Jesus celebrated life. There is no hint in the Gospels that Jesus preferred death more than life. He embraced dirty and rowdy children; he touched and healed the diseased, welcomed society's outcasts, and challenged traditions that appeared to interfere with pious living, like picking grain on a Sabbath. He told stories to make the living think and some of them sounded so absurd that they brought smiles and frowns to listening faces.

Jesus did not encourage people to die so that they could enter life eternal or be resurrected from the dead. Rather, he brought Lazarus to life and canceled death for the woman's child. The stories of Jesus were about ordinary scenes in ordinary life, a wayward son, a shepherd, a business man hiring temporary help, giving aid and comfort to an injured man on the road, and so forth. His use of humor and drama was for day-to-day events, the routines of life, not for a future resolution beyond the grave. Jesus himself lived his life for the living. He did not preach at funerals or sit with mourners at wakes as those who later followed his way do.

Jesus reacted to death in his own personal life. In a violent world, those in power did not hesitate to kill. Caesar ordered the execution of Pontius Pilate some years after the death of Jesus because Pilate ordered the deaths of so many. The infamous story of Herod, the younger, ordering the beheading of John the Baptist at the request of Salome demonstrates casual abuse. So, whenever Jesus opposed those in power he threatened his own life. His crucifixion, along with all those others who were hung on crosses at the same time, was not for a capital crime measured by today's standards, but for offering a possible threat to the Roman Empire. In essence, Jesus was executed for an unspecified threat against Rome that may or may not have been genuine. He died because those in power saw him as a possible threat, not a real one.

As the Gospels portray Jesus, he sent Judas from their dinner table to betray him. Jesus just asked him to do it quickly because it was not something pleasant to look forward to. Jesus stilled the sword-filled hand of Peter at the arrest and healed the wounded guard's ear. In the Gethsemane prayer, he asked for freedom from his impending death, finally relenting by suggesting that he would obey God's will. Of the final words of Jesus, "Father, why have you forsaken me?" are memorable. It is difficult to judge the historical accuracy of these events, but together they preserve an image of Jesus that accurately reflects his reluctance to die.

Jesus did not want to die, but he did not shun it either. He did nothing to extend his life. He did not defend himself at his trial, although probably not an historical event but it does reflect the memory of the later church concerning how Jesus would probably have acted. He stopped Peter from attacking the soldiers to protect him. Did he look ahead to life after death or was he satisfied with his life to the point that he no longer had to cling to it? We can never answer these questions, but when we reflect upon his life, he was fulfilled; he kept his faith with his Father; loved his followers, and was loved in return; he brought a new message of the Kingdom of God for all who paid attention; he lived without greed or human ambition. There could be no more for him, even in the ideal hope of Heaven.

Jesus did not find value in living an idle passive life. He lived vitally and vigorously; Jesus lived as he walked miles upon miles, spoke intimately with his closest followers, told fascinating stories to all who listened, healed the sick, preached sermons of good news, and fended off enemies with gentle humor and sharp responses. To die and live in bliss, as we humans have defined heaven over the centuries, would have bored him. Indeed, it would have hurt him, for he would neither be active nor spread the Kingdom of God. The meaning of his life was on earth and living among people who hungered and thirsted for what he offered. Obedience to his Father meant Jesus served people in their lives, not deferring it to beyond the grave. The true miracle was not afterlife, but continuing his ministry throughout the difficult years, centuries, so that we today can and do encounter the same Kingdom of God that Jesus offered in the first century.

Jesus did not die with regrets over the quality of his life. He had done what his life and ministry demanded. People had responded to him and accepted the Kingdom, freed from the servitude of the human condition including the inequities of society. Jesus died a horrible death enduring the physical pain of his wounds and the excruciating pain imposed by slowly suffocating, but his life had been successful. There was nothing he could do to be more successful. Jesus had no regrets over his life.

This is a gift of the Kingdom of God. Those who receive the Kingdom of God know they are loved, have complete dignity, and are content with their place in the world. They do not have to be wealthy or powerful, famous and adored by thousands, beautiful or handsome to the eye or physically superior. Rather, they know they have lived a life that reflects God's glory and love. There is no need to live forever in bliss. It is enough to have lived in the Kingdom of God.

Eternal life is not a necessity, but may be an unsought bonus. Those who *need* to live eternally have not truly experienced Jesus' Kingdom of God. Those who have lived in the Kingdom may be blessed in eternity, but do not need it. They are satisfied.

Chapter Fourteen
HOLY SCRIPTURE

It was a shabby home in central Florida. Its badly weathered front porch led to a screen door with the screening torn and its springs rusted. Inside, the house was furnished with 1950s style wire furniture covered with vinyl in worn bright colors. There was a mantle atop a well used fireplace with an open Bible resting alone on the top. Walking over to it, I noticed that it was worn and opened to Psalms.

The gentleman who had invited me into his home saw me looking at the Bible and said, "I never close my Bible. It is the Word of God and should always be open. The Word should always be exposed to the light of day. Nothing should ever close it from the world." He repeated, "I always leave it open."

This man had a deep respect for the book that he believed held the revelation of God. It was his Holy Bible. For some churches opening the Bible at the beginning of the service indicates the beginning of worship. This kind of respect reflects an attitude toward Scriptures that it is most reverent and pious. Let me suggest a different but just as respectful and reverent approach to the Christian Scriptures.

The Bible is a book of faith. Over many centuries, people of faith have recorded their experiences of God and faith. To understand this we have to use our imaginations and travel back to a time when modern science was still prenatal, not yet born, and communications between nations was slow and cumbersome. The center of community life was stories. Writing was rare and shared by only a few scholars. Most people were illiterate and unschooled. At days end, near dark because they used all of daylight to work, families and tribes gathered to talk and share. The day's events would be shared highlighting some special things. But, as is the way, when people gather and talk, the day's events were frequently compared to other past events that were similar.

Stories were compared and, sometimes, exaggerated. Old events grew and became larger until a local flood spread to encompass the entire area and beyond. As some stories became folklore, questions rose fed by the folklore. To answer the questions that defied logic and understanding, people of faith relied on their faith; God became the answer. We must be careful for it sounds as if the stories were fabricated, folk lies. Not so. The stories to answer the questions were honestly answered from the knowledge and understandings they had. To use Noah's story again, the ancients knew that rain caused water to rise in the streams and rivers. It made sense that if enough rain fell there could be a catastrophic flood. The answer was logical and based on observation, but why?

Why would the forces of the world cause it to rain so heavily that people are killed, plants drowned, and animals slain? Again, observation plays a role. People could not have done this, not the animals or other known forces. The cause must come from a far greater power. Only the holy could effect such a dramatic climatic change, but, again, why?

In the Old Testament the story about the flood offers a reason; the Jewish people had done evil and broken their covenant with God, so God punished them. Using God and faith to answer the mysteries of their world brought order and sensibility to chaos and despair. Faith replaced mystery and horror with reason and hope. God became a reality in their lives.

They did not understand the world through scientific exploration. Rather they looked inside and outside for reasons that made sense to them. God offered them explanations of the wonder and mysteries of the world. This was a genuine approach for the world stretched the human spirit and mind.

—•◦•—

The ancient Scriptures also offered people a way to live meaningful and just lives. They understood God in relationship to human events, in balance with the great events of the day as well as the tiny personal actions that affect day-to-day living. Life found meaning, not merely explanations. These were reasons to live in better relationships to family, friends, and cultures. Good living meant more than abundance and well-being, but also ethical and moral behavior. The Bible stressed this so that the faithful saw themselves, not merely as individuals with needs and wants, but as people encountering each other in ways that added meaning to their own lives. People became more than individuals, they became communities, tribes, and nations. The Jews became a unique and special people, those selected and elected by God.

———

Scriptures presented history, not as a sequence of events, but as how people interacted with each other and as a community in relationship to the divine. Wars were not simply wars but God's reaction and judgment. The winning nation was blessed by God and the losing nation damned or punished. Life was a spiritual journey that involved every aspect of life in the most ancient accounts,

God was the God of Israel and the other nations had their own gods. The Jews saw themselves as a nation that was on very intimate terms with God who had an impact on everything. The God of Israel was frequently in conflict with other gods such as Baal. This was not monotheism, but multi-theism. In later years, belief in Israel's God expanded and was understood as a single deity for all the world so that the gods of the other countries became false gods or idols, no longer competition. Monotheism was born.

———

Scriptures also brought together the wisdom of the people. Wisdom was not a human construct, but insights from people whose thoughtfulness was embraced and inspired by God. Nothing in their lives was separated from their relationships to God. Wisdom was more than human thought, it was inspired human thought. Scripture brought this wisdom together and made it available to people of faith. This brought not only divinity into wisdom but added an authority to wisdom it would not have had otherwise. Wisdom transcended time making it available for all generations, even ours today. As the generations passed and experiences grew, this validated their wisdom. Some of this wisdom was codified into law, the law that formed the foundation of the Hebrew people. Formally this became the Torah, the Law, and the first five books of the Old Testament.

There is also beauty. The Psalms are poetic, using a form of poetry that is no longer used, even in Hebrew; still there is a majesty and meter that sings to the sensitive reader. The Psalms are holy poetry, an experience in worship where one loses oneself in God and where the God out there becomes the God in here. The Psalms take holy history and bring it alive in the hearts and spirits of the faithful. The poetry of the Psalms took ancient wisdom and leaped the centuries to become a holy experience for today.

The Old Testament, especially for Jews, offers a sense of identity. The story of the Jewish people takes them back to mythic origins and moves through holy and living history, Sometimes the history is slanted by religious concerns and judged by faith, but the grandeur of the movement of the Jews through time is impressive and adds a strong identity for them as God's chosen people.

The Prophets shouted their words calling the people back to a holy path, back to a more righteous way, and forward to better lives and a better nation. The prophetic tradition appears to have waned, if not perished completely in the modern age. Few nations or people call for justice any more. Greed and power have replaced this sense of indignation against injustice and corruption. Justice is measured by profits and fairness by wealth. There is no pious call for everyone to be treated equally, but rather politics, medicine, and law respond to subtle and legal bribery rather than human need. Popularity has replaced righteous indignation. We vote for comfort rather than integrity; we drive gas-guzzling automobiles rather than care for the health of our air; we imprison rule-breakers rather than heal broken souls.

We need to return to Scripture in a healthier and holier way to recapture the God who loves and inspires us, the sense of awe before our world and find our God. Scriptures should be a guide for today, not a nostalgic look at an old and bygone age. Scriptures have not lost their power; we have lost our sense of wonder and faith.

For Christians, our holy Scriptures have another section, the New Testament. Although not as complex as the Old Testament, the New Testament uses the Old as a resource. The New has six narrative books, the four Gospels, the Acts of the Apostles, and Revelation (Apocalypse). There are letters (epistles) and at least one sermon (Hebrews). The primary sources from the New Testament on the life of Jesus of Nazareth are the four Gospels.

These Gospels are truly inspired. Although the names of the authors are not contained internally in any of the Gospels, I will use the traditional names of Matthew, Mark, Luke, and John for convenience even though they are not necessarily accurate. In the earliest Christian communities from about 70 C.E. to 120 C.E., the various communities met a variety of problems that demanded that the story of Jesus be recalled and repeated. As suggested above, these were not uniform communities, but diverse, and each dealt with its own unique problems. Mark's community was not the same as Matthew's, Luke's, or John's. So each writer wrote for the Christians he lived and worked with, to meet their needs, to assuage their doubts, to build unity among them, and to strengthen faith. Rome was their common political and religious enemy.

They could easily have used one of the Gospels as the common "holy" Gospel to reflect the life of Jesus and its impact on the writer and his readers. One would have been enough. After all, for Christians, there is only one Bible. For many years there was only one acceptable translation for English-speaking people, the King James Version. But the editors of the Greek New Testament, those who collected the various books and brought them together, realized that human beings are diverse and the message of faith must be as diverse as the people. So there is not one Gospel, but four, to address differing environments.

The New Testament responded to different people with different needs. This is the wisdom of God, to meet people where they are rather than where they are not. To follow this faithful wisdom is to understand that Jesus did not tell one creative and all-encompassing parable, but many of them with completely different slants, characters, environments, and problems.

This genius of diversity did not end with the closure of the New Testament canon, which formalized the books that were included and closed it to future additions. This closure did not end diversity. Rather, diversity continued by interpreting the Gospels and other New Testament books differently. The same passage in a Gospel, for example, meant different things to different people or groups of people. The interpretations reflected the different needs and environments of the Christian communities, beyond the New Testament age.

The message of John the Baptist offers a simple example of this. Some Christian interpreters see the harsh words of the Baptizer just before the baptism of Jesus as an echo of the message of Jesus himself. The world was filled with sinners who needed saving. Others understand the same passage as a sign of the passing of the old for the new, the Old Testament for the birth of the New Testament. Another is the Bible itself. Is the Bible a human and historical book or is it, proverbially, a dictated message of God. No one argued that the Bible was actually dictated by God, but that each word and each jot was inspired by God and therefore must be literally true. Others argued that the writers were inspired, but the words themselves were not the words of God. Still others believed that the key to its authority is the final acceptance by the Christian community; people of faith wrote or edited it but its final value was based on how the Christianity communities accepted and understood it.

These differing interpretations led to denominationalism well before the Reformation of Martin Luther and John Calvin created a formal split. Severe differences went beyond biblical content and debated doctrine as well. The so-called docetic debate (was Jesus human or God disguised as a human) questioned whether Jesus was totally Godhead or was there a truly human side. This book argues that the human Jesus is more central to faith than the Christ of the early church, which indicates that this debate has never been completely settled.

Scripture, as we see it today, meets people from just about every Christian theological perspective from hardcore biblical fundamentalists to Roman Catholicism's emphasis on the equality of the Bible and tradition. The basic truth that God's love is expressed eloquently in the Bible transcends theological and interpretive differences. Love, however, does not necessarily mean the same thing to all. Greek, the language of the New Testament, for example, has three words for love, each defined the same, but the connotations differ, *agapè*, *philos*, and *eros*. The holiness of the Bible must pass through human hands and minds. Translations from the Hebrew and Greek shift from age to age as language changes and translators make subtle and different emphases. Even the ancient manuscripts have variations between the many copies of the Hebrew and Greek texts.

Celebrate these differences. God's Scripture is not static and forever buried in the past, but is a living document that constantly interacts with people of faith. God is not a stone tablet forever frozen but a reflection of a living God forever changing. God's revelations are not fossilized like extinct animals but still move among and within us.

Even the most somber writings in the New Testament tell us much about our human encounter with the divine. Paul in his letters deals with confrontation and hostility, with different approaches to faith, and with friendship. He was an interesting man who was handicapped in some way, the "thorn in his side." The handicap is not specified clearly. One scholar suggested a few dozen years ago that the thorn in his side was his arrogance. This might be true when you read his letters and realize that he always claimed that he was correct and everyone else wrong. Paul did not compromise or listen to alternate viewpoints. Obviously, the later church agreed with him because they included so many of his letters in the New Testament. Also, a few other New Testament writers claimed to be Paul or wrote under the authority of his name. He made theology interesting and combatitive.

If you like war stories where the good guys win, read Revelation (Apocalypse). This book is filled with ugly and uglier images for evil, a monster with seven heads and a torture pit filled with fire and brimstone. The armies of Christ vanquish the enemy and the good guys, who cannot save themselves, are saved by the holy armies. Celebrate the message that those who cannot adequately help themselves that holy help is coming, the armies of Christ are coming. Celebrate that winners do not have to be Type A personalities; Matthew wrote that the meek shall inherit the world. Others can be winners, too. In a world dominated by competition, where giants run on grassy fields and hardwood floors, fleet feet run on cinder, where knockout power makes winners, and where voluptuousness is crowned, there is hope that the ordinary and the less than spectacular will stand just as tall before God.

Jesus offered the same thing when he gave the Kingdom of God, and it is without violence. Faith speaks to all, those who need heroes to save them and those who accept the God within as a source of vitality and well-being.

Scripture can act as a safeguard against excess. Because Scriptures of all faiths form the foundation of their dogmas that grow and develop, these holy books are the sources to visit to validate questionable teachings. The American militia movement confuses faith and patriotism. The Muslim fundamentalist movement sends the faithful to kill themselves and others in suicide bombings. Voices cry into the spiritual ears of the insane to kill their families for God. These excessive behaviors are not acceptable in most religions today, but not because their Scriptures, when taken literally, forbid them. Indeed, looking at them from the Christian biblical texts, most can be defended. The God of the Israelites slew their enemies and a pair of daughters seduced their father. Dying as a martyr is well documented in most religions. Jacob obeyed the voice of God to sacrifice his son at the altar. Revelation threw scads of people into the fire.

The question becomes interpretation, interpretation, interpretation. Scriptures are written, but people get in the way. We read the words of faith and wisdom and look behind them for hidden meanings and ideas that fit within our personal theology and philosophy. We highlight obscure passages we like and ignore those we do not. We take a verse and remove it from its setting so it can say what we want it to say rather that what it does say. We follow a particular cause and find Scriptural evidence to support it, even when the support is weak or not at all.

Faithful people, using the same Scripture, argue from opposite perspectives. In the Old Testament, for example, if we look at the seven day creation story, does seven days mean seven twenty-four hour time periods or are does time mean something different, like 100 years or a millennium? Or is the seven days a symbolic statement that is meaningless in relationship to normal time periods?

In the New Testament, are the parables of Jesus understood as stories with very specific meanings not to be interpreted or are they open to different interpretations for each generation of believers? These are not easy choices, but they suggest how Scriptures can be abused or misunderstood.

An argument can be made that all of these quite different interpretations are legitimate. God lives in everyone's heart, and Jesus offered the Kingdom to those who accepted it, so would not God through Scripture speak to each in a different voice? This is always a possibility. Indeed, this makes more sense than that only a single interpretation is valid. The parables work this way, as we have seen. The stories Jesus told were open-ended so that they related to each specific person from every possible environment.

Celebrate this! There is nothing wrong with reading the Scriptures of your faith and finding meaning for yourself. When you read and something embraces your heart, this is good. When a passage appears as an omen for you, take it seriously. Finding meaning or guidance in Scripture uses Scripture well. There is simply no need to be only a Scripture student. There is more than enough space in faithful lives to become personally intimate with Scriptures so that it captures our hearts and minds, not for learning, but for inspiration and to deepen our spiritual lives.

This is the way it should be. We seek not only enlightenment and wisdom but religious enrichment and personal growth.

There is a huge difference between how an individual approaches Scripture for personal enrichment and growth and expanding this to become doctrine for everyone. The individual assimilates Scripture in a way that meets specific individual wants and needs. This is precise and not transferable to another. Even in a moment of sudden awareness, this dare not be confused with seeking knowledge and enlightenment. Seeking knowledge and enlightenment moves away from the heart, spirit, and feelings into the head and mind as an intellectual pursuit. We need to share our feelings about faith as well as our knowledge of faith and Scripture. All of these can be shared with others and become part of the environment of a community faith. The community of believers become the interpreters, not an individual.

Differences between faithful communities create schisms. The Orthodox religions broke with Rome; Martin Luther questioned Rome and the Reformation birthed Protestantism. These religious differences became doctrinal debates that have haunted the Christian faith for centuries. The Spanish Inquisition was an attempt to keep the faith pure and free from false beliefs and used torture and execution as punishment for religious impurity, but tortures and executions can never be holy, the intent of God.

When individual meanings are imposed on others as if they were universal interpretations, this confuses faith even more because these meanings may relate only to an individual interpretation and neither to what the passage itself intended when first written nor what faithful communities believe. This tears a hole in our understanding of Scripture, because a meaning that very, very few can identify with becomes an official interpretation, or an obscure and relatively unimportant biblical phrase becomes a prime doctrinal principle.

Be leery when someone says with great authority, "The Bible says." This strongly suggests that the person is making a pronouncement of absolute truth. Jesus suggested to us through his parables that absolute truth is not the way God speaks to us. Rather, God speaks to individual hearts and spirits knowing that these are as different as people are different.

The authority of Scripture is designed to meet the needs of so many different and unique personalities and situations that absolutes become counter-productive; they lead us away from the truth that God speaks to us.

The richness of the Scriptures of any faith bind the faithful and the religion's principles, but it can also be badly abused and cause friction within the faith. The rampant denominationalism of Christianity bears witness to this reality. Denominationalism and separateness gain strength when interpretations become absolute and do not recognize or respect alternatives.

After all has been said, however, Scripture forms the foundation of our faith, no matter what the faith may be. This foundation should elevate faith from human capriciousness and aberrations and purify it for the ages. Unfortunately, we humans keep tinkering with it and reinterpreting it to meet our prejudices. Scripture has the potential to unite Christianity, but we keep messing around with it and remain divided.

Somehow, we have to find a way to unite our heads and our hearts so that we can bridge the growing gap between us. Perhaps, if we follow the thought and teachings of Jesus, we will find Truth and become one.

Chapter Fifteen
CELEBRATING FAITH

Faith celebrates life. Life can also celebrate faith. We experience this in many ways, but the best known are public worship and private reflection. These may merge during worship, and should, but still remain distinct entities in our lives. The approach here looks at Christian worship and suggests ways to approach worship to reflect the Kingdom of God and respect the traditions that have kept Christianity alive and vibrant for centuries. There are two primary forms of public worship with many gradations between, the Eucharist (Mass) and the Word (focus on preaching). The approach in this book explores the ingredients of worship, the Eucharist, the Word, Scripture, prayers, hymns, fellowship, and the setting. Following this, I briefly give my personal reflection.

Public worship needs form. Some conservative Protestants argue that the Roman Catholic Mass is too formal and predictable and that there is no room for self-expression in such a rigid structure. This forbidding claim is belied by the strict structure of one of the simplest Christian services, the revival meeting. Everything takes place sequentially and is as structured in its own way as the Mass.

Worship demands order and structure. For most of us to successfully participate in public worship, we need to feel comfortable. A strange and uncomfortable environment tends to alienate us from the event and we are left empty, unfulfilled, and sometimes angry.

When we step into a church we want to feel good about it. We want the service to be familiar. The music should stir us inside, either spiritually or nostalgically. As we settle in, we relax and our minds open and our hearts are receptive to what will happen. Ritual prepares us to worship whether it is "high" church with strong formality or "low" church with its structured informality. Structure permits us to let go of worries and preoccupations that disturb us and frees our minds to explore and our spirits to receive inspiration and be renewed.

Structure is a bridge to the past evoking forgotten memories and feelings and mixes past and present in ways that can offer new insights. It is difficult to separate nostalgia and religious feelings because they are so closely related in our experience. For example, when parents have an infant baptized can they truly disentangle their emotional love for the child from the holy feeling of the moment and the wonder of the experience? Fortunately, we do not have to separate and analyze these feelings. The God within is part of our wholeness, not our separateness. God in us is not like clothing that can be donned or shed at will. God is integrated into our core being. He is there whether or not we recognize or feel her. He is part of our total being.

Structured worship helps integrate these mixed and confused feelings. These feelings reinforce our faith and become part of it. Hence, our faith is personal, unique to each of us and different from everyone else's. In this way, we gather in public for both an intense personal experience and, at the same time, a shared group experience. The interaction frees us to adapt to new experiences.

There can also be a down side to this, for the repetition of structure makes some rigid in their expression of faith and worship. It can be hard to adapt to new worship patterns. The common refrain, not exclusive to worship centers, "We never did it that way," can block growth and freeze our religious experiences into the past.

The structure of worship envisioned here must make sense from several perspectives such as personal experience, community, symbolism, and responsibility. Each person worshipping should feel the presence of holiness. There is no way to clearly identify holiness for it can be just about anything from a sense of unworthiness to elation. Each person's experience will be unique for it originates in how a person feels about herself. Feeling good about one's self is quite different from feeling wretched. So, worship has to find a way to incorporate both positive and negative personal experiences.

No one lives in isolation. We have families and friends, extended relatives and work environments, groups like fraternities and sororities, interest groups such as bridge parties, political affiliations and drinking buddies, and we have churches. For the most part, church fellowship is quite limited. Seldom is there personal intimacy between individuals. We may hug someone as we "pass the peace," but we know nothing or very little about the person we hug. We may not even know their name or where they live.

Public worship needs to extend these shallow relationships so that we can and do support each other. We strengthen each other's faith, offer spiritual or psychological support, and even physical support for those in need. An hour worship on Sunday can do little to make this happen, but it should help to make extended intimacy and trust a genuine possibility.

Symbols promote faith by offering specific images from the Cross to an open Bible, the communion table, stained glass windows, clergy robes, hymnals in the pews, and so forth. Symbols are present whether intended or not. Icons in the orthodox tradition are rich with symbolism, but so is the utter plainness of a Quaker meeting house. Symbols are symbols, not the real things. So, symbols take on different meanings. Compare a highly adorned church with the barrenness of a Quaker meeting house. The dramatically contrasting styles symbolically mean the same thing—the presence of the divine, God. An empty Cross refers to the resurrection for some and for others the suffering and death of Jesus. Symbols are not universal, what they mean for worshippers depends upon their individual personality, background, environment, and experiences.

Responsibility adds still another dimension for public worship. Public worship is community, people sharing faith and God with each other. One cannot regularly worship with others and act as if he is alone and that it is only his own personal experiences. Jesus lived a communal life, in relationships with others. The only exceptions were the times he went off by himself to gain strength and wisdom. Otherwise, he debated with lawyers; lifted his voice to teach and tell stories; he touched the ugly and unwanted; he healed those trapped in disease; embraced runny-nosed children; and walked toward death knowing it would help others.

To worship God responsibly, worship must focus on God and others. Without others, God becomes an idol that stirs our egos and satisfies our wants. Without others, the meaning of the life of Jesus is rendered trivial. God sent his son into the world to offer us the Kingdom, to give hope to the hopeless, raise the lowliest to spiritual heights, and to give us courage to live a more spiritual life in a secular world.

Public worship needs to be responsible in a like manner to the lifestyle of Jesus of Nazareth. Those who worship must be responsible to God and for each other including those we would not normally associate with. Worship needs to cut through cultural curtains that frequently separate us, rich and poor, upper and lower class, Irish redheads and Arabs with beaked noses. This is critical for cultural curtains place between us barriers of racial and ethnic prejudices, economic stratifications, religious differences, educational inequities, and political diversity. Often these differences go unnoticed because churches have become, in many cases, extensions of our culture. Denominations frequently are separated not only by religious doctrine, but also by class and other social criteria. Religious doctrine is often confused with cultural standards. Patriotism is frequently confused with religious ideals and popular cultural causes substituted for spiritual philosophies.

So, in addition to being responsible for each other, be responsible for the Christian worship environment. Never let it become merely an extension of the surrounding culture. If worship does not confront and challenge the prevailing culture, the chances are that the worship has yielded to the pressures of society. The best example of this is the churches that were filled with "Christian" slave owners. There are references to slavery in the Christian Bible noting that it existed during biblical times, but nothing in the Bible justifies owning another human being. These churches reflected the prevailing culture, not the message or style of Jesus.

The principle here cannot be more specific because the varieties of religions and internal differences within religions suggest that to keep worship as pure as it can be in a human world depends upon the theology of the organization.

The Eucharist celebrates the Last Supper of Jesus with the Twelve. Paul expanded it into a community ritual. In the Upper Room portrayal of the events, Jesus used the words "in memory of me." This was extended as worship began to celebrate Jesus hanging from the Cross. Suffering became central, and the Eucharist became the ingestion of the body and blood of the crucified Christ. As time passed and the remembrance of the Upper Room became dimmer and dimmer, the shared meal became far less important and the transformation of bread and wine into the genuine body and blood of Christ became the focal point. Paul's interpretation of the events became most important.

In the Gospels, Jesus said "in memory of me." How much of the actual scene as the Gospels portray it is accurate and how much reflects the faithful thinking of Christians living in the first century is conjecture. The point here is that Jesus offered the bread and wine as a memorial, not as actual flesh and blood. Looking at the life of Jesus, the memorial set in a framework of respect and love is more accurate. To remember Jesus in the flesh would be to see him walking and talking with friends and followers, embracing a pock-marked body, touching a person in pain, putting soft, moist clay on blind eyes, welcoming a hated tax-gatherer like Nicodemus to dine in fellowship with him and his associates, and of gently engaging a lawyer who wants to trap him into making an illegal statement. This was the man who told the parable, perhaps several of them, of the "Great Banquet" that invited the uninvitable to dine together. Jesus saw sharing a meal as one of the great levelers of society, bringing together the pious and the impious, the elite and the lost, the wealthy and the poor, the healthy and the ill, the clean and the unclean.

Blood was life for the ancient people. When Jesus said "this is my blood," he was not talking as much about blood fluid but of the animated life. Blood was equivalent to energetic life, the acts of living vigorously and of being active. To sip of the wine in memory of him was to see him in a faith that was active, not passive, as daring to risk because of the strength of faith, and as being bold rather than cowardly in living faith.

The Eucharist must reflect this. It should not be bowing and kneeling and receiving literal flesh and blood, but an opportunity to share in the memory of the great spiritual son of God. It is also an opportunity to boldly greet and welcome those who surround us as we eat and to invite the barn worker who cleans up after animals to dine with the white-shirted executive from a large corporation.

The Eucharist is commonly called communion with a slightly different emphasis for the bread and wine which are not usually understood as the literal body and blood of Christ, but as the symbolic body and blood. Still the emphasis on communion, communion with God and the children of God needs more emphasis, so that it truly becomes a shared meal. When the Eucharist/communion descends from its holy throne, which reflects royalty from the Middle Ages (notice the ornate priestly robes) more than genuine piety, and truly enters the world of ordinary people, it will better reflect and respect the life of Jesus.

Celebrate communion by lifting our heads joyously, shouting our inner joy, hugging someone we don't know, and welcoming the Kingdom of God into our lives by imitating Jesus. Feel the power of God within by opening our hearts to new and different experiences, by feeling the divine as we interact with God's children rather than piously closing our eyes and bowing our heads, and living inside our own little secret and holy world. Jesus never hid. He retired from public exposure from time-to-time to meditate and renew himself but he never hid. He faced friend and foe, those who supported him and those who undermined him. Jesus embraced strangers, those he did not know; he touched the sore festered lepers (probably not true leprosy as defined by modern medicine), allowed scruffy children on his lap, dined with an unclean and hated tax gatherer, argued with lawyers, and walked with all manner of people from an impoverished widow to a wealthy and a foolish young man.

Baptism is a rite of passage — passage into the family of God. As such it is a community activity not as a family gathering after worship or even in a home. It is never done in isolation. Baptism is rich and could be incorporated into each time we worship. For example, welcoming us all back into the faithful family is rich in imagery and meaning. Baptism can also be rich in nostalgia as we fondly remember our children's baptisms. More than this, it is where the Christian community accepts responsibility for those still too young to accept responsibility for themselves. This is the kind of responsibility that people of faith should share with all of our people regardless of age.

John's Gospel opens with the words (Revised Standard Version), "In the beginning was the Word, and the Word was with God, and the Word was God." The meaning of the Greek that is translated as "Word" is *logos*, and it is pregnant with meaning. In modern Christianity it has come to mean several things: Christ, the Bible, and the preached word. Many religions and sects use Scripture and preaching as central to the practice of faith.

My tradition strongly stresses Scripture. The Christ, as presented here, is the Risen Lord who transcends time and space to become a part of the today's world in faith as well as first century Judaism. He still inspires as well as informs. Jesus is the motivator and teacher behind faith. For public worship the Bible and the preached word together transmit faith. To understand this better, we dare not separate them. Truly, the Bible cannot be taken literally without destroying it and losing the underlying message of faith. Within its covers lay the core revelations of our faith. Some may be housed in historical-type narratives, others in poetry and song, still others are theological treatises, mythology and other stories, but behind all is a faith that reveals God. The Bible is a holy book because it inspires and creates awe; it has transformed generations of people, and influenced world powers.

Preaching has interpreted faith from the beginning. Sermons interpret Scripture, church dogma, current events, ethics, morals, and faith. Preaching should have an authoritative basis to keep sermons from degenerating into blatant personal opinion or culturally induced prejudices and bigotry. For me, as a Christian, the ultimate measure of preaching is the life and teachings of Jesus of Nazareth. My own method of preaching was to specifically interpret a passage of Scripture from the lectionary for each week. The lectionary is a system, shared by many denominations, that selects reading from the Old Testament, the Gospels, and the letters and other writings in the New Testament. This adds discipline and order and also reflects the church calendar effectively. It also tends to avoid the more difficult, less popular, more controversial, and obscure Biblical texts.

Regardless, Scripture and preaching are linked by tradition and form a major part of public worship.

Music has been rich in the Christian tradition and other religious traditions as well. Over the centuries some of the greatest music in the Western world originated in faith. Within classical music there is much religious music that has filled the churches ever since. Folk and Gospel music entertains us on radio and in churches adding a new flavor to an ancient custom. Music fills a deep spiritual need that combines religious thought with nostalgia, and crosses many human barriers such as denominationalism. In some denominations, music forms the heart of the service when the liturgy or service is chanted.

Hymns provide mutual participation by the congregations and clergy and embraces our feelings as well as our faith. The music stirs us as do the poetic words. The poetic words can be problematical for there can be a disjuncture between the words and how we each interpret our faith. Martin Luther, the great reformer, wrote a magnificent hymn, "A Mighty Fortress Is Our God," which was used by the first Roman Catholic Mass in English in the United States. It refers to the "enemy" (Satan, Devil) as if it is a powerful force that humans cannot fight successfully. In the Bible, only the Book of Revelation stresses demonic power in this way.

"Amazing Grace" calls us wretched. This contradicts the message and manner of Jesus, yet the hymn is a favorite and once reached the charts that rate the popularity songs. It was my father's favorite hymn, but I still cringe when the negative theme is repeated and wish I had an opportunity to rewrite the poetry to match more closely Jesus and his love of and respect for his people. It would be great to change the word "wretched" into something like beloved.

The Gospel hymn, "In the Garden," has a beautifully sweet melody, a ballad, and poetry more suited to romance than to the Kingdom of God. It grabs our hearts with a sentimentality that belies the banality of its words.

Music can be so powerful and much Christian music stresses our helplessness rather than our strengths and potential. Jesus saw human potential when he preached and told stories that recognized us as thoughtful and sensitive people. Certainly we are flawed, none are perfect, but there is the possibility of doing good and caring about others, and of overcoming the temptations that entice us and the greed that lies so close to the surface. This attitude of Jesus needs to be captured in music.

Because some music is so strongly identified with religions, for Christian, Muslim, Hindu, and most other religions, writing new melodies is always necessary and desirable; it may also be wise to use some existing traditional music with new words. For Christianity, this could mean new poetry for existing melodies such as Beethoven's "Ode to Joy." Perhaps we can rework the words to cast new thoughts that reflect the attitude of Jesus towards his followers.

Another approach is to reinterpret existing words. The great biblical myths have added such depth and meaning to faith that these need to be interpreted to better fit our understanding of faith.

Music adds to the celebration of faith. Music helps to break through the solemn mood that marks the seriousness of worship. Worship should bring us joy, feelings of elation and happiness. Music helps make this happen. Music elicits strong emotional responses including joy and sadness. Ideally, worship should elicit strong positive feelings.

Prayer plays a prominent role in public worship. Liturgical prayers focus on familiarity through repetitiveness. The Lord's Prayer and the Roman Catholic Rosary best illustrate this, and liturgical prayer also stresses seasonal topics. These are critical for they demonstrate the strength of prayer and familiar prayer patterns help us to open our hearts and spirits without trying to be original or creative. We can relax and let words and thoughts flow easily.

There should also be space for quiet time and for personal thoughts that should not necessarily be shared with others. Quiet is very difficult for many people. Sound engulfs us. Radio is never silent. Neither is television. Some people always have a radio or television turned on to ensure that sound always surrounds them. Yet, there is strength in silence. Meditation thrives on silence; it allows inner thoughts to be heard. To avoid uncomfortable silence, churches frequently have quiet music played during meditative times. Of course, this does cover the accidental noises that interrupt our thoughts, noises like shuffling feet, coughing, and other sounds that a congregated group of people tend to make. Regardless, we need time to move inside ourselves and shut out the world so that our own inner life can expose itself to us.

Mostly, public worship needs several approaches so that it embraces the needs of each individual during the service.

Personal reflection is part of public worship but also can be a daily private practice in the lives of many people of faith. We teach children to pray before retiring for the evening, but this tends to be formulaic and may or may not continue during their adult lives. The Rosary, though not as frequently used today as in past years by Roman Catholics, is a formulaic prayer that uses repetition. Other formulas create reflection based on daily Bible readings or reflective aids such as small booklets of meditations and prayers for each day. They can quiet the mind and provide ideas to reflect upon. Use them well, especially the meditative booklets so that you understand their biases and do not become reliant upon them and stifle your own thoughts and beliefs. Jesus did not demand conformity. Do not hesitate to disagree or let your meditation wander to where your mind and heart want to go.

Jesus told stories that frequently made no sense. These have the power to startle the mind and open it to something quite different, to innovative ideas and new possibilities that transform us and truly make us new. Now, we tend to use materials that reinforce our thinking rather than awakening us to a new vision and new realities never before considered. For prayer to be at its very best it has to transform us, slowly or startlingly rapidly, into new beings in the Kingdom of God. Too often prepared devotional writings talk about the Kingdom of God as something that will happen in the future rather than as an immediate experience that truly grabs and moves us now, at the present moment.

Jesus began some of his parables with "The Kingdom of God is like…." Then, he would tell a story that more often than not made no logical sense according to the customs of his day or ours. If only we could read them as new stories we have never heard before. Prayer can do this, for we can put aside what we know and let our minds and spirits float. True, we can never escape who we are and our memories are always there to keep us where we are. This does not have to be a spiritual prison; we can probe the borders and beyond, and stretch our minds and spirits. In place of accepting what a written meditation offers, read and explore it thoroughly and skeptically, look where you have not looked before and question the assumptions you have held and the assumptions the writer puts into it. Look at the parables of Jesus for models of innovative exploration. Why would a conniving steward be rewarded rather than the prudent one? Why would the faithful and obedient son be given no celebration when his run-a-way younger brother has a feast? Why should workers who labored from dawn to dusk be paid the same as those who worked only an hour? Look for something you have never seen before. Look for absurd answers to everything. In other words, let the passage speak to you anew, completely new, not with regurgitated material from another that you have heard many times before. Let Jesus reach through the centuries to open your mind, spirit, and ears to a new sound, new thoughts, and new spiritual insights.

This can also be done by silently retreating into yourself until the outside voices and the mind are stilled to free new inner voices and new ideas. This takes training, that is, lots of practice for this to happen, but it will happen. If you persist it works quite well opening new personal vistas and religious insights. It follows the way of Jesus who wandered into the wilderness to be refreshed and renewed. The voice of God can be heard best when human voices are stilled including your own.

Chapter Sixteen
A PORTRAIT OF JESUS

Christians have been discussing Jesus in great detail for nearly twenty centuries with as much disagreement as agreement. This long, long discussion has been about the Christ, the Risen Lord, experienced by the faithful from the earliest Christian era to the present. This is especially true for those near the beginning when the Gospels and other New Testament books were being written. Outside of the four Gospels almost nothing has been written about the human Jesus that dates within fifty to eighty years from his death. The so-called biographies and traditions created about him have dealt with who they wanted Jesus to be, based on their experiences and hopes within their faith; Jesus as a human being has been neglected.

The primary focus of this work is to look at Jesus as a human being based on what his parables suggest. This focus is quite valuable for it sets the tone for the kind of person he was in life and in his encounter with people. He liked and trusted people without preconditions and without considering their importance, their status in life, their ugliness or beauty, their health, or their economic status. The Gospels are limited in what they can tell us about him as a person because they are preoccupied with the impact he had on Christians during the years after his death until the time the Gospels were composed. Their faith and their hearts dictated how Christians understood him. This also set the tone for the centuries from then until now.

Paul, the earliest writer in the New Testament, mostly ignored the human and wrote about the plight of sinful and weak humans needing the forgiveness and salvation that Christ Jesus, the Risen Lord, offered. Paul, in my opinion, believed that people had to have the correct belief in order to know their sinful condition and to understand that their salvation was based on the death and resurrection of Christ. This was not a portrait of Jesus, but of Paul's theology probably developed parallel to the formation of the followers of Jesus into a church.

On the other hand, there is ample evidence that hints at what kind of person Jesus was. His parables reveal much as has been pointed out throughout this work, but there are other clues as well from other scenes and events recorded in the Gospels. Not all of them are historical in the modern sense, that is, during the first century history was more than a chronology of events. It included constructs of what it must have been like. Legendary information was frequently integrated into history so that it appeared as fact. We are more careful today.

This portrait is "informed" by history but includes supposition based on general knowledge. For example, my central premise that the parables suggests that Jesus liked and respected the people he encountered cannot be supported by historical quotations or factual data. Rather, it is based on inferential information and conclusions.

Nazareth was the hometown of Jesus. It was a small village not far from Sephoris, at one time a major city. Nazareth was poor and inhabited by peasants. It was too small and insignificant to have a temple or resident priests. Tradition suggests that Joseph, Jesus' father was a carpenter and there is no reason not to accept this. Carpentry was not the lowest of the skilled trades, but close to it. So Joseph earned enough to get by doing rough woodwork, but not enough to save or have any extras and certainly no luxuries. It was not a life of extreme poverty, but severely impoverished nevertheless.

Jesus grew up in a poor town and in a poor family. The nearest urban area was Sephoris, but culturally and economically it was far enough away to suggest that Jesus had little, if anything, to do with the city. It is not mentioned at all in the Gospels, so Jesus probably did not mention it as he entered into his life's work and ministry, nor did he include it in his travels. As a child Jesus played in dusty streets with neighboring children who were as poor as or poorer than he was. It was a hard life and he probably began working at an early age to help his father support their family. This is especially true because he was the oldest child in a family with several younger children.

Growing up poor in a village without a temple meant that his family, friends, and neighbors provided most of his early education. Learning to read was not an option because only the higher class people could afford an education and, still, most of the upper class could not read either. His knowledge of his Jewish faith and the Bible came from lessons taught and stories told. This does not at all make him either ignorant or intellectually slow. He memorized what others with more resources would read. He built his intelligence around learning quickly and retaining what he learned. He exercised his intelligence with insight, wisdom, and wit.

Most significantly, perhaps, Jesus learned his faith and his understanding of the world with eyes, ears, and mind tuned to poverty and human need. He understood an economic system that benefited the wealthy and suppressed the poor, where debt was exacerbated by heavy taxes and land owners demanding greater profits from their tenant farmers and slaves. Small farmers continually were forced to sell their property to meet these heavy financial demands. Unfortunately, this frequently drove them even deeper into debt and further into poverty.

As artisans, the family of Jesus was safer than most from the growing poverty of neighbors and friends, but this did not reduce the awareness of desperate times becoming more and more desperate. He looked at those around him, the friends he grew up with and the neighbors who shared meals and shelter with each other, and saw pain and injustice.

When he became an adult and began his ministry, it is notable that most of his associations were with people from impoverishment and those who struggled daily to buy food and maintain shelter. He, in spite of his great wit and thoughtful responses, never related well with the well-to-do and powerbrokers. He was always a man of the earth, never in a proverbial ivory tower. His idealism was always tainted with realism and country wisdom. He understood the tension between the powerful and the powerless, between the rich and poor, and between the well educated and those with street knowledge, to use a modern idiom. Hard work did not mean success; most often it met with greater debt and fewer resources as the power brokers and landowners, usually landlords who lived in cities in grand residencies, gained more power and greater wealth.

He worked most closely with the kind of people he knew well and understood their problems and their world. Jesus was a man of the earth, not of the sophisticated urban environment.

———•◦•———

Jesus had a personal magnetism that drew people to him; he had a charismatic personality. As he walked the country roads and visited the small rural villages, people came to hear his stories, listen to his sermons, and question his ideas. Some were attracted by his personality; others were repelled by and envious of his attractiveness. Others were drawn to him because of the rumors that preceded him and the reputation he gained; some were repelled because they thought his ideas wrong and against their everyday practices ("We always did it that way!").

It is possible that Jesus would have gone unnoticed if it were not for his charismatic personality. No one would have paid attention to a homeless wanderer who walked the countryside in rural Galilee telling stories and doing miraculous deeds. There were lots of "magicians" plying their trade. But, when one of them had a special appeal that attracted crowds, this caused a reaction. People gathering to see Jesus neglected their work while they listened to him. This was noticed and stirred curiosity. Soon, news of his fame spread and others noticed. This led to his confrontations with representatives of the various political, religious, and economic authorities, those who worried about anything or anyone who disturbed the routine of life or interrupted business. Being a charismatic person drew audiences for Jesus, but also created some enemies along the way.

———•◆•———

He was a spiritual mystic who intensely and intimately felt the presence of God. There are a couple of occasions where Jesus, while praying, called God "Abba, Father." Abba is the word used in Jesus' world and language (Aramaic) for Daddy or Papa. It was more than calling God his Father, but calling him this in the most intimate and personal way. This is so intimate and so personal that it violated the general rule for the terms the Jewish world called God that were used during Jesus'. God was addressed in awed language and, at one time, they avoided speaking the name of God altogether. The name of God was a tetragrammaton (four unpronounceable consonants) that is usually transliterated in English as Yahweh or, in more modern times, Jehovah. In the ancient world the Jews preferred not to say the name of God aloud. Jesus countered this tradition by addressing God by name, the most intimate name, Abba.

Extraordinary intimacy with God is mystical. It is far more than knowing or even experiencing God. Abba suggests that Jesus could rest his head in the lap of God, that is, totally trust and feel and know God's presence; this is far more intimate than any religious experience that most experienced. Jesus did not feel just the warmth of God, but felt God totally. Jesus was not in awe of God but felt comforted and cherished by Abba, his Father.

Jesus also had mystical experiences or intimate visions of God. The story is told in Matthew, Mark, and Luke about the temptations. Matthew and Luke offer great detail while Mark appears to mention it only in passing, the reference is weak and brief. As the story is told by Matthew and Luke, after forty days and nights without sustenance, Jesus had a vision of demonic temptations that he had to confront and conquer. Jesus was tempted to perform a miracle by making bread from rocks; then was lifted to the top of the temple to jump and not be hurt; then to the top of a mountain where he was offered all he could see. To do all of these on the fortieth day would have been more than miraculous. Also, if the Devil lifted and moved Jesus around at will to the various places that were too high to easily climb in a short time, this gave the devil a huge amount of unearthly power.

After forty days, Jesus saw this vision of his human potential to act with greed and to abuse power; he conquered the temptations within himself that would be extremely hard for most people to say no to. Jesus experienced within himself characteristics so rare that they lifted him above normal human experiences and brought him closer to Abba, Father. Add to this relationship with God the many times he went into the wilderness to pray alone, to increase his spiritual strength and be renewed within himself and the God within, and to continue his work among the people who mattered so much to him, The base for his faith was the intimate and mystical relationship between himself and Abba, Father.

There was far more to Jesus than his intimate and mystical relationship to Abba, Father. His intense liking of people, especially those without power and on the fringes of society reveals another characteristic, his willingness to support weak people. Poverty and disenfranchisement from the culture and especially the economic and political power made these people the prey of the wealthy and powerful.

Jesus said, "Blessed are the meek," an absurd remark no matter who considers it. Jesus was not at all meek. He confronted those who disagreed with him, defended the poor widow, and walked without fear to his death. Jesus struggled for the meek, not the powerful. Jesus suggested that it was the impotent who would inherit the earth. Strange to say this when the world then and now is controlled by the powerful. The competitive nature of the world honors the athletically powerful as well as the economically powerful, but seldom honors those with inferior athletic skills, no economic power, and are spiritually weak. But Jesus defended and called the losers of his world the favored of God.

Jesus was a social revolutionary. He looked at injustice and cried No! Jesus looked at poverty and shouted No! From his impoverished youth, he understood the issues, but, more than the issues, he felt the pain and deprivation that injustice and poverty imposed on people.

Jesus was not an insurrectionist, that is, he did not attempt to start a revolution that would strike down the causes and those who caused injustice and poverty. He did not lift a sword to cut off evil, nor did he form a band of guerillas to fight for the powerless. Nevertheless, he challenged some of the principles that held the peasants in virtual servitude by challenging authority and privilege. He asked a wealthy man to part with his riches, but he could not and walked away from Jesus and discipleship. Jesus walked with his friends on a Sabbath and pulled grain to eat and the authorities challenged him. His response was that hunger needs to be dealt with no matter the day.

He wanted a better life for people, especially those with few resources. Unlike the Messianic hope of the Jewish people who awaited a David-like messiah to rise up with an army and cast out of Israel the Roman conquerors, Jesus understood that the problem of oppression was more than the Roman occupiers. Oppression involved both, outsiders and insiders, the Romans and the imbalance of the Jewish religious and economic systems at that specific time in history.

True, a rebellion, properly armed and with enough forces, may have freed them from Rome, but would it have freed them from injustice and oppression? It seldom does. History suggests that one oppressive group tends to replace another group as the oppressors; sometimes the reformers become corrupt often in the name of justice.

Jesus looked in another direction. He looked at the Kingdom of God. Many words have been written about the Kingdom of God, and many have analyzed it far too much. During the time of Jesus the idea of kingdom meant ruling a country by a person of special birth or special appointment such as a king. This happened in Israel when David became King and Solomon, David's son, inherited the throne and when Caesar appointed Herod the Great, a half-Jew, as the king of Israel.

In a like manner, a kingdom of God would be a country ruled by God. A kingdom was ruled by a king. A kingdom of God is where God is king. The Kingdom of God that Jesus offered was where God ruled or reigned. Jesus offered them a life that God ruled, not as a future hope, but as a present reality. Jesus invited them into a kingdom where God ruled rather than the oppressive rulers in Israel at that time. Politically, Rome ruled Israel by maintaining control over all local power systems from the secular kingship to the religious institutions. Those who accepted the Kingdom of God found something a bit different. It was not a political restructuring of Israel as was expected by the Jewish expectation of a David-like Messiah, but a restructuring of the individual, a discovery that living in God's Kingdom restructured the person so that his or her approach to living was more powerful than the outside political or religious powers.

Because Jesus encouraged his audiences to use their own intelligence, thoughtfulness, experiences, prejudices, and faith when hearing his words, the experience of God ruling in their lives was not uniform for it related to each person individually and personally. Together they recognized God ruling in their lives, but individually the experience was unique to each. This challenges human imaginations for we want most things to be straightforward and uniform so we know what to expect. Despite our expectations, each individual experiences the Kingdom differently even when the difference appears to be minor. It is not predictable.

There are no portraits of Jesus. No one painted pictures of a peasant, especially a rural peasant. Nevertheless, thousands of portraits have been painted between his death and today. Some became extraordinarily famous and captured the imagination of a generation. Earlier in my lifetime one portrait could be seen everywhere; it appeared to be ubiquitous. It was in shades of brown and a touch of yellow. Jesus did not look Jewish, but European with an aquiline nose, hair carefully brushed with a golden radiant sheen, and a visage of utter peacefulness. Although he was robed as if from the first century, the painting (print) reminded me of oils from the Middle Ages and Renaissance where Jesus and other biblical characters were dressed in the clothing of the artist's age.

This picture was not Jesus or anything close. So, I really do not know what he looks like, and my artistic talent is below amateurish. Still, my image of him is based on my visualization of period clothing from the first century as best I know it, but it is also a moving image. It is as if one of his most important characteristics has taken over in my mind. Jesus, during his life's work, had no home and he walked the roads of Galilee incessantly. His strides were long and sure and his feet covered with dust and somewhat gnarled from their lack of protection from the heat and road surfaces. His hair was combed roughly with a patina of dust covering its blackness. Weather lines creased his face and humor lines spider-webbed his eye's edges. A scraggy beard hid a chiseled chin. Large, muscled, and calloused hands hung from the edges of his burlap textured peasant robe.

Although his strides were long, they were unhurried and casual like he had no place where he had to be. Dark eyes stared ahead as if looking for hazards. He does not walk alone, but with several other men who chat quietly among themselves, leaving Jesus to think his own thoughts.

When they approached a small village or town, Jesus paused and visited with anyone he found. The conversations began as ordinary talk about weather or local happenings, but soon he would ask pointed questions that evoked curious responses. Jesus had a way of asking innocent questions that revealed something about the person or the town or about anything, and this stirred more than casual interest from the person with whom he was chatting. Jesus' ability to evoke a friendly response opened up opportunities to tell a story or make a witty aphorism such as "Blest are the poor in spirit for they shall inherit the earth." This made little sense to the villagers, but stirred their interest in Jesus, a strange man and, perhaps, a sage.

It took little time to gather a small audience. My vision does not include a booming voice that could have reached the outer limits of the village, but a soft voice with a hint of a lisp causing people to listen more carefully and softly stressing a point rather than loudly. His presence was commanding in spite of an average stature. His voice, eyes, and gestures embraced his audience. Jesus' eyes never penetrated menacingly into people but welcomed them warmly as did his gestures which were rather slow flowing with his words more than emphasizing them.

What was most startling were his private conversations with individuals. His eyes never left them and distractions never diverted his eyes. When he spoke to a person it was like the rest of the world did not exist. Jesus totally focused on that person. For most people this concentration was welcomed and warmed them, but for a few it caused them to squirm and fidget. For the latter it was like Jesus invaded their space making them uncomfortable and intimidated. For the others it was like he invited them into his space.

When curious children scurried around, Jesus messed their hair with affection and squatted to be at their level. He answered their terrible questions like, "What are you?" with gentle humor and honesty, never hiding truth nor apologizing for it. Frequently, parents warned their children to keep away from Jesus because someone had seen him touch a leper, who could only live by begging, whose pock-scarred face repelled and frightened. Even when people gave charity to a sick person, it was more often than not tossed from a distance to keep from getting too close and becoming infected. So, children, be careful around Jesus because you never know where he's been or whom he's touched.

The sick sought him because he never rejected or turned away from them. He tenderly touched them and spoke with kindness and compassion. When the rumors spread and preceded Jesus on his journeys, some came to him for healing. They had heard that he had done miraculous things before and wanted his help. These, he embraced and spoke words of comfort and hope, and some were healed.

Not all was serious, however. Jesus told jokes about himself and his closest friends like "Peter, a fisherman, is so afraid of water, I'd have to walk out and save him." Unlike his former mentor, John the Baptist, Jesus liked good food and sipped wine with friends.

He was a memorable person who not only drew people to him as he offered them a new life under the Kingdom of God, but left his mark on them. They remembered his words and deeds, his great wisdom and warm friendship, his wit and gentle touch, his willingness to embrace the ugly, unclean, and contemptible. Jesus was unique. He lives through the centuries beyond his death to offer new values to life that sustains and enriches all regardless of their powerless or poverty. He offers a new life under the rule of God. He lives today making us better, more precious, and filling us with new life.

Chapter Seventeen
A NEW KOINONIA?

Not too many years ago, it seemed like everyone published a book criticizing the church. The American Christian scene demanded renewal. It never truly happened. Perhaps, significant renewal never occurred because the books criticized rather than offered a fresh approach. This book was written to offer a different perspective on the meaning of our faith and a different look at Jesus Christ. I wanted to make this work a positive and spiritual journey toward renewing faith. It is natural to include some criticism as a part of the argument for returning to the human Jesus as the model for our faith rather than the model developed by the early church. For this chapter, I will move from the premises outlined in the rest of the book to a vision of how this perspective on faith can create a holy fellowship of believers.

The various groups of Christians and their institutions are called churches. This word has many burdens for it has numerous meanings gathered over the years. The most prominent is a religious institution: The Roman Catholic Church, The Episcopal Church, The Presbyterian Church of American, The United Methodist Church, and so forth. Related to this is the local building/congregation: Saint Agnes Roman Catholic Church, First Presbyterian Church, and so forth.

The core of a fellowship of believers based on the model of the human Jesus should have a name that is not primarily recognized as an institution. I selected *Koinonia* because it is the Greek word in the New Testament that means fellowship, a close group of followers of Jesus who gathered to share faith and each other. *Koinonia* allows us to develop a new fellowship based on the criteria of the life of Jesus rather than trying to reform an existing institutional church. Also, there is the strong belief by this writer that God reveals himself to people through their own ability to assimilate the revelation. Traditional Christian faith is as valid to some as the faith expressed in this book. Hinduism has attracted millions with hope and faith nurtured by their traditions and way of life. So it is with the multitudes of faiths that inhabit our world. *Koinonia*, as expressed in this work, is another alternative for those who follow Jesus and want a faith more in tune to our modern world without giving up the ancient wisdom of Jesus and how he lived his life as a guide for living.

Jesus lived a life in flux. He began his life as the son of a craftsman, perhaps a carpenter, raised a peasant Jew in the impoverished village of Nazareth, later he followed the strict and rigid teachings of John the Baptist, started his own ministry, formed his own tiny fellowship of twelve (perhaps a symbolic number), and continued to adapt to each situation that confronted him. When healing was required, he healed; when teaching was needed, he taught; when compassion was necessary, he spoke gently and touched warmly; when he wanted to alter the orientation of others, he told stories (parables); when confronted with hostility, he responded appropriately. Jesus never organized a formal group. He had his twelve closest followers, but even here the number may reflect the Twelve Tribes of Israel more than twelve specific followers, especially when the names are not exactly the same in the different Gospels.

The key is fellowship, a relationship between believers that supports everyone, welcomes everyone, and loves everyone. The New Testament contradicts itself sharply. The model of Jesus is clear; he loves and reaches out to everyone, especially those rejected by the culture and the religious, political, and economic hierarchy. Matthew in Chapter 18 cites a way to expel recalcitrant members of the "church." This is most interesting because the church did not exist until it was created after the crucifixion and resurrection and account of the day of Pentecost. Jesus did not found a church; he did found a koinonia, a fellowship of followers. When Jesus met those who did not fit in, he healed them of obstructions to faith and invited them into his fellowship. He welcomed the unwanted, a radical contradiction of the words found in Matthew where he explained a way to expel the unruly and unwanted. When in doubt, choose Jesus over the Gospel writers.

His followers were pretty much like any other human group. There were disputes and mumblings between them. The force that overcame all of these disgruntled moments was the charisma and leadership of Jesus. He wanted his friends to share as one, the strong helping the weak and the weak helping the strong. Strange, is it not, how Jesus saw the weak as good, not bad, people to be recognized not belittled. He saw positive things where most others saw nothing or negative things. Jesus saw beauty in people festered with ugly sores.

This is the heart of *koinonia*, seeing the beauty and good in people and places others cannot see. Seeing beauty and good is difficult, and some believe boring. Is not an adventure story more interesting than romance for most of us? Or, the action cartoons of fighting evil more captivating than purple dinosaurs? Or, hell more interesting than heaven? We read Dante's *Inferno* rather than his other poems such as the one about heaven. People tend to look for the hidden motive behind good deeds, always suspecting a payoff. We tend to trust goodness far less than badness. With people who are evil, we have an idea how they will act or respond. But we say things like "They're not for real" about good people. Strange, isn't it?

Ideally, in *Koinonia*, the level of trust is so great that we would even give our lives for it. Jesus (in spite of the newly discovered *Gospel of Judas*) trusted his enemies so much that he lost his life because of them. The followers of Jesus follow one of the most difficult discipleships there is, because we are called upon to befriend and embrace the most heinous without embracing their corruption. We are called upon to love all, as in *agapè*, a selfless love. It is easier to love the adorable and sweet, the beautiful and handsome, but to love those we would rather detest is difficult. Jesus, being the very special person he was and the special and beloved son of God, easily loved the repugnant, but my guess is that he did what most of us should do, he recognized that his love was not sentimental; it did not rely on "liking" or "feeling good," but was a free obligation of his life's work and, therefore, an obligation of faith. It is seldom easy to be worthwhile, but it is critically important and demands to be done.

Not all will join this fellowship. Even Jesus could only gather a relatively small group of followers, and we should not recruit to enlarge the size of the group. Beyond the Twelve, Jesus did not do any recruiting that we know of. Rather, he told his startling stories to stir up minds, preached his difficult sermons of living, and taught those who gathered about him. We do not need to convert the "lost" souls of the world, because they are loved even when they are totally blind and deaf to this love. It is their freedom to respond to or reject this love. God loves without conditions; Jesus loved without conditions. To evangelize, to win lost souls, is to deny the power of God's love, which reaches past barriers that human wisdom builds to separate the good from the bad and the different from ourselves.

No faithful person can truly believe that God's love is limited by what we humans believe, that God loves those who follow the teachings of Jesus more than those who follow the teachings of the Buddha or that Christians are more loved than the followers of the Prophet Muhammad. This reduces God to human stature and is, frankly, insulting. Only Christian arrogance can create a concept of God that is so exclusive that most of his people throughout the world are barred from his magnificent love. No! God's love is far greater than our human capacity to use our minds to think or conceive ideas.

Koinonia leadership is organic to the group. There is no "holy" church, but a fellowship of believers. This fellowship spawns leadership. Leaders come from within the group and are not imposed on it. This opens a critical question. Koinonia is a group of faithful people who must share and expand the faith and our knowledge of it. One of the responsibilities of leadership is to learn, learn, and learn even more — to learn enough to properly instruct and, then, to learn from those whom the leader teaches.

———•◦•———

Koinonia should not be rigidly institutionalized. There need not be a "set in stone" dogma, but flexibility to reflect the pliability and resiliency of Jesus as he adapted throughout his life to changing conditions, interactions, and new insights. The only dogma would be standards and theologies that reflect the way of Jesus such as: love and respect everyone and do no intentional harm. *Koinonia* reflects the culture that surrounds us. An American *Koinonia* would differ significantly from a Brazilian or Norwegian or Vietnamese and still hold the same core belief in God as revealed in Jesus of Nazareth.

Flexibility means creating as few rules as possible and, then, ensuring that they can and will be changed when necessary or desired while still adhering to the pattern of Jesus' life.. It is clear that the world and its peoples have changed over the centuries and millennia. Although within the relatively short time of recorded history humans have apparently changed little, there has been some change. The average life span has expanded greatly. We think of Jesus as a young man at thirty, but the average death for people during that age was around thirty. Jesus was on the older side of middle-age. The average size, weight and height, of people has grown considerably. We know little about the human brain and no one measured comparative intelligence between the time of Jesus and today, but it seems logical that our brain power has increased on average, however little it may be. (Individually we can't compare: Galileo vs. Einstein or Michelangelo vs. Picasso. It doesn't work.) Because humans tend to grow and mature, so should our faith, and so *Koinonia* should be free to grow and mature. *Koinonia* must be open to change and be versatile.

Society changes. Schools often have dress codes. Just a generation ago schools could not have accommodated youth belting their trousers several inches below the hips. The national sentiment against an unjust war in Vietnam of the 1960s was followed by an invasion of Iraq. Attendance in churches has dropped dramatically while the flavor of fundamentalism has grown. *Kiononia* must be open to change and versatile.

There must also be a structure to hold it together. Even Jesus did not ignore structure. He gathered around him the seeds for his work to continue beyond his lifetime. Although we know little about the actual interactions between Jesus and those in his inner circle, the Twelve, as they walked together, they learned, but they also reacted. They were not just passive listeners, but took on tasks for themselves. The only firm knowledge is that Judas managed the money and Peter appears to have been closest to him. The struggle between James and John suggests that there was a hierarchy of some sort. Jesus had a small organization of his closest disciples who learned and grew. It never became a church or even a huge and faithful following, but a small intimate group with little to distinguish between them. Only Jesus truly stood out from the rest.

We must also contend with our humanity. People cannot maintain, grow, and pass on to others anything without some structure to identify and unite it as recognizable and useable. There must be something to grab hold of and join. Without structure there is little to identify with and become a part of. The difficulty is that structure also encourages ambition. Even the early church struggled with this issue. Paul confronted Peter and the Jerusalem Church to debate whose interpretation of faith would dominate. Some modern churches lock in leadership and lose some flexibility by elevating some to be bishops and even Popes.

At this point my primary understanding of Jesus fails me a bit. Jesus is not a leader whom we can reliably imitate. Those with the natural charisma to gain faithful followers have tended to abuse the talent (James Jones of mass suicide and David Koresh of Waco). Even those leaders who have been democratically elected can find their egos getting in front of their talent. To exactly imitate Jesus as the model for leadership cannot be done, but we can find insights from his style of leadership as we know it.

There are some insights that might give us some clues. Jesus never commanded anyone to follow him. Rather, he invited them, and some asked to join. Not all could meet the standards he required, to leave what they were most familiar with and take off in a new and unknown direction was and is incredibly difficult. The so-called rich young ruler, for example, could not leave his wealth. Jesus invited everyone to follow him, but hinted what the true cost of discipleship was. We have tended to make the cross a barrier by suggesting that we take up the suffering of Jesus as the price of genuine discipleship. Jesus, on the other hand, tended to suffer little during his lifetime and the true cost of his discipleship was moving into the unknown world and giving up what was most comfortable and familiar. He gave up his family and a relatively stress-free life of working with wood.

Leadership does not necessarily demand pain and suffering, but it does demand taking risks and moving beyond the familiar. Leaders need to inspire their followers to break new ground in their lives, open their minds to the new and unexplored and move from what is psychologically and spiritually comfortable into the new, unknown, and uncomfortable. This is what Jesus did; our leaders can do this. Jesus left behind the familiar faith of his parents and friends as well as the specific and rigorous teachings of John the Baptist, and moved into the dangerous world of gentle rebellion against the status quo and of finding friends who were powerless and impoverished, ugly and disliked. Jesus dared to risk himself.

———◆———

Evil haunts humankind. To deal with the evil in human hearts, called sin, the church developed confession (reconciliation). All denominations practice confession, although the practice is not uniform. Roman Catholics, who believe the church to be a divine institution, have their priests forgive the sins of penitent sinners. Most Protestants do not share the belief in the holiness of the institutional church and it cannot, therefore, forgive sins. Protestants believe that confession is an act between the individual and God. There is community confession with formulaic prayers of confessions or those composed by a church's pastor or religious leader, but it is still an act between an individual and God.

Koinonia takes a slightly different approach believing that it (*Koinonia*) is not divine and that forgiveness is a reality of the love of God, not a response to a human plea. For the Christian, forgiveness is genuine and real, not because we are truly bad people. Enough of this! Jesus loved without reservations or concerns about the motivations of others. He just loved. His huge capacity to love, unfortunately, did not remove evil from the world or from the human heart.

Koinonia is a fellowship based on faith and supports its members by recognizing that, although we are forgiven because God's love is far greater than our capacity for evil and sin, we need to live as good a life as we can. We must understand that living in forgiveness demands recognizing this and living accordingly. We do not live to gain forgiveness, but live because we are forgiven. In *Koinonia* none are preoccupied with our sinfulness. Instead, we celebrate the freedom to live that forgiveness has given us.

———•◦•———

Living in forgiveness frees us to dare to live. We dare to take risks in life for others and for ourselves. Those who worry about their sin may be sin free but are nonetheless imprisoned by sin. Timidity becomes a pattern for living. For the timid it is better to avoid sin than risk damnation. Those in *Koinonia* are free to risk, to walk boldly through life doing good without fear of tripping on the curb of evil. Most worthwhile endeavors require risk. Opening a new business risks failure. Raising a family has so many risks that it is sometimes a wonder that people dare to have children. The same holds for Christianity. One cannot truly be a follower of Jesus without taking substantial risks. Think about Jesus as he faced enemies each day walking the byways of the ancient world. He touched the pock-marked and diseased without hesitation, endangering himself. Jesus welcomed, according to tradition, Mary Magdalene, a harlot, as a friend whom a crowd would have willingly stoned. He dined with Zacchaeus, the hated tax-gatherer, threatening that the pious and judgmental would hate Jesus because of the terrible people with whom he associated..

Jesus could not have continued his work without taking huge risks that, finally, killed him. We cannot follow him without taking risks, without living a life in forgiveness, and without knowing we live fully in the love of God. To befriend a poverty stricken person in rags and a dirty face when we are well dressed and in a hurry is not easy. There is a gap to be leaped over. That leap is risky. This same principle applies to all we do in faith. To reach the prisoner, the diseased, the super-wealthy, and the person down the street anguishing over sudden unexplained death, we must risk ourselves.

We risk making mistakes, but must take the risk nevertheless. This may the hardest, for it means that we risk our self-esteem and failure. Failure pricks at our sense of well-being and sends wrong signals to others. But, we live in love and forgiveness and so we risk.

This we celebrate!

Dining as a group is a central act of people everywhere. Family meals, more common a generation ago than today in the United States, celebrates family. Table talk gives families an opportunity to share the day, tell stories, impart values, and express love. It is around the family meal that parents and children talk about events of the day, important relationships, and the work or school day providing an outlet for frustrations. As we chat around a table we gain insights from others. It could also be story time, telling about grandparents and aunts and uncles and nearly forgotten cousins. Family legends are often born and sustained over pot-roast and mashed potatoes or Caesar salad and yogurt.

Sipping our soup we laugh as we reveal the day's blunders and follies; giggle over shared jokes and tall tales; and chuckle as we share foolish memories. Life becomes a little bit better.

Families share ethical, moral, and religious values as problems are confronted and solutions sought. A child shares an event at school or on the playground and the whole family expresses opinions and values, faith and ideals that implant principles for the future. All of this together expresses the love or lack of it in a family and forever changes their future, however subtly.

Modern family life tends to neglect the family dinner where we can eat leisurely and talk. School schedules, commuting time, and other social demands steal this casual and meaningful time shared. It is a great loss.

The family meal has a long tradition. In Christianity's parent, Judaism, it was where the faith was kept alive and where the rituals and stories thrived. It is what Jesus requested when they went to the upper room in Jerusalem for their last shared meal together. The New Testament only records a final meal, but there were many shared meals over the time Jesus and the Twelve were together. Mealtime may have been one of the most significant teaching times for Jesus and his friends.

Meals were critical for Jesus. The story of the fishes and loaves was a sermon turned into a meal and a meal turned into a sermon. Luke records parables that centered on feasting. The last supper established the memorial meal, communion. Paul cited the memorial meal as central for the celebration of the faith – a feast of love.

With his parables, Jesus introduced another dimension to shared meals. In the parables, the invited guests, those who met all of the religious and social criteria, declined to attend. The banquets were filled with people from the streets, that is, those who may or may not fill the needed religious purity standards for Jewish meals. Dining together now included the spiritually unclean, the culturally crude, and the financially impoverished.

Koinonia should include dining together. This is more than a ritualistic communion or coffee and donuts for those who remain following a worship service. It should be a meal where human interaction takes place, friendships made, ideas and concerns shared. This requires more than most churches presently ask of their people, and it requires some adaptation. But faith without intimacy is weak because trust and mutual reliance are missing.

Because *Koinonia* is based on faith in Jesus and fellowship with others, the fellowship must be far more than casual; it must be meaningful and spiritually and emotionally intimate. This may be the most difficult aspect of *Koinonia*. Intimacy is incredibly hard for it requires a personal openness that most people do not prefer and some appear incapable of.

Intimacy is based on trust. Trust is related to faith. We believe in God and trust in Jesus as the ultimate guide for holiness and genuine humanness. In faith we can take the next step to trust. The fellowship of *Koinonia* frees us to be completely open to and with others. We can share our thoughts and secrets and hear their thoughts and secrets. When meals bring together people from widely different lifestyles, economic backgrounds, educational levels, and social standards, intimacy becomes far more difficult and far more necessary.

This is an ideal based on faith and is very hard to achieve. It can be done when *Koinonia* creates a setting and atmosphere to encourage it. Eating together may be a way to achieve it. Sitting and talking freely with others may be more natural while sharing a meal. Talk does not end with dessert. It continues as interest in each other increases. It also becomes more intimate as relationships grow and deepen. There is a danger that this may create cliques that break the fellowship into smaller and more exclusive groups. This is to be avoided.

There is no part of this that is easy; it is extremely difficult. There also have to be ways to keep those who cannot make the leap into trust within the broader fellowship until shared faith slowly removes barriers to trust. Unfortunately, there will be betrayers within, such as Judas Iscariot betraying Jesus centuries earlier. These betrayals are temporary setbacks, and need not interfere with the process of developing fellowship and deepening trust.

Life is education. We learn as we experience new or different things. Learning and becoming more informed has always been part of the Christian life. The earliest church had its catechism as shown in some of the earliest writings (*Didache*). The Bible and established tradition have formed the basis for Christian education. The Bible is the core document of our faith, and traditions are the practices and doctrines that developed over the centuries, frequently informal, often written into the canon of the various denominations. Church history, especially denominational history, becomes part of the tradition.

Christian education focuses on children and youth, but includes adults as well. We want our people to understand the faith and to know about their specific religious heritage. *Koinonia*, of course, has no history, but the traditions that are part of church life and that crosses denominational lines is important, for it confronts us regularly. Religion has a special place, or more accurately, many special places in society. Roman Catholicism has gotten much press, mostly negative, in the last few years. Publicity like this makes us aware, consciously or unconsciously, of the weaknesses of the various denominations.

Members and participants in *Koinonia* must be able to put their faith in perspective. This is especially true because *Koinonia* rejects many popular beliefs. The primary source of our faith is the Bible which is interpreted differently by different traditions, looking at the life of the human Jesus and following his teachings and his pattern. This requires looking at the four Gospels with new eyes and with a specific bias, that is, that these tiny books are the product of writers who were influenced by their fellow believers long after the death of Jesus. This means that, to understand our faith, we must attempt to separate what most accurately reflects the life and words of Jesus from the additions by the writers based on their faith and the influences of their contemporaries.

This puts aside the belief that the Bible is itself totally true and totally accurate. This great and inspired book is not perfect for it was composed, Old and New Testaments, by people of faith who were also people of their own generations. None of the writers were magical seers who wrote for unknown centuries far in the future such as ours. The Bible was written by faithful people who were as flawed and human as we and could not see into civilizations and societies not yet born. To take the Bible literally and as absolutely and perfectly correct is to commit idolatry. The Bible is how faithful people expressed their faith; it is not a god, not even a lesser god.

Still, the Bible, specifically the Gospels, is the best record we have. It just needs to be read more closely and with more discrimination. *Koinonia* leaders must be thoroughly knowledgeable concerning biblical criticism and research, what archeology has discovered, and what historians wrote and continue to write about the ancient world. Learning of our faithful biblical roots is a continuing quest. It does not end, but is a lifelong endeavor.

Faith is the core of Christian education and is the model for understanding our faith throughout this work; we begin with Jesus. Jesus struggled with his faith. Living in an impoverished community like Nazareth, he was nurtured on Judaism as passed on to him by his parents and with little input from priests or rabbis. This was traditional Judaism. Sometime later in his life, he turned to the radical teachings of John the Baptist, who condemned the Jewish people for straying from the way of God. John was a very strange man who shunned normal behavior. He wore uncomfortable clothing and probably ate no meat, but thrived on insects and wild honey. John called people from their wicked ways to be baptized by him to remove their sins and enable them to restart their lives. Symbolically, baptism recalled the passage of the Jews from enslavement in Egypt to cross the sea into a promised land and into a better relationship with God.

Jesus followed John for some unknown period and learned from him. Where or how the break between them happened is unknown, but their mutual opponents compared them, sometimes to point out the contrast. John ate no bread and drank no wine; Jesus ate too much and drank wine. John talked of baptism to purify, and Jesus offered a Kingdom to all, even the unpure. These contrasts highlighted the probing faith and mind of Jesus. His devotion to God was complete, but his approach changed dramatically throughout his lifetime. Jesus won the Kingdom of God by learning from his family their Jewish religious traditions, studying under the radical John the Baptist he learned of disagreements within Judaism, and then arrived at his own unique understanding of God. His understanding was born from his relationship to God, his Father, but before it became clear, before he was ready to meet and be baptized by John, his one-time mentor, he studied his faith, so that when he finally understood it clearly, it was clear enough to build his life completely around it.

Faith is a life-long study. It begins in the home under the tutelage of parents, becomes broader as we sit at the feet of others with greater wisdom, and matures as we sit with peers and look even more closely at the implications of our faith for living. Study is seeking to understand our faith and gain enlightenment.

Communication is critical. Communication with God is complex, for we pray words to God, but as we speak them we see no response, no eyes to reflect mood, no lips to smile or frown, and no nods or head-shakes. We pray to an invisible God. The early church found the memory and image of Jesus something to fill in the missing images of an invisible God. Later, some of those early Christians, who were believed to be superior, were elevated to sainthood (the earliest use of this term referred to any practicing Christians, not special ones). These elevated saints became the object of prayer for certain segments of Christianity. These substitutes for God are inadequate at best and idolatry at worst.

Nevertheless, praying draws us closer to the invisible God and the God within. As we seriously read a prayer, create one from our own mind and faith, or let our minds meditate with imagery or nothingness, we get into the mood of prayer, which changes us so that we are receptive to different experiences; we are freed from the ordinary and regular to become unique and different and sensitive to a voice otherwise unheard. *Koinonia* strengthens this when the participants reinforce and strengthen each other. A fellowship of believers sharing faith and prayer together is synergistic, that is, as they unite they become more than they are individually or collectively. Prayer in *Koinonia* is powerful especially when recognized that it is a relationship with God rather than a shopping list of wants. Prayer awakens the God within and, because God is always one, we are in tune to the Holy.

Science is perceived as discounting the Holy. It does not. Science simply does not study the ineffable or the unknown. Science studies the brain

but doesn't understand it; psychology studies our feelings and the interaction between emotions and the brain. Both address the mind, but it remains poorly defined and not understood. Our faith is like this; it is poorly defined and not understood. It is poorly defined because of the many
expressions of it from the so-called sophisticated religions such as Christianity, Judaism, and Islam to raw and primitive expressions like animism.

Koinonia is a fellowship of those within Christianity who question some
of the beliefs that appear to contradict reality. Faith should not contradict
reality, but enhance it. Take a simple pleasure — looking at the colors of
a sunset through foliage shading a small lake. This scene can be seen from
several perspectives. Let me cite two: scientific analysis or as beauty. The
difference is clear. A scientific analysis would consider the rotation of the
earth, the atmospheric refraction of light, the content of the lake, and the
photosynthesis of the foliage, to name a few. An eye for beauty would not
analyze anything, but internalize the beauty of the gradations of light, the
framing of the picture by the foliage and the shimmering reflection off
the water. The scientific analysis is easy, just research the available
information. Beauty is something completely different for it measures the
complexity of the human mind. Color, the sky, the foliage, and the lake
combine with warmth or cold, the sound of wind and water, and the
fragrances that permeate the scene; these enter the person in a way that
causes an emotional response. The response cannot be predicted for each
of us is different and the image can settle peacefully within or stir an ugly
memory and incite terrible and fearful feelings.

The scene is reality but our response is something more than reality
for it is unpredictable and strong. Prayer in *Koinonia* is similar because it
evokes feelings and emotions within as the wonder of God moves us in
unpredictable ways. As we feel the loving and accepting presences around
us, we find that the experience of holiness clarifies and fills us. We feel, not
only the presence of those around us, but the God within unites with the
God without and we are enriched spiritually.

Jesus is the inspiration for *Koinonia*, but he is also present in it. Jesus as the son of God was present in human form to reveal the goodness of God. We form a *Koinonia* fellowship to celebrate the life and ministry of a man who leaps through the ages and becomes a part of our fellowship. His words and actions, the memories shared in the Gospels embellish the life of Jesus to meet our needs; these things come alive in a faithful community, in *Koinonia* fellowship.

Jesus brings us together as he gives us the Kingdom of God, a kingdom not of royalty and politics like the Herods, the Caesars, the kings of today, the dictators who rule, or even the democratically elected presidents; it is a kingdom of the spirit of God for justice and prosperity and peace in a world that struggles for right but fails. The Kingdom of God, through Jesus, reigns in our hearts and minds. It is an ever new day that dawns as the Son rises. It is our Kingdom, the Kingdom of God.

Nothing makes sense unless we compare and judge everything against the life, words, works, and teaching of Jesus. It becomes a resurrection experience as Jesus lives today and as we bring him alive in our faith and fellowship. *Koinonia* brings alive our faith and our understanding of life.

This is the ultimate victory; the Kingdom Jesus continually presents to us an opportunity to move beyond the ordinary and into the extraordinary world of faith and service. This celebrates all that Jesus has given us in the Kingdom. It lifts life to a new and exciting meaning and purpose that transforms all who sincerely join the fellowship of faith.

Chapter Eighteen
AFTER THOUGHTS

This has truly been a "labor of love." As an ordained minister of a major denomination, my life has been centered in the Christian church, mostly in small parishes in relatively rural settings where the great bulk of my work was with people, dealing with day-to-day concerns and with occasional life-changing crises. This ministry was a joyous experience that gradually shifted as my own awareness changed.

What caused this change is beyond my complete knowledge and understanding because much happened in the unconscious that brought together a lifetime of experiences. I can, however, point to a few things that did make a difference and moved the change along. One occurred while driving one Sunday evening and listening to a missionary on a radio religious talk show. The missionary was talking about his work with a primitive tribe of natives deep in the Brazilian rain forests near the Amazon River. He described the people as extremely primitive, impoverished, and worshipping gods found in nature, the trees and rocks, the moon and sun, animism. Poverty had driven these people to raid other tribes to steal their food and kidnap people to cannibalize. The other tribes retaliated with their own raids. It was an ugly cycle of raid responding to raid and constant fear exacerbating their poverty and hunger.

The missionary explained the dangers of being killed and eaten as he brought the message of the Gospel and salvation to them. I could hear the pride in his voice as he shared the sacrifices he made to bring his marvelous message to these primitive and pagan cannibals. The host prompted the story by interjecting questions to illuminate the audience. One question the host asked was how the missionary ministered to their poverty and hunger. The response startled me. The missionary explained that their poverty and near starvation was not a concern; it was their souls he wanted to save. It was okay to suffer and die as long as they did not go to Hell. This life is but temporary; Hell is eternal. This startled me for it did not make sense to intentionally allow suffering to continue when something could be done about it, or, at the least, trying to do something. This did not sound like genuine Christian principles, at least to me. The memory of this stayed with me and haunted me for years, and still does.

This raised a couple of contentious issues. Are those who do not know of Jesus and the Christian message automatically condemned? Is God so harsh that he does not bring the message of salvation to those who live in remote places? This is not the loving and benevolent Father of Jesus of Nazareth.

Later, I was confronted by the charismatic movement in my small parish. This initiated theological guerrilla warfare that split the church. A single parish could not sustain a congregation that was severely split by different brands of Christian thought. Upon reflection, I confess that those who participated in the charismatic movement were far more thoughtful and more emotionally committed to their way of thinking than the "average" member of the congregation. The average members were committed to a more sentimental approach that included Sunday school lessons, memories of key events of their church from favorite hymns to the baptism of their children and nephews and nieces, and the way things were as they remembered them.

What bothered me most was the vehemence of the struggle. It soon became ugly. Rumors were spread; alliances molded; strategies developed; and back-biting perfected. Christians could not be "Christian" with each other.

This experience scarred me. Not too long after I returned, part-time, to school to earn a newly developed degree offered by seminaries, the Doctor of Ministry. The classes stimulated me and after a couple of years, I began work on my doctoral project. I developed a program to be used in a local parish (a neighboring church of a different denomination in the same community) — storytelling focused on children. I had long presented children's sermons, but decided to use the parables of Jesus as the model to communicate with children. This meant a shift from sermons to stories. My study of the parables became serendipitous, a completely unexpected and delightful study.

For the most part, the Gospel writers put the parables in contexts that served their purpose to develop a theological Jesus who related directly to the communities of the Gospel writers. Most parable endings were added to fill the religious leanings and spiritual needs of the writer and his readers, embellishments that helped the Christian movement grow and prosper. Over the centuries these embellishments buried the original parables with interpretations that varied from allegories to reading the parables as actual historical events rather than stories.

Wow! I truly became excited as I reread the parables with a different perspective, struggling to read them as if I had never read them before; to see them as fresh stories; to hear them as if Jesus spoke to me. The morals disappeared and I received and understood new meanings that were exciting and fun. The title of my project was born: *Serendipity.* Reading parables tantalized me for interpretations that had been "set in stone" fell to the side and now new worlds opened. Rereading a parable became a new experience every time, for I now knew that Jesus intended that the parables tease my imagination and force me to rethink everything I believed. Jesus trusted me to use my own head and heart to open up possibilities that met me where I was and the person I had become over the years of my growth and development.

From the parables I returned to the Gospels for another look. As I read, I felt empowerment overtake and engulf me. I was no longer a sinner fighting for salvation, but a loved person free to follow Jesus and thankful and grateful for his love and trust.

This was not a process that happened quickly. It was gradual. This process resulted in this book. The book is neither a theological thesis nor an academic study. Scholars will probably rip it apart for there was no great study, heavy reading, or intense research, but an awakening built upon my experiences both personal and educational. My education was mainline, so the premises of this book violate what I learned from my teachers and texts of past years. I like to think that I grew beyond them, but I probably just broke from them. Or, better still, they spawned my growth, made it possible because of their teachings and visions.

The development of the thought for this work percolated for many years, some of which was unconscious. The process of writing helped me to bring to consciousness the major differences in my approach to Jesus Christ from what I had been raised with and learned. Re-finding the human Jesus as a model reinvigorated me.

I blame no one for the content of this book. If I am to be accused of heresy, and I will be, the blame lies entirely with me. However, what is written here is what I believe to be an alternate approach. It addresses the two incidents that bothered me throughout the years as the ideas percolated. The narrow-minded idea that saving people from sin is more important than caring for their bodies is flawed. The love of God is far more powerful than our human capacity to sin. This love conquers our sin in a definitive way. A loved person who fully realizes this love is a free spirit who lives a victorious life. Those South American indigenous people were as loved by God as the piously misguided missionary.

More important, Jesus healed the sick. At no point did he neglect a suffering body. Jesus never made "conversion" a condition for healing. Never!

The intolerance for divergent views within Christianity is genuine and real. It is just as real as the intolerance for other religions. As I struggled in a relatively small church with the crisis of theological division that ripped into the heart of the life of the congregation, I was forced to rethink my own prejudices. My life had been centered on the church, locally, denominationally, and ecumenically. Most of my time and energy focused on the local church, so serious divisiveness boxed me into a corner because I truly cared about the ideals of my faith. I discovered I was a theological bigot at the same time I accused others of the same crime.

This demanded that I challenge my own faith and thought. It pushed me to reconsider some interesting internal conflicts. I was and am opinionated about faith and politics but am also committed to the great idea and strength of minority dissent, that is, the need for the voice of alternate ideas and ideals. How does this impact my faith? Could I seriously live with religious thought that was significantly different from my own?

Yes! was the resounding answer. I could respect and live with contrasting opinions because I respect people. Not everyone, nor should they, agrees with me. Tolerance, for me, can be difficult because some ideas are not easy to accept, and this demands discipline; I must be tolerant even when I don't want to be. Where does debate fit into this? I love engaging ideas including religious ideas. We can only engage alternate ideas when we are prepared to listen to what others are saying.

How refreshing it would be when differing Christian theologies can genuinely communicate and hear what the other says. It would be a start. So that one day, perhaps, different religions can talk without the barrier of believing that there is only one way that God speaks to people, their way.

This book is my journey in faith. I am a person of the present time, not from the first century, so I have to understand my faith as a person of today, not from centuries past. For example, the first Christians thought as Jews, so all of the initial concepts about Jesus were understood as Jews, not Gentiles. The Gentile interpretations would become significant only with the ministry of Paul. After Paul, the Christian world would be divided between the Greek speaking world and the Jewish world, between those who followed Paul and those who followed James the brother of Jesus and Peter in Jerusalem.

As the Greek speaking world dominated, especially after the time of

Constantine, the influence of Greek and Roman thought took over New Testament concepts. This continued until the modern day where the terms have slowly been modified by today's world. We cannot recapture the world of the Old and New Testaments without imposing modern thoughts and values on them. One quest of the book was to find a way to return to Jesus with as much accuracy as possible (total accuracy is impossible).

This book chose the human Jesus as the way to return as closely as possible to the ancient world where our Christian faith was born. This was a conscious choice that liberated me to discover a new awareness of the love of God rather than a god of retribution. Now faith frees me to act as I understand Jesus taught so many centuries ago. I can never be perfect, but I can dare to act like I am a Christian. I can take chances for my faith and for all the children of God, not merely a select elite few.

Experiencing my resurrected Lord is not some ineffable spirit that stirs my feelings, but Jesus speaking to me through the centuries to use the God within to empower me to be faithful. The Holy Spirit is that which animates me to respond to the trust that Jesus has shown me. This is not a captivity of the spirit where I respond exactly from a pre-written script, but where I, as a specific individual, use my brain, my sensitivities, my talents, and the God within to work in faith.

Not too many years ago, Heaven was portrayed typically by the motion picture industry as serene people floating in clouds with faces that reflected the bliss they felt. This is glorified pap feeding us boring visions where all people are the same. This denies the life that Jesus has given me. I am not living a boring life, anything but. As important, I remain an individual creature, unique and different, someone special. Any vision that reaches beyond this life is speculative.

Another delightful thing I found in my faithful quest was that Jesus lived in the moment and encouraged others to do the same. He made today's living meaningful and fulfilling. He gave us the Kingdom of God as an experience and promise for today. The idea that salvation was a delayed experience just doesn't ring true as I read the words of Jesus. So, when I rely on Jesus as my guide and strength, I can find the resources for living today, right now, in my present life. I think of my family. It may turn out that my family will support me in my old age, yet my more genuine experience of them is now, today. Today, I simply cannot enjoy what will happen tomorrow. Today, I enjoy today.

Bad things do happen. We do confront tragedy and misfortune. More often than not, we suffer though these experiences, we do not enjoy them. So, as we endure, we anticipate what tomorrow will bring, ease from suffering, wrongs made right, and tragedy turned into victory. However, this does not change today's suffering. Sometimes desperation in the moment shouts out to end it all, and even death becomes a welcome retreat into nothingness.

Yet, if we turn to the inner God and the living Jesus, we can find the strength to know that we will triumph. Our fortune may be lost, our health gone, but the inner strength and courage to sustain us in the worst conditions enriches us. There is a noticeable and significant difference here in contrast with "being saved." Here we are given the resources to do it ourselves, an extension of the love and trust that Jesus always demonstrated with his original followers. It is not God taking over and doing it for us.

Resurrection is living in the moment triumphantly. We are not passive automatons preprogrammed and without control over our being, but people acting faithfully and boldly. This is the victory, and it is ours.

Jesus reigns, not as a benevolent dictator, but as our leader showing and guiding us through the joys and pains of day-to-day living. We become victorious. It is not God winning the battle of Armageddon, but us winning against the powers that would suppress and destroy our humanity. We do not need to be rich for this, or successful, but live with all the grace that Jesus has given us in the Kingdom of God.

I think back about the Brazilian missionary who cared only for the souls of the primitive natives and now know how misguided he was not to have seen the total person he was working with and ministering to the whole person. My split parish may have been better able to talk about God including dissonant opinions and to heal themselves if they had experienced *Koinonia*, the Kingdom of God. New insights are rare and I will never be the same as I was as I grow into this new vision of Jesus.

It is a true blessing.

———————•••———————

In religion point-of-view is everything. The Bible is an excellent example of this. How we view and understand the Bible is often how we view and understand our faith. The viewpoint of this book is clear. The Bible is a book of faith gathered, written, and edited by people of faith; it contains Truth but also the flawed and very human perspectives of the various writers. Although the Old Testament, per se, has not been referred to very much, this perspective is true for both old and new.

Within this point-of-view there are differences. For example, I have searched for the words that Jesus himself spoke for the authority that brings faith alive for me today. On the other hand, I could have chosen to use the viewpoint of Mark, the earliest of the Gospels. Mark has no resurrection scene and appears to have little respect for the Twelve disciples. Matthew takes some of Mark's material and portrays the Twelve as far more capable and understanding. Or, I could have left the Gospels and concentrated on the viewpoint of Paul who only has one reference to the human Jesus and it quotes him for the institution of communion.

There is no uniform way to approach the biblical material. This accounts for part of the reason, if not all of it, for denominations and theological divisions. All of these viewpoints are valid for those who follow them. Because God speaks so that all his people can hear and understand. There are many ways for us to listen, not a single unified way. This extends to other religions beyond Christianity making them valid expressions of God. Humans cannot limit the voice of God.

However, as I strive to come as close to the Truth of God as I can, I find the most relevant revelations come from Jesus and his teachings rather than how Matthew, Mark, Luke, and John interpreted the life of Jesus. This is especially true for me because each writer told the story differently emphasizing different things and different time sequences. The Gospels are not a single voice, but internally contradictory, and do not reveal the life of the human Jesus, but reconstruct the time and situations of each of the writers.

I chose a faithful path to walk, a way to spiritually travel in my quest to understand my relationship with my Lord Jesus. The way took me in a different direction than I had traveled before and opened new insights and understandings for many critical Christian issues. Nevertheless, it is where I begin as I think about my faith. Perhaps, the most important thing I have learned is that God believes in me, and Jesus spelled this out clearly. God loves and does not try to put ignorant or unresponsive people in Hell.

All of us confront evil and sin daily, but through the power of the God within, as Genesis explained to us, and the Kingdom of God Jesus brought us, we are victorious, not because we fear eternal punishment, but because we are loved. I seek forgiveness constantly as I move about my life from day-to-day, but it is more thanksgiving for forgiveness and new life and because my life is better and more fulfilling. It can be that way for everyone because the Kingdom of God embraces all.

There are a couple of issues that need to be dealt with: the many sayings of Jesus that I have not considered and the discrepancies between the Gospel narratives. These considerations are important for they are in the New Testament Gospels and are the basis for much Christian thought over the centuries. One of my difficulties is that I am not a New Testament scholar with the time and resources to carefully read the scholarly works of some great and careful thinkers over many centuries but especially the twentieth century. My thoughts developed as a result of relatively independent study and thought. Nevertheless, I have spelled out in this book and rejected some approaches to the Christian faith that have long been accepted by millions of the faithful and clearly expressed by some fairly sharp and very faithful minds.

The New Testament was composed by humans who received a message from those who were close to the actual life and events of Jesus of Nazareth. The first of these New Testament writers was Paul, the Apostle, whose letters preceded the Gospels by some twenty years. The Gospels were written after the fall of Jerusalem in the war that began in 67 CE (Common Era). Hence, the writers of the four Gospels were not the original followers of Jesus, but wrote some forty years after the crucifixion. They used materials, more than likely stories and sayings passed down through the generations from mouth to ear and mouth to ear.

In addition, the writers were educated people with a facility for Greek. The original followers of Jesus were working-class, peasant Jews who spoke Aramaic and probably knew some Hebrew. There is no indication that any of them even knew Greek, although they probably knew some conversational street talk Greek. They had no use for it in the rural communities or in Jerusalem where some Roman soldiers may have been quartered. Also, it is extremely probable that the original intimate followers of Jesus could not write. They were illiterate. None of them could have written the Gospels.

The story of Jesus is not and was not an historical biography. The

Gospel writers put together remembered words and remembered events to inspire faith. These tiny books passed on the traditions about Jesus as they filtered through the minds of faithful human beings who experienced Jesus as a reality in their lives based on their experiences of the Risen Lord, the Lord of faith and resurrection. There is certainly fact mixed in, but the core is still faith expressing faith, faith sharing faith, and faith inspiring faith.

The reality of this is clearly shown in the writings of Paul. He was the first of the New Testament writers and paid no heed at all to the historical Jesus. The only time Paul quotes Jesus is during the institution of the Lord's Supper and, then, the words are tinged with post resurrection faith, feelings, and thoughts. I wanted to get as close as I could to the human Jesus, to meet the man rather than his life filtered through generations of faith. What I wanted is probably impossible to have because no New Testament writer was truly interested in the man, they wanted to fully realize and experience the Son of God, the Risen Lord. Historical information is scarce and seldom as reliable as we would like.

The layers of faith have become seriously distorted by the centuries between the actual life of Jesus and today. This distortion is quite clear. All one has to do to see it is carefully look at the denominations rampant today. Roman Catholicism remembers the Lord who suffered for our sinfulness and remember by eating his physical body and blood. Many, many layers of traditions have developed over the centuries since. Baptists remember the same sacrifice but focus on the Bible as the only way to understand our religious heritage and faith. Tradition means very little. Calvinists (Presbyterians, Congregationalists, etc.) know that God's greatness, especially his knowledge of all that was, is, and will be predetermines our spiritual fate, our salvation or damnation even as we were born. The quality and content of our lives may reveal our future, but do not determine it. Pietists (Methodists, Wesleyans, etc.) concern themselves primarily with living piously as we forever seek perfection as the gateway to salvation.

The result of my search to clarify my faith led me to focus on the outstanding upside of Jesus, his willingness to love and trust us far more than most Christian teachings permit. The center of faith has been on the willingness of Jesus to suffer and die to forgive our sinfulness. This stresses the horror of human failure and the potential to suffer through eternity for our failures. Yet, Jesus did not come to save a few and punish all others. Jesus came to empower us all.

This raises the second question, the emphasis on life eternal. This has always suggested that our present life's only purpose is to prepare for the next. This degrades the value of human life now, in this time. It is like saying that the value of childhood is only to prepare for adulthood. No, children are valuable for who they are as children. There is potential in every child, but there is also potential in every adult. I truly believe that human life is not merely a preparation for another life, for we are as valuable now as we ever can be.

God did not create us as inferior beings to test us for our worthiness for tomorrow. He created us as precious beings. This life is important. It is what we have. Jesus offers us the Kingdom of God now, in this life; this is strength for living, not for dying. This is the joy and victory of the Christian life.

Printed in the United States
128995LV00003B/13/P

9 781606 930915